TALES FROM A WICKLOW TEA ROOM, 1898–1960

MICHAEL
FEWER

Tales from a
WICKLOW
TEA ROOM

1898–1960

BEEHIVE

WALKING GUIDES
The Wicklow Way
Irish Long Distance Walks: A Guide to All the Way-marked Routes
The Way-Marked Trails of Ireland
Irish Waterside Walks
Ordnance Survey guide to the Wicklow Way
Ordnance Survey guide to the Western Way South
Ordnance Survey guide to the Beara Way: West Cork/South Kerry
Waterford Walks

GUIDES
Day Tours From Dublin

TRAVELOGUES
By Cliff and Shore: Walking the Waterford Coast
By Swerve of Shore: Exploring Dublin's Coast
Walking Across Ireland: From Dublin Bay to Galway Bay
Rambling Down the Suir: The Past and Present of a Great Irish River
Michael Fewer's Ireland: People, Places, Walking and Wildlife
Europe's Atlantic Fringe: Exploring the West Coasts of Portugal, Spain and Ireland

ANTHOLOGY
A Walk in Ireland

BIOGRAPHY
Thomas Joseph Byrne: Nation Builder
J.B. Malone: The Life and Times of a Walking Pioneer and Explorer of the Nearby

ARCHITECTURAL HISTORY
The New Neighbourhood of Dublin (with Maurice Craig and Joseph Hone)
Doorways of Ireland

CHILDREN
Naturama: Open Your Eyes to the Wonders of Irish Nature
My Naturama Nature Journal (with Melissa Doran)

HISTORY
The Wicklow Military Road: History and Topography
Hellfire Hill: A Human and Natural History
The Battle of the Four Courts: The First Three Days of the Irish Civil War

NATURE
A Natural Year

For my beautiful grand-daughter, Alexandra Jane

Published 2023 by Beehive Books
7–8 Lower Abbey Street, Dublin 1, Ireland
info@beehivebooks.ie
www.beehivebooks.ie

Beehive Books is an imprint of Veritas Publications.

ISBN 978-1-80097-072-4

Design and art direction by Lir Mac Cárthaigh
Printed in Ireland by Walsh Colour Print, Co. Kerry

Beehive Books is a member of Publishing Ireland.

Beehive books are printed on paper made from the wood pulp of managed forests. For every tree felled, at least one tree is planted, thereby renewing natural resources.

CONTENTS

ACKNOWLEDGEMENTS

I have enjoyed chatting through the ether these last two years with Tom McGuirk, without whose encouragement, assistance and stories this work would not have been possible. I also had the invaluable help of Gloria Smith of Glencree, and the encouragement of Niamh McNamee and Val Kiernan of the Glencree Centre for Peace & Reconciliation, and Brian Dunne of the Wicklow Uplands Council. Thanks are due also to Aideen Ireland, the late Gregory O'Connor, and the staff of the National Archives. It was encouraging that Síne Quinn and Lir Mac Cártaigh of Beehive Books 'got it' and it was a pleasure to work with them during the publishing stage. Thanks also to Fiona Dunne, editor, and Eileen O'Neill, indexer, and to Éanna Ní Lamhna, Manchán Magan, John Quinn and Kathleen Watkins for endorsing the book.

Thanks to my friend Dick Cronin for translating the entries in Irish. Jonathan Williams, as always, was behind me right through, never without an encouraging word. A special thanks to Teresa and my friends and family who have had to put up with months of me nattering on about the wonders I was discovering in the visitors' books.

AUTHOR'S NOTE

All efforts were made to track down signatories but it was not always possible to identify them, so I only write about those signatories whom I have been able to locate. Where no mention is made of a signatory's birth or death dates, it is because it has not been possible to ascertain this information. Long gaps between entries are due to very badly damaged or missing pages. Visitor book entries have been largely replicated, including idiosyncrasies of spelling, but for ease of reading have been made as uniform as possible without disrupting the sense of the original. '[*Sic*]' has been added only in the case of blatant errors, since there is considerable variation in how place names and people's names are spelled throughout the visitors' books.

Glencree, Co. Wicklow

INTRODUCTION

Glencree, less than 10 km south of the Dublin suburbs, is a scenic valley extending eastwards from two dramatic and beautiful glacial lakes, Upper and Lower Loughs Bray. The potential of the valley was noticed early by the Norman occupiers of Ireland when it was clothed in an ancient oak wood, untouched by the O'Toole clan, the Gaelic owners of the land. Ignoring, as was their way, the O'Tooles, the Normans declared it a royal deer park and royal forest, and eighty red deer were imported from the Royal Forest at Chester to stock the park, which was said to have been enclosed by a ditch and bank. The lands to the north, in Glencullen, were owned by St Mary's Abbey in Dublin, the abbot of which was an avid deer hunter. Records show that in 1291 he and his friends strayed into Glencree and were accused of hunting 'with nets and other engines, and with greyhounds, and of taking wild beasts and working his will with them, to the great injury of our lord, the King'.

In 1806, an army barracks was built at the head of the valley to watch over the Military Road. It became disused by the 1820s and, in 1858, a reform school was established there, which was run by the Missionary Oblates of Mary Immaculate, a Roman Catholic order. It ceased operations in the 1940s, and in 1946 the old reform school, as part of the Red Cross's Operation Shamrock, became a reception centre for child refugees from Germany. Some were orphans, but many had parents who, in the aftermath of World War II (WWII), were unable to feed and look after them. When they had been brought back to health, they were fostered out to Irish families all over the country. The most recent use of the Glencree buildings was when an organisation called Working for Peace provided refuge for people affected by the Troubles in Northern Ireland, which became known as the Glencree Centre for Peace & Reconciliation.

Towards the end of the nineteenth century, the valley of Glencree was in the ownership of Lord Powerscourt, a descendant of Richard Wingfield, 1st Viscount Powerscourt, who cleared what remained of the O'Toole clan from the valley early in the seventeenth century.

It is possible that Wingfield brought in settlers from his estate in Benburb, Co. Tyrone, to repopulate the area, which is how the Gallaghers, Quinns and McGuirks, a subsept of the O'Neills of Tyrone, may have come to Glencree.

Around 1830, a cottage orné or hunting lodge, designed by Irish architect William Vitruvius Morrison, was built by Sir Philip Crampton in a sheltered site overlooking Lower Lough Bray. At an elevation of 1,250 feet, Lough Bray Cottage was reputed, at the time, to be the highest inhabited dwelling in the Wicklow Mountains. Here, according to contemporary travel writer James Fraser, Crampton 'occasionally retreats … from the fatigues of his professional duties'. Crampton, born in Dublin in 1777, was an eminent surgeon and anatomist, president of the Royal College of Surgeons in Ireland on four occasions, and surgeon general of the British Army in Ireland.

It is thought that a stone, thatched gate lodge was also built around 1830 or a little later and it seems that from at least the 1870s the McGuirk family lived there. The land about the gate lodge, while including scenic Lower Lough Bray, and overlooked by beetling Eagles Crag, was termed a 'rocky, heathy pasture' on a nineteenth-century Powerscourt estate map and would have been little use agriculturally for other than mountain sheep. Less than 24 km from the centre of Dublin city, however, the two picturesque lakes and their surroundings had become an attraction for tourists and excursionists by the end of the nineteenth century.

Around 1880, Mary McGuirk and her husband, Arthur, decided to augment their meagre income by providing teas for visitors to the scenic lakes and travellers in the Wicklow Mountains. Their cottage was the last roadside dwelling on the Military Road until the Glenmacnass Valley, about 20 km to the south. Mary and Arthur McGuirk's son Thomas married Mary Jane Toole from Glencree around 1896 and, when she moved in, she assisted her mother-in-law, then aged seventy-five, with the tea room. Arthur died aged

The McGuirks' cottage, c.1890

Mrs Mary McGuirk, the tea room originator, with her grandsons, Arthur and Tommy, about 1900

ninety in 1901, and Mary was unwell for a number of years up until her death in 1910 at the age of eighty-one. Mary Jane had two boys: Arthur, born in 1897, and Thomas, born a few years later, so, for a period at the turn of the century, there was little space in the two-room cottage. Teas were served in the kitchen/living room. In spite of this, the McGuirks used occasionally take in paying guests, and some accommodation was later provided in an adjacent timber hut. This practice continued up until 1957.

The hours were often long: many entries in the visitors' books suggest that McGuirk's often stayed open as long as there were visitors to serve. In December 1937, for instance, a group of six had 'a good solid feed' after midnight Mass at the chapel in the nearby St Kevin's Reformatory School, or Glencree Reformatory as it is also known.

The fare provided by the McGuirks was clearly of high quality and is consistently praised in the visitors' books, the quality being maintained and possibly improved by the succeeding McGuirk women. They made their own bread in the traditional way, in a pot over the open fire. They kept hens and sometimes geese, so there was no shortage of fresh eggs, and they had beehives that provided honey. Homemade jam, probably mainly blackberry, blackberry and apple, or fraughan, was a treat for city folk, and McGuirk's tea was legendary and frequently referred to as 'refreshing', 'excellent' or 'splendid'.

Mary Jane's younger son, Tommy, died in 1942, and in the same year her other son, Arthur, married Mary Gallagher (known as Mona) from Glencree. She was the second-eldest of eleven children, and the only girl. Until her marriage at the age of forty, she had looked after her ten brothers and was an accomplished woman, not only an expert at needlework, but an excellent baker of bread, sponges and fruitcakes. The people in Glencree still talk about her great bread. It is said that Arthur married her to look after his mother and to help her with the tea room, and it certainly was Mona's skills that sustained and enhanced the reputation of the tea room. It cannot have been easy for her, because her mother-in-law was said to have been a formidable woman but, with little help from Arthur, she excelled at carrying on the tradition.

The prominent Dublin physician Bethel Solomons was a frequent visitor; when Mona was pregnant with Tom, Solomons organised for her to come into the Rotunda Hospital so that he could personally look after her for the birth. In later years, Mona McGuirk developed chronic bronchitis, and the tea room closed when she had to stop serving teas late in 1961.

When I was researching my book *A Walk in Ireland* in 1998, I came across a number of references to walkers in the Wicklow Mountains enjoying refreshments in Mrs McGuirk's tea room. It seems that callers were requested to sign their names in a visitors' book, and contribute comments on the quality of the welcome and fare they received. It was not an uncommon tradition in more grand circumstances: guests' or visitors' books became popular in the mid-Victorian period in hotels, inns and restaurants. The McGuirks' cottage, however, was a long way from the grandeur of places such as Dublin's Shelbourne Hotel, and I'm sure that some visitors to the tiny tea room were surprised to receive such a request. Intrigued by the references I had found to Mrs McGuirk and her visitors' book, and by the idea that it might still exist, I began to make enquiries about it in Glencree.

Visitors' books normally have a relatively low survival rate. Important ones usually suffered from the plundering of famous names by autograph hunters: a famous example was a page taken from the guestbook of a Chamonix hotel in which the poet Percy Bysshe Shelley had written his name, describing himself as a democrat and an atheist. Most visitors' books, however, end up being

The McGuirks' visitors' books

dumped. Two years after making enquiries about the McGuirks' visitors' book, I had almost given up hope when I received word that not just one but eight volumes of visitors' books existed, and were in the care of Gloria Smith and her husband, Paddy, who lived near the old barracks in Glencree.

I made contact with Paddy and Gloria and went to visit them. Paddy was a sheep farmer, and a great friend since boyhood of Tom McGuirk, the last surviving member of the McGuirk family who ran the tea room. Tom lives in Canada: his partner, Jan, is Gloria's sister. Imagine my delight when the books, which had been carefully stored in supermarket bags in the Smiths' attic for years, were produced. The earliest volume, from the 1880s, had long ago been destroyed by damp, but most of the rest, from 1898 onwards, were reasonably well preserved.

With Tom McGuirk's agreement, the Smiths kindly loaned the books to me to peruse, and I found them fascinating. Handwritten historical material always has the power to transport one to the place and time in which the words were inscribed on the page – many of the unique personal communications written in these books were redolent of the holiday atmosphere and the companionship of friends and family the writer was experiencing at the time. Most of the volumes are not formal, register-type books with pages divided into columns for date, name, address, nationality, but provided completely blank pages that allowed for comments, line drawings and verses, in addition to names and addresses. Although Mrs McGuirk simply asked that her visitors might comment on the service and fare they received, many could not resist going further, offering up a variety of additional personal details.

While some entries are quite stilted and self-conscious, others are deliberately frivolous and used by visitors as a rare opportunity for public self-expression, literary or artistic, or to record their sense of personal achievement after long treks or cycles over the mountains or along the rough Wicklow roads. Some visitors left descriptions of their travels, poems in English and Irish, portraits of their companions, and other sketches and drawings. Walking clubs used the pages to give a brief report on the route they had taken that day, and listed the names of their members who took part. Cycling clubs similarly wrote of their journeys, the quality of the roads and their pride in the excellence of their 'machines'. The Old Crocks Cycling Club, Loraine Cycling Club, Anti-Idlers Cycling Club, and the Howth Cycling Club were just some of the popular clubs that visited Glencree during the first few decades of the twentieth century. It seems clear that some visitors thumbed through the previous entries in the book before they 'signed in', and in some cases a snide comment or a bon mot can be seen to have been added to an earlier entry.

In the main, the entries are spontaneous, written snapshots of moments of contentment and enjoyment in the lives of people long gone and, for many, long forgotten. Some of the names, however, were familiar to me, people whom I knew had become quite prominent, famous or, indeed, infamous, in later years, but I was also curious about the many others whose names, handwriting or comments suggested they were worth finding out about. It wasn't long before I realised that the books as a whole constituted a unique, valuable and often quirky insight into social, political and cultural aspects of modern Irish history from the late nineteenth to the mid-twentieth century.

What was also intriguing about the entries in the books was the opportunity, for individuals who would later become prominent, to see what company they were keeping at the time of their visit to McGuirk's. For example, we can see who accompanied Arthur Griffith on a Cumann na nGaedheal charabanc outing to Glencree in January 1901, and who accompanied Oliver St. John Gogarty and his wife, Neenie, to McGuirk's in the summer of 1913.

I found names that at first glance seemed to be relatively unique but often turned out to be quite common. For instance, seeking out

Fashionable cyclists at the end of the nineteenth century

information on R.W. Rowe, who signed the book on Good Friday 1902, one has to trawl through a long list of people with precisely the same name, including a Royal Navy stoker 2nd class who died in action in 1918, a semantic scholar who produced learned papers such as 'Morphology of perimsial and endomysial connective tissue in skeletal muscle', a naval captain who wrote *The Shiphandler's guide for masters and navigating officers, pilot and tug masters*, and a geologist who wrote *Soil Survey of the Caribou Area, Maine*.

Other entries enable us to see certain people in a different light. The Major C. Harold Heathcote of Richmond Barracks who enjoyed taking tea with his wife on 20 August 1916 turned out to be the officer who had commanded the firing squads that executed Patrick Pearse, James Connolly and others after the 1916 Rising a couple of months before.

Many who signed their names felt it necessary to include additional details, such as their rank or station in life. For instance, on 1 August 1898, N.C. Geoghegan signed the book as 'Attorney Gen. Dublin'. Charles J. McCarthy visited McGuirk's on a number of occasions and, as well as giving his address, on one such visit added 'Dublin City Architect'. In March 1902, cyclist Louis M.J. Halligan of 3 Connaught Terrace, Dalkey, records that his qualifications include LRCPI (Licentiate of the Royal College of Physicians of Ireland) and LRCSI (Licentiate of the Royal College of Surgeons in Ireland).

Many of the entries are windows into the energetic cultural and political developments that occurred during the sixty-odd years that the books encompass, such as the upsurge from about 1900 onwards in the enthusiasm of Gaelic revivalists and nationalists for writing their names in Irish, in addition to poems and descriptions of places and companions. This continued until the 1950s, when the practice began to die out. A dramatic reduction in the number of English visitors can be seen during the period of the War of Independence and for several years afterwards, but by 1926 they are back again in

List of names in the *Cló Gaelach* script, January 1901, from the McGuirks' visitors' books

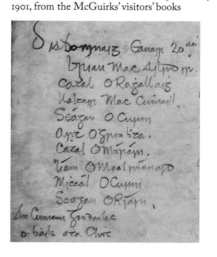

good numbers: by the 1950s, they represent a large proportion of the summer visitors.

Although there were three Mrs McGuirks over the period of the tea room's existence, they become, in the eyes of the visitors, a singular Mrs McGuirk who enjoys consistent and considerable praise for her oft-mentioned kindness, hospitality, and baking and cooking abilities, which gave this tiny rural cottage a remarkable reputation.

What follows are the stories of some of the people who took tea at McGuirk's over the years, and of the world they inhabited. There are many more people with intriguing or familiar names that I attempted to track down but failed to find. Gaps between entries are mainly due to runs of damaged pages. There are names that readers will readily recognise, but there are also those whose more obscure stories were revealed when I investigated their histories, finding myself unfolding the course of one human life after another, with all their successes and failures, in many cases more than one hundred years later. It was a strange feeling, seeing them in the moment of their light-hearted and enthusiastic handwritten contributions but knowing what their futures held, and how they would end up.

McGUIRKS' VISITORS' BOOKS, 1898–1960

As will be seen, the majority of those who signed the visitors' book in the early period are from a wealthy Anglo-Irish background. Most of them attended Protestant schools and those who went to university usually attended Trinity College Dublin, at the time unavailable to Catholics. In the earlier decades, the entries display a solid sense that Ireland, for many of the Irish, was very much part of Britain. Many of the young visitors to McGuirk's did not hesitate to join the British Army when war broke out in 1914, and many of them did not survive. Throughout the period, however, increasing numbers of Catholic middle-class visitors are arriving in McGuirk's, and the use of the Irish language is becoming more prevalent.

From the 1870s onwards, a general rise in living standards, together with the growth of free time and spending power, encouraged city people to venture out into the countryside on day trips and holidays. Railways provided cheap transport for the working classes, and in summertime brought large numbers of Dubliners to the seaside resorts along the north and south coasts of Dublin Bay. By the late nineteenth century, groups of better-off people took day trips in charabancs, the forerunner of today's touring coaches: open coaches with capacity for over twenty passengers and with a canvas hood that could be hauled into position to give shelter when it rained. These vehicles were joined on the country roads by cyclists and walkers, and tea rooms began to spring up to provide these explorers of the countryside with somewhere to relax in comfort and enjoy refreshment along the way.

Illustration of a steam train, early-twentieth-century, by George Fagan

There was a great surge in the popularity of the bicycle in the 1890s. Bicycles of varying types had been in use in Ireland since the 1860s, and the first cycling club in Ireland, the Dungarvan Ramblers Cycling Club, was established in 1869. In the early years, cycling remained an exclusively male-dominated, upper- and middle-class activity. The original 'bone-shakers', cumbersome machines propelled by pedals attached to the front axle, were superseded in the early 1870s by the 'Ordinary', popularly known as the penny-farthing. These machines were not for the timid: a fall from one could easily be fatal, and the young men who rode them scoffed at the idea of brakes.

By the beginning of the 1890s, the bicycle had developed to more or less the configuration that we know today, chain-driven with two spoked wheels and pneumatic tyres. They were initially called 'Safety' bicycles but, unlike the Ordinary, they became enormously popular because they were suitable for 'properly' clad women to ride with modesty. It was the first bicycle type to be mass-produced, and as such was within the financial reach of many. These new cycles were looked down upon, however, by 'Ordinary' stalwarts, until William Hume rode a pneumatic-tyred safety bicycle at Queen's University Belfast sports day in 1889, and scored easy victories over

those riding Ordinaries. The pneumatic tyre, developed by John Boyd Dunlop, a Scottish veterinarian and inventor who spent most of his career in Ireland, made all the difference.

The American publication *Munsey's Magazine* pointed out in 1895 that what was 'merely a new toy' for men was, for women, 'a steed upon which they rode into a new world'. It is clear that, while cycling soon became a vibrant part of cultural and social life in Ireland, it was particularly embraced by women because of the freedom and independence it provided. A publication with the title *The Wheelwoman and Lady Cyclist*, 'The Only Ladies Cycling Paper', came out in 1896, with articles about notable society lady cyclists and suitable clothing for cycling. There were those (mainly men) who believed that cycling might intoxicate women to perform immoral acts. Some trumpeted that riding bicycles would destroy a woman's femininity by giving her muscular arms and legs and tempt her to wear masculine clothes: women cycling would lead inevitably to immodesty, promiscuity and infertility. Women's bicycle saddles were even causing consternation in medical journals: some medical men considered saddles to be potential stimulators of sexual desire for women and it was thought that the action of pedalling created rhythmic movement of the clitoris, thereby arousing sexual feelings. Some companies, such as A.G. Spalding & Bros, were quick to cash in on the controversy by producing special saddles for women, 'relieving the sensitive parts of the body from pressure of any kind', and labelled 'Anatomical' or 'Hygienic'.

All these concerns were soon swept aside. The usually conservative Dr Seneca Egbert of the University of Pennsylvania Medical School wrote, in 1890, with regard to women cycling, that 'it gets them out of doors, gives them a form of exercise adapted to their needs, that they may enjoy in company or alone, and one that goes to the root of their nervous troubles'. Amalie Rother, a cycling devotee who clearly had no 'nervous troubles', said in 1897 that

> an experienced female cyclist can only be amused by the question, 'skirt or trousers?' A woman has exactly the same number of legs as a man ... and should clothe them sensibly, giving each leg its own covering rather than placing both into one. Has it ever occurred to anyone to put both arms into one sleeve?

The women's rights activist Susan B. Anthony observed that 'cycling did more to emancipate woman than anything else in the world'.

Regarding developments in Ireland, the *Weekly Irish Times* commented on 13 July 1895 that the 'girls in town here are having the bicycle fever pretty badly – they are teasing their fathers and mothers and husbands and brothers to buy them a pneumatic steed, and those who have learned to ride, and some who haven't, may be seen whizzing in all directions about town'.

Long bicycle rides from Dublin out into the countryside became very popular and McGuirk's tea room benefitted greatly from the boom: in addition to male cyclists, they catered for several women's bicycle touring clubs. There are many enthusiastic passages in the visitors' books written by cyclists who stopped for tea in great good humour, and with pride taken in the distance covered. According to the signatures, men and women cyclists seem to have been equal in numbers and they often named their bicycles as they would have named a horse, as Nelsons, Astons or Balmorals.

It is likely that many of the early cyclists who came to McGuirk's had a copy of the popular *Cyclist & Pedestrian Guide to the Neighbourhood of Dublin* by R.J. Mecredy, which was published in 1891. Mecredy was writing for the *Irish Cyclist and Athlete* magazine from 1885, and by 1890 had bought the paper and become its editor. He won the 40 km English tricycle championship in 1886 and, in 1890, on a Humber machine with Dunlop tyres, won all four English cycling championships. Mecredy later moved on to motor cars and became their most influential advocate; he is often described as the 'father of Irish motoring'.

Glencree from Mecredy's guide of 1891. Much of the valley in this scene is forested today

In his *Cyclist & Pedestrian Guide to the Neighbourhood of Dublin*, Mecredy advised his cycling readers where to go, and where the best roads and scenery were to be found. With regard to the Military Road from Rathfarnham to Lough Bray, he describes the stretch over the 'wild and sterile' Featherbeds in the 1890s as sandy and covered with loose stones and protruding boulders; almost unrideable. As soon as the highest point at 1,600 feet is reached, however, 'the surface improves … In wet weather it is extremely sticky, and during continued drought it is loose, but at other times there is a narrow strip at the edge which is almost as good as a racing path, and coasting in perfection can be indulged in.' 'Coasting' is presumably the term he uses for 'freewheeling'. He describes the road to Enniskerry from Glencree as 'never good for a tricycle, and at all times requiring care and skilful management … deep sandy ruts abound'.

Mecredy waxes lyrical about the beauties of Lough Bray and its lofty cliffs, and has no problem recommending his readers to enter the private grounds of Lough Bray Cottage, 'a fairy retreat' that would be impossible to surpass. He refers peckish readers to McGuirk's, 'where refreshments, in the way of tea, homemade bread, fresh eggs and butter can be obtained'.

A.F. Harding (centre right) with the Welsh rugby union team that defeated the All Blacks in 1905

It is thought that although visitors' books had been kept from the opening of the tea room around 1880, the earlier volumes were destroyed by damp, and some of those that survived were badly damaged. The earliest readable volumes date from the second half of the year 1898, and bear the title 'Lough Bray Visitors Book Please Sign Your Name' in simple script.

11 June 1898
Miss F. Church
W.W. Carruthers
A. Denker
Ida Gamble
Charles Gamble
Veronica Gamble
A.F. Harding
L.A. West
Miss C.G. Shaw
Mr. & Mrs. B. Hilliars

Mrs McGuirk's thoughtful attention contributed towards making this a very pleasant days [sic] outing.

These visitors left their names in the visitors' book using Mrs McGuirk's indelible blue pencil. The only name that I could track down is Arthur Flowers Harding (1878–1947), an English-born rugby player who played for and captained the Welsh international rugby team. He was on the team that beat a touring All Blacks side in 1905, after which he emigrated to New Zealand, where he lived for the rest of his life.

15 June 1898

Edward H. Taylor *29 Lower Baggot Street*

Grave of Sir John Ross (left), Dunmoyle, Co. Tyrone

Edward Henry Taylor (1867–1922), born in Wicklow, was Professor of Surgery at the University of Dublin, 1906–16, when he became Regius Professor of Surgery. He was an outstanding surgeon who, two years after his visit to McGuirk's, wrote, with William Haughton, a paper, 'Topography and the convolutions and fissures of the brain', that is still referenced today. He was a colleague of E.J. McWeeney, Ireland's first professor of pathology at the Catholic University, who also frequently took tea at McGuirk's.

23 July 1898

Hon. Mr Justice Ross *Dublin*
J. Harrison *Dublin*
Richard Rogers *Dublin*
Katie Rogers ditto
Mrs Harrison

Excellent Tea, beautiful day. Splendid fishing, enjoyed day, got wet but hurragh for a nice tea.

Sir John Ross (1853–1935), born in Derry, attended Trinity College Dublin where the future Lord Glenavy, Lord Chancellor of Ireland, and the Irish unionist politician Edward Carson were contemporaries. He became a Member of Parliament (MP) for Londonderry in 1891 and in 1896 was the youngest judge ever appointed in the United Kingdom and Ireland. He was created a baronet in 1919. Responsible for drafting the 1904 Land Act, as a judge he had a reputation for fairness. He succeeded Lord Glenavy as Lord Chancellor of Ireland in 1921, a post he held for only one year as it was abolished when the new Free State government took over.

Author Joseph Sheridan Le Fanu by his son
Brinsley Le Fanu

25 July 1898
H.V. Le Fanu
C.A. Le Fanu
E.C. Le Fanu
J. Royse
O. Royse
A.L. Foljambe
F.S. Le Fanu
T. Le Fanu

Although I cannot identify all the individual Le Fanus in this group, they are probably descendants of Thomas Philip Le Fanu, father of the famous writer Joseph Thomas Sheridan Le Fanu. The T. Le Fanu at the end of the list is probably Thomas Joseph Le Fanu, who was educated at Haileybury school in England and then Cambridge; at the time of this visit to McGuirk's, he worked in the Chief Secretary's Office in Dublin Castle, before becoming secretary to Chief Secretary for Ireland Augustine Birrell in 1910. The list of names is written in one hand, probably his, which might explain why A.L. Foljambe, in spite of the second initial being L, is most likely Arthur William de Brito Savile Foljambe (1870–1941), who was born in Sussex, England, and, at the time of this visit to McGuirk's, was aide-de-camp to Lord Cadogan, Lord Lieutenant of Ireland. Foljambe fought in the Boer War, returning to Ireland as State Steward, 1906–8. In 1907, he inherited the title of Earl of Liverpool and in 1912 was appointed Governor and Commander-in-Chief of New Zealand.

J. Royse and O. Royse are John MacDonnell Royse of 49 Eglinton Road, Dublin, and his sixteen-year-old daughter, Olive. Royse was married to the Hon. Louise Mary Monck, second daughter of Viscount and Viscountess Monck.

Many of the entries are effusive in their praise of Mrs McGuirk and her hospitality. Although society was very class-conscious at the beginning of the twentieth century, the use of terms such as 'old friend' for Mrs McGuirk by members of the upper-middle class seems to transcend class distinction. Other examples of this include 'Mrs McGuirk's teas as usual splendid'; 'treated with usual kindness'; 'treated very kindly'; and 'best of tea and lots of very good butter and cake'.

J.F. Keatinge's shop (right) in Grafton Street, Dublin, around 1947

5 September 1898
J.F. Keatinge
Mrs McCready
Ada McCready
Christopher McCready
Cyril McCready
Annie McCready
Enid McCready

Cycled from Kilcoole to Roundwood, Luggala, Sallygap [sic] to Lough Bray en route to Kilcoole – very hot day – delightful ride.

During these last years of the nineteenth century, many cycling visitors were proud to describe the route they had taken.

J.F. Keatinge and family were enthusiastic cyclists and regular visitors to McGuirk's for decades. Seven years after this visit, J.F. Keatinge established the well-known J.F. Keatinge and Sons, a plumbing and decorating business with premises in Grafton Street. He was also a Justice of the Peace: the firm he founded was still in business in 1990. His son, Charles T. Keatinge, was a Fellow of the Institute of British Decorators, and wrote a paper in 1900 for *The Journal of the Royal Society of Antiquaries of Ireland* entitled 'The Guild of Cutlers, Painter-Stainers and Stationers, or the Guild of St Luke the Evangelist'.

Drawing of hill walkers, November 1900

Hill walkers were also frequent callers at McGuirk's. Country walking in Ireland was a pastime mainly enjoyed then by educated, middle- and upper-class people, and ramblers' clubs such as Na Sléibhteágaigh and the Brotherhood of the Lug were established in the early twentieth century. These clubs were almost always composed of men, quite often civil servants and members of the legal profession. The Brotherhood was founded on the summit of Lugnaquilla in 1903 by five friends and is still active today. It became common for hill walkers to record in the visitors' book the weather conditions on the day of their visit, the route they had taken through the mountains, and points of interest along the way, as the next pair of companions does.

29 October 1898
A.W. Donaldson
C. Jamieson

Walked from Rathgar, got here 7.15 – very wet – after usual substantial Tea, left for home again – on foot – Full Moon not visible. (NB speciality Blackberry Jam.)

St Stephen's Day, 1898
Ohno Hash C.C. [Cycling Club]
M.W. Robertson
L.C. Longstaff
R.J. Mecredy
M. Hubert Greene
Charles C. Figgis
Cecil G. Thompson
W.A. Higginbotham

This group from the strangely named Ohno Hash Cycling Club includes Richard James Mecredy (1861–1924), writer, journalist and author of the *Cyclist & Pedestrian Guide to the Neighbourhood of Dublin* (1891).

1899

28 January 1899

J.M. Aimers
W. Danby Jeffares
Wm Conolly
Alex Mulhall
S. Kane
B. Cooke

Sketch left in 1899

Had a very nice evening on the whole, at present suffering from the effects of a large tea – started at 3.15 from Rathgar, arrived here at 6.15. Had it rather bad in roads from the summit of the mountain down to here & anticipate worse going back on account of the snow which has lain here since Monday last and has frozen hard since and is freezing still. The ruts and holes are awful! Indulged in a small impromptu snowball fight on the way, but are reserving our chief energies for 'Don' who we expect to meet us on the way home.

I could only track down two of this group: Walter Danby Jeffares (*d.* 1900), who attended The High School in Rathgar, Dublin, and died in action in the Boer War at Driefontein, and J.M. Aimers, who lived on Highfield Road, Rathmines, and was an early owner of a private telephone.

25 March 1899

A.W. Donaldson   *Rathgar*

Here for tea 10.05pm, stayed till 11.30. Walked today from Bray (8am) via Glen of the Downs, NTMt Kennedy [Newtownmount-kennedy], Roundwood to Richardsons, got there 2.50, left there 5.15, Glenmacnass Falls 7.10, Sally Gap 9.10 – total 50 miles.

This entry is evidence that McGuirk's was open to visitors at all hours. A.W. Donaldson, a prodigious walker, alone or with friends, was a frequent caller and early in the new century became a founding member of the walking club Na Sléibhteágaigh.

5 May 1899
Thomas Smalley
W. Merriman Thompson
Wm F. Beckett
Harry C. Nealon
J.M. Aimers
Robert Woods

William Francis Beckett (1871–1933) in this group was an up-and-coming quantity surveyor and son of a successful building contractor who built the National Library in Dublin. Two years after this visit to McGuirk's, he married Mary Roe and they had two sons, the second of whom, born in 1906, was the playwright Samuel Beckett. William Beckett was a jovial character who loved the beauty and peace of the Dublin and Wicklow mountains and enjoyed walking and cycling there. When he was old enough, William took his son Samuel walking with him, exploring Tibradden, Glendoo and Killakee, and beyond McGuirk's tea room as far as the Sally Gap. They talked and philosophised as they went, and Samuel discovered in the moorland wilderness the peace and inspiration that would sustain him in future times. Aspects of mountain landscapes, the great rocks, the skies and the vegetation frequently surface in his writings: even as an exile in old age, Beckett said that 'the old haunts were never more present … I walk those backroads, with closed eyes'.

McGuirk's was, for some reason, particularly popular among the medical profession at the time. The last named of this May 1899 group, Robert Henry Woods (1865–1938), was a regular visitor to

McGuirk's and an early Irish biophysicist and otolaryngologist who specialised in the head, neck, ear, nose and throat. He subsequently gained an international reputation and was elected president of the British Laryngological Society. He stood in the 1918 Irish general election as an independent and was returned as a representative for Dublin University.

20 May 1899
Donn Piatt
M. Hayden
H. Sigerson

Donn Piatt photographed between 1865 and 1880

Arthur Donn Piatt (1867–1914), born in Washington DC, was the United States vice-consul in Ireland. A year after this visit to McGuirk's, he married one of his companions on this day, Hester Sigerson.

M. Hayden was Mary Hayden (1862–1942) of Dublin, educated at Alexandra College and the Royal University of Ireland, graduating with a Master of Arts (MA) in modern languages. She became a campaigner for women's rights at university and was a member of the Dublin Women's Suffrage Association. A good friend of Patrick Pearse and his family, she was a member of the Gaelic League (Conradh na Gaeilge), but opposed violence and the 1916 Rising. Appointed Professor of History at University College Dublin (UCD), she wrote *A Short History of the Irish People* (1921) and her published diaries are a window onto Victorian Ireland with its wealthy middle classes, country gentry, artists and writers.

Hester Sigerson (1870–1939) was born in Dublin to Hester Varian and George Sigerson, who was a doctor, poet and senator. A writer, she published works on the republican Anne Devlin and the revolutionary, writer and poet Charles Kickham, as well as two books of poetry: her poetry was included in both W.B. Yeats's and Padraic Colum's anthologies of Irish verse. A member of Cumann

The neo-classical front of Bolton Street Technical School, designed by Charles J. McCarthy, now part of Dublin Technological University

na mBan, she had two children with Donn Piatt: Eibhlín Piatt Humphreys and Donn Sigerson Piatt.

8 July 1899
Charles J. MacCarthy [sic]
Walter Innes Pocock
James Duncan
Ellen Duncan

Rode from Dublin via Glendhu and Feather Bed Mountain en route for Glendalough.

Charles J. McCarthy (1858–1947) (this list of names seems to have been written by the last-signed, Ellen Duncan, and she misspelled McCarthy's name) was Dublin City Architect, 1893–1921. He started out apprenticed to his father, also an architect, and he inherited his father's practice after his death in 1882, and was responsible for buildings such as Bolton Street Technical School and Kevin Street Public Library in Dublin; the Presentation Convent in Dingle, Co. Kerry; and the Church of the Star of the Sea, Courtown, Co. Wexford. He was chosen from a list of ten to become Dublin City Architect in 1893, and during the course of his tenure he designed and oversaw the erection of 1,700 houses, and was in charge of the reconstruction of the O'Connell Street/Abbey Street area after the 1916 Rising. He married Clara Louise Christian, a painter and friend of the writer George Moore, in 1905, but she died a year later in childbirth. He retired early due to poor health in 1921, but enjoyed a long retirement living at the Stephen's Green Club.

Walter Innes Pocock (1859–1913) was born in Bristol, England, and studied anthropology at Trinity College Dublin. At the time of his visit to McGuirk's, he was working as a higher-division clerk for the Local Government Board, which was attached to Dublin Castle and exercised British government control over Irish local authorities. He retired in 1900 and returned to Bristol, where he died.

James Duncan was the husband of Ellen Duncan, and worked with the Teachers Pensions Office.

Ellen Duncan (1862–1937) is one of the very few female visitors to McGuirk's about whom we know more than we know about her husband. She was a journalist, art critic and first curator of the Municipal Gallery of Modern Art (now Dublin City Gallery The Hugh Lane). A founder of the United Arts Club in Dublin, she came to prominence when she curated two radical art exhibitions in Dublin in 1910 and 1912, showing the work of artists that hadn't been seen in Dublin before, including Cézanne, Picasso, Matisse and Van Gogh. As curator of the Municipal Gallery, she was later closely involved in the Hugh Lane paintings bequest controversy between Ireland and Britain.

Clonmell House, 17 Harcourt Street, Dublin, was the home of the Municipal Gallery of Modern Art, from 1908 until 1932

5 October 1899

Mr & Mrs Palmer	*Hyderabad, India*
Miss G.E. Going	*Cahir, Co. Tipperary*
Miss Isobel Taylor	*London*

This Mr Palmer was possibly the great-grandson of General William Palmer, confidential secretary to Warren Hastings, who, with Robert Clive, is credited with laying the foundation of the British Empire in India. General Palmer's son, also named William, was commander of the cavalry in the Nizam's Army in 1799, and fought with the army of General Wellesley, later Duke of Wellington, to win significant victories against the Nizam's enemies during 1803 and 1804. General Palmer founded the Palmer and Company bank in 1810, which was subsequently immersed in a series of scandals in the 1820s. William Palmer died in 1867: the 'Mr Palmer' above could be one of his sons, William or Edward, who were educated in London at the Nizam's expense.

Photograph by Fr Edward Sherwin showing Dr E. J. McWeeney inspecting a copy of the 1916 Proclamation on railings at St Stephen's Green, Dublin, in 1916

Miss G.E. Going was one of the Quaker Going family of Cahir, Co. Tipperary, who became the owners of Suir Mill in Cahir in the late 1790s and lived in a fine house called Alta Villa, which had been built by Charles Going of Mountrath, Co. Laois. The other Quaker milling families in Cahir at the time were the Grubbs and Walpoles. The Goings lived at Alta Villa until the mid-twentieth century.

1900

13 January 1900
E.J. McWeeney
George K. McWeeney
R.B. Joyce
Robert Woods
J.M. Aimers

Edmund Joseph McWeeney (1864–1925) was a distinguished doctor who helped to establish the science of pathology in Ireland. In 1884, he received a first-class honours degree in literature and pathology, after which he obtained a degree in medicine at the Catholic University School of Medicine. He worked in Vienna, and then in Berlin with the German physician Robert Koch, who had identified the bacteria that causes tuberculosis; on returning to Ireland he was appointed Ireland's first Professor of Pathology at the Catholic University. He published at least fifty-five learned papers and contributed to many more. He lived at 86 St Stephen's Green.

He carried out the autopsy on Thomas Ashe, a member of the Irish Volunteers who died on hunger strike in Mountjoy Prison in 1917, and found that the cause of death was forced feeding, the only medical evidence not disputed at the Coroner's Court. A polymath,

McWeeney was a founder member of the Dublin Naturalists' Field Club and a specialist in fungi, adding 252 new species to the 530 already known in Ireland.

George Kendellen McWeeney was his brother.

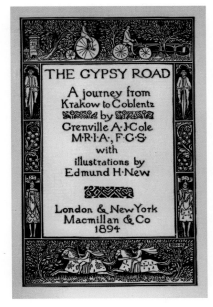

The Gypsy Road, a travelogue by Grenville Arthur James Cole

5 April 1900

Helen Laird
W.S. Atkinson
Geo. Pethbridge
J. Stephens
J.A. Cunningham
C.A. Harrison
R.B. Forster
A. Livingstone
Grenville A.J. Cole

Geological Field Class, Royal College of Science for Ireland, took tea and went on to Luggala.

This group of geological students was led by the last on the list, Grenville Arthur James Cole (1860–1924), an English geologist who, from 1890, was Professor of Geology and Mineralogy in the Royal College of Science for Ireland. In 1893, he undertook a cycling tour of Germany and Poland and wrote a travelogue entitled *The Gypsy Road: A journey from Krakow to Coblentz* (1894). He was a staunch supporter of women's education, and taught for three years at Bedford College, the first higher education college established for women in Britain. He became director of the Geological Survey of Ireland in 1905 and wrote many learned papers in addition to eight other books, including the popular *Handbook of the Geology of Ireland* (1924).

16 April 1900
J.A. Wheeler
M.J. Dillon
Seamus A. Macrost   *Baile Atha Cliath*

The last signatory above was the first of many visitors who were proud to use Irish in McGuirk's visitors' book.

22 April 1900
Mrs Lane-Poole   *Enniskerry*
Stanley Lane-Poole   *Trinity College, Dublin*
Rosamund Lane-Poole   *6 Hume Street, Dublin*
Guybon Daraint   *HMS Prince George*

While women feature just as often as men in the visitors' books, it is usually only the male signatories that I can locate in the various biographical dictionaries: women not only had to change their names on marriage, but rarely, in the early twentieth century, did they become 'noted' personalities in other than the arts or as the wives of prominent men. Typical of how most women of the time had little more status than being their husband's wives, searching for Mrs Lane-Poole I found that she turns up on a British Museum website as Mrs Reginald Lane-Poole, and the only information available was that she was 'Female' and, under the heading 'Biography', that she was described as 'Widow of Henry Lane-Poole'! From another direction I unearthed a little more: her name was Charlotte Wilson before she married, in 1879, Stanley Edward Lane-Poole (1854–1931), an English orientalist, author of many books and Professor of Arabic at Trinity College Dublin, 1897–1904. Only in his biographical details did I find that Charlotte died in 1905. She did, however, bear a daughter (Rosamund) and three sons, one of whom died young.

Her son Richard (1883–1971) joined the Royal Navy in 1898 and served through World War I (WWI) and WWII, retiring as a vice-admiral and Knight Commander of the Order of the British Empire. Her other son, Charles (1885–1970), lost his left hand in a shooting accident and went to Paris to study forestry in 1906. After graduating, he worked as a forestry officer in South Africa and Sierra Leone. On a visit back to the family in Dublin in 1911, he met and married Ruth Pollexfen, a cousin of W.B. Yeats whom we shall meet again under her married name, Ruth Lane-Poole.

Of Guybon Daraint I could find no trace, but his ship, HMS *Prince George*, was a battlecruiser; commissioned in 1895, it saw service in the Dardanelles during WWI before foundering off the coast of the Netherlands in 1921.

20 May 1900
Mafeking Relieved Hurray!
W. and Mrs Hobbs, London, and party, enjoyed a most refreshing cup of tea and were very pleased to see an old friend again.

The attack on Game Tree Fort during the siege of Mafeking. Illustration by H.C. Seppings Wright

It is notable that major current affairs and events in Ireland and the world are usually left unmentioned in the visitors' books, as if, up there in the rarefied and calming air of the mountains, in a holiday ambiance, such things were not considered important. There were, however, some exceptions to the rule, as when the Hobbs family cannot resist announcing the end of the Siege of Mafeking during the Second Boer War: Mafeking was a trading town close to the Transvaal border in South Africa, which the Boers laid siege to one day after the South African Republic declared war on Britain on 12 October 1899. The siege lasted for 217 days and was finally lifted by a British force on 17 May 1900. While the whole matter was of little significance, it was sold to the British public as a military victory and great rejoicing took place when the word got back. The worst of the Boer War, little of which was publicly known at the time, was yet to come, particularly the establishment of concentration camps

The Royal Botanic Gardens, Ceylon (Sri Lanka) today

to house the women and children of the Boers. By November 1901, 117,000 Boers were held in these camps, of which over 20,000, mostly children, died.

1 July 1900

Professor Marcus Hartog

C.J. McCarthy FRIA — *City Architect*

C.H. Oldham Barrington — *Lecturer*

James Duncan — *(nobody in particular)*

Ellen Duncan — *(Leader writer)*

One wonders what this group of companions had in common. Marcus Hartog (1851–1924) was a natural historian and educator, born into an academic family in London. Cambridge-educated, he went to Ceylon in 1874, where he remained for three years as assistant to the director of the Royal Botanic Gardens. On his return, he lectured in natural history at Owens College, Manchester (now the University of Manchester), before becoming Professor of Natural History at Queen's College, Cork (now University College Cork), a post he held for twenty-five years. He supported the non-Darwinian evolutionary ideas of the English novelist and critic Samuel Butler, and wrote a supportive introduction to Butler's book *Unconscious Memory* (1910). He also contributed to the *Encyclopaedia Britannica* and the *Cambridge Natural History* (1895).

Charles J. McCarthy, whom we have met previously, this time proudly added his qualification (Fellow of the Royal Irish Academy) and official title.

Charles Hubert Oldham (1860–1926) was educated at Kingstown Grammar School in Dún Laoghaire and Trinity College Dublin, from where he graduated in 1882 as Senior Moderator, and with the Large Gold Medal in experimental physics and a gold medal in mathematics. While in Trinity he founded the Protestant Home

Rule Association and, a little later, the Contemporary Club. As a lecturer under the Barrington Trust, he addressed meetings all over the country, imbuing his audiences with the principles of liberal enlightenment. His success was so notable that he was appointed principal of the new Rathmines School of Commerce. He became the first Professor of Commerce at the foundation of University College Dublin in 1909, which chair he vacated in 1917 to become Professor of National Economics.

21 September 1900
H.S. Guinness – Very excellent tea and cake.

Henry Seymour Guinness (1858–1945) was a son of Henry Guinness of the Guinness Mahon merchant bank and he enjoyed a busy and varied career. An engineer by profession, he worked in the Indian Public Works, 1880–95, and was a lieutenant in the Burma State Railway Volunteer Rifles during the Anglo-Burmese War. On his return to Dublin a year before this visit to McGuirk's, he was appointed High Sheriff of County Dublin and a director of the Bank of Ireland. In 1920, when most of the local authorities in the south of Ireland had Sinn Féin majorities, the British-controlled Local Government Board withheld rates from the councils, so they had to make other arrangements for finance. W.T. Cosgrave, then Minister for Local Government in the Dáil Éireann government of 1919, sought instead a financial accommodation with the Bank of Ireland, and Guinness was one of the directors of the bank that provided the necessary finance, tantamount to a vote of confidence in the possibility of Irish independence. Two years later, when Cosgrave was president of the Executive Council of the Free State government, he nominated Guinness to a seat in the new Irish Senate (Seanad Éireann).

October 1900

Mrs W.D. Handcock   *Sallypark*
Miss Geraghty
Miss Lily Tabuteau
Miss Eileen Hargrave
Miss G. Hargrave

This Mrs Handcock (*d.* 1920), née Eleanor Olivier Rooke, was the widow of William Domville Handcock (1830–1887) of Sallypark, near Firhouse in Dublin, which was built *c.*1770 by the Earl of Clanwilliam but was bought by William's grandfather in 1796. William was the author of *The History and Antiquities of Tallaght*, first published in 1876, an important work on the history of the area. After his death, Eleanor continued to live at Sallypark until her own death. The two Hargraves were her companions and housekeepers, and the second listed, Gussie, inherited Sallypark: Eleanor Handcock wanted her to marry her nephew, Rev. Charles Rooke, who was on the first Irish rugby team to win the Triple Crown in 1894. This union never took place, however, and Gussie married a Major Medicott instead. Sallypark is a nursing home today.

1901

In 1892, the academic, linguist and Irish-language scholar Douglas Hyde delivered a paper to the Irish National Literary Society entitled 'The Necessity for De-Anglicising Ireland', which led to the establishment of the Gaelic League in 1893. The League was a social and cultural society that promoted the Irish language and Irish-language publications, the best known of which was *An Claidheamh Soluis*, which was edited by Patrick Pearse. Irish-language schools and learning groups were widely established throughout the country, and large numbers of people embarked on learning Irish and, as much as was possible, on using it in their everyday lives.

An issue of *An Claidheamh Soluis* from January 1900

From about 1900, this increase in the use of Irish is reflected in the visitors' books: a good proportion of the names of visitors from now on were the Irish versions, often accompanied by the customary praise for the fare enjoyed, and sometimes by poems, all *as Gaeilge* ('in Irish').

20 January 1901
Brian Mac Ailindir
Cathal Ó Raghallaigh
Walter MacCumhall
Seágan Ó Cuinn
Art Ó Griobhta
Cathal Ó Moráin
Liam Ó Maolruainaigh
Michál Ó Cuinn
Seagán Ó Ríain
An Cumann Gaodhlac ó Bhaile Atha Cliath

Lá Fluic ar Fad. Fuairamar Fáilte agus Fiche ó chlann Mic Eirc. Dfhánamar le uair no mas sin agus an gaoth ag éirigh go hárd. Ba maith linn an tamharc ón doras.

Arthur Griffith

This charabanc group were Cumann na nGaedheal members from Dublin who must have arrived in poor, windy weather. Loosely translated, their note reads: 'Wet all day. We received a great welcome from the McGuirk family. We stayed an hour or more as the wind was rising hard: we all enjoyed the view from the door.'

The only name in this group that I recognise is Art Ó Griobhta, or Arthur Joseph Griffith (1871–1922), writer, newspaper editor and politician, and one of the two founders of the political party Cumann na nGaedheal ('Club/Society of Gaels'). He had returned two years earlier from South Africa, where he had supported the Boers against the British, and founded the weekly *United Irishman* newspaper. A few months before this visit, he established Cumann na nGaedheal to unite nationalist groups and associations. Six years later, Cumann na nGaedheal joined with other clubs to become the political party Sinn Féin.

Sinn Féin had little involvement in the 1916 Rising; it was misnamed the Sinn Féin Rebellion by the British media. Griffith was elected to the Dáil in June 1918 while in prison in England, and on his release served as acting president of the Dáil while the president, Éamon de Valera, was in the United States. Appointed Minister for Foreign Affairs in 1921, he was chosen by de Valera to lead the delegation to London to negotiate a settlement with Britain. The resulting Anglo-Treaty with Britain, which he and his delegation signed, led to the outbreak of civil war, and two months later, suffering from stress and overwork, Griffith had a stroke and died, aged fifty-one.

2 February 1901
(Queen Victoria's Funeral)
A.W. Donaldson
A.W.L. Barlee

Walked from Terenure, got here 6.05 pm.

As a sea change in Irish politics and culture was occurring, and until the Easter Rising of 1916 and the subsequent War of Independence, most ordinary Irish people thought of themselves as Irish by race, but British by nationality. While many of the Irish who joined the British Army at the outbreak of WWI did so for economic reasons, many of the upper and professional classes, who would have insisted that they were Irish, joined up out of loyalty to Britain. Regular visitors to McGuirk's, such as the hill walker A.W. Donaldson, were at the other end of the spectrum from Cumann na nGaedheal, and felt that Queen Victoria, who had died on 22 January 1901, should be remembered.

Queen Victoria's funeral cortege, London, 2 February 1901

12 **March 1901**

W.F. Bailey   *Dublin*

G.H. Bailey   *Dublin*

William Frederick Bailey (1857–1917) was an eminent barrister and well-known figure in Dublin cultural life. A Fellow of the Royal Geographical Society, he was also a member of the Royal Irish Academy and a governor of the National Gallery. Under the second Irish Land Act of 1881, he was appointed one of three estates commissioners in Ireland and, as such, was one of three senior civil servants tasked with proposing a boundary between Ulster and the rest of the country, should the southern counties achieve Home Rule, laying the groundwork that underpinned the establishment of the Irish border by the Boundary Commission in 1926. Bailey's proposal, which followed physical geographic features, ignoring existing administrative boundaries and, in places, existing Catholic/Protestant majorities, was rejected. Bailey was one of the most noted travellers of his time, counting North, Central and South America, North and South Africa, and Central India among the places he had visited. He was a friend and useful supporter of Hugh Lane in his efforts to establish a new art gallery in Dublin.

G.H. Bailey, his brother, was a scientist who wrote on the subject of chemistry, his best-known work being *Bailey's Elementary Chemistry* (1910).

William Frederick Bailey, *c.*1916

3 **April 1901**

R.H. Crofton

J.M. Aleam

From Edmundstown to Glendalough – in hope.

Richard Hayes Crofton (1880–1968) was born in Dublin and educated at St Columba's College and St John's College, Cambridge.

After joining the British colonial civil service, he worked in Hong Kong and Zanzibar, where he was assistant Chief Secretary. He wrote a number of books, including *Adventures in Administration* (1927), *The Old Consulate at Zanzibar* (1935), *A Pageant of the Spice Islands* (1936) and *Zanzibar Affairs 1913-1933* (1953).

21 April 1901

Miss Philips	*Salisbury*
F.F. Devine	*Tullamore*
Fetherstonhaugh KC [King's Counsel]	*Dublin*
Miss A. Fetherstonhaugh	*do [ditto]*

Geoffrey Fetherstonhaugh (1858–1928) was born in Co. Mayo and graduated from Trinity College Dublin with an MA in 1883. He became a barrister at law in 1895 and was subsequently appointed KC. He was elected Unionist Party MP for North Fermanagh in 1906. Members of the British Parliament are not allowed to resign, but an appointment to a Crown office of profit disqualifies an MP from sitting. Non-positions such as 'Steward of the Manor of Northstead' were invented in order to allow resignations, and Fetherstonhaugh used this ruse to resign his seat in 1916.

11 May 1901
Dr and Mrs Hastings-Tweedy
Had excellent tea and cake.

Dr Ernest Hastings Tweedy (1862–1945) was a gynaecologist and Master of the Rotunda Hospital who became noted for performing a primitive surgical procedure called a pubiotomy, an extreme surgery involving severing the pelvis of a woman in labour in order to deal with a difficult delivery. He was the author of the textbook *Practical Obstetrics* (1910).

Ink and wash drawing by an unknown artist showing the Lying-in Hospital and the Rotunda, Dublin, in the nineteenth century

9 June 1901

Ethel S. Whittle	*Warrickshire [sic]*
Ellen Duncan	*Dublin*
C.J. McCarthy	*Dublin*
Herbert Wood	*Dublin*

We have already met Ellen Duncan and Charles J. McCarthy.

Herbert Wood (1860–1955) was born in London and received a BA from Oxford in 1883. In 1884, he joined the Public Records Office in Dublin, which was accumulating, arranging and cataloguing the archives of Ireland. Wood specialised in the records of the medieval period in Ireland and, in 1912, was assigned to compile a guide to the records held in the Public Records Office, but the onset of WWI delayed the work and it was 1919 before his 334-page guide was finally completed. Wood was made Deputy Keeper of Public Records in 1921, in time to see the Public Records Office and its irreplaceable contents destroyed when the Civil War broke out the following year. His guide to the records had been completed just in time, so at least what records had been destroyed had been catalogued. Wood retired in 1923 and returned to England.

23 June 1901

Mrs Frank Joyce *Good food, good pie, warm welcome*
Robert Lloyd Praeger *ditto, ditto*

Robert Lloyd Praeger (1865–1953) was an Irish naturalist, librarian and writer whose most well-known work was *The Way That I Went* (1937), a potpourri of facts and reminiscences concerning the topography, geology and natural history of Ireland. He was born in Belfast and, despite having a degree in arts and engineering, took up a post at the National Library of Ireland in Dublin in 1893. He had always been an enthusiastic botanist, however, and sought a way to further his interests in the subject. In Dublin, he mixed with a coterie of kindred spirits, and became involved in the Dublin Naturalists' Field Club. By June 1901, when he visited McGuirk's, he had just published his first important botanical work, *Irish Topographical Botany*. Between 1909 and 1911, he led the Clare Island Survey. In 1923, he retired from the National Library to enjoy a thirty-year-long retirement, during which he wrote numerous learned papers, as well as a number of books. He was president of the Royal Irish Academy, 1931–4, and the first president of both An Taisce and the Irish Mountaineering Club.

A 1900 Royal Enfield Quadricycle in the Beaulieu National Motor Museum, UK

14 July 1901

Robert Skelton *Aungier Street, Dublin*
William M. Conway *S. Great George's Street*
    On Motor Quad

This pair must have caused quite a stir: motor cars of any type were rare at the time. The first car imported into Ireland was a Benz Velo in 1898, but cars were extremely expensive and initially viewed by most as an eccentric craze. By 1904, only thirty-eight motor vehicles were registered in Ireland. The 'Motor Quad' mentioned here was a Royal Enfield Quadricycle, really a motorbike with four wheels: at the time, the next best thing to a motor car. The driver sat at the back, with the single passenger on a seat in front of the handlebars.

The vehicle cost £110 and 5 shillings in 1901, and *Autocar* magazine reported that 'a sound quadricycle properly driven is a good touring machine, and one that can go practically anywhere'. A vintage example was recently sold for €55,000.

Sketch of a horse and carriage, September 1901

5 August 1901
Mr & Mrs F. Frood & maid   *Booterstown*
Mr & Mrs W.D. Himsworth & family   *Blackrock*

Some of the entries in the visitors' books underline the 'upstairs, downstairs' culture of the time, which, within a couple of decades, would largely come to an end. The Froods travelled with their maid, but saw no necessity to record her name.

14 September 1901
Shooting Party
Ellen Grace Barton   *Batsford, Herts*
R.J. Barton   *Dublin*
RJB had 1st shot.

R.J. Barton had an address at Sorrento Terrace, Dalkey. His youngest son, Vivian, joined the Royal Field Artillery as a second lieutenant in June 1916 and was killed in action in France in September 1917, aged thirty-four.

2 October 1901
Surgeon General A. Sibthorpe CB [Companion of the Bath]
The Misses Sibthorpe (his sisters)
Miss Taylor   *London*
Miss Dalton   *Dublin*

Charles Sibthorpe (1847–1906) was another of the distinguished Irish medical men who frequented McGuirk's. He was born

Charles Sibthorpe

in Dublin and, after studying medicine at the Royal College of Surgeons in Ireland, joined the Indian Medical Service and was appointed Resident Surgeon to the Madras General Hospital and Professor of Pathology at Madras Medical College. He was later appointed Professor of Ophthalmology, Anatomy and Surgery and in 1894 was appointed Surgeon General with the government of Madras, a post he held until 1900. In 1880, despite his years in India, he was elected a Fellow of the Royal College of Physicians of Ireland, and in 1897 was awarded a CB (Companion of the Bath). In 1885, he was staff surgeon with the British forces in Burma when that country came under British rule. At the age of fifty-three, he retired back to Ireland where he lived with his sisters in Dublin. He died five years after this visit to McGuirk's.

1902

23 March 1902
Dr F.C. Purser
R.M. Gwynn

It is likely that these two arrived on foot, as both were enthusiastic hill walkers. Francis Carmichael Purser (1876–1934) was born in India, and attended school at the Grammar School, Galway. He received a degree in medicine from Dublin University in 1901. He played rugby for Ireland in 1898, was a major in the British Army during WWI, and received an MBE (Member of the Order of the British Empire). He was president of the Trinity Football Club, 1920–2. In 1933, he was appointed King's Professor of Medicine at Dublin University, and was an honorary professor of neurology, specialising in brain injuries. He was awarded an OBE (Officer of the Order of the British Empire) in January 1922. The artist Sarah Purser was his aunt, and Olive Purser, one of the first women to enter Trinity College Dublin and the first to become a scholar there, was a cousin.

Robin Malcolm Gwynn (1877–1962) was born in Co. Donegal, educated at St Columba's College in Dublin and attended Trinity College Dublin at the same time as Francis Purser. His mother was a daughter of Irish nationalist MP William Smith O'Brien. Gwynn graduated in 1898 with a BA, followed by an MA in 1906, when he was elected a Fellow of Trinity. The following year he was appointed lecturer in divinity and was ordained a priest in 1908. He never served in a parish and devoted his life to education and working with the poor of Dublin. He was a founder member of the Social Service (Tenements) Company, which provided housing for poor families, and the Trinity College Mission, which assisted the slum dwellers of Belfast. After the Dublin Lockout in 1913 and the police brutality towards strikers, he joined the Industrial Peace Committee and was involved in the foundation of the Irish Citizen Army. He was an accomplished cricketer, and once had the distinction of bowling out the legendary English cricketer W.G. Grace Jr.

Rev. Robert Malcolm 'Robin' Gwynn

6 April 1902

Rev. C. Shanks   *Bray*

Mrs McGuirk looking A1 as ever and reminding one as ever of old times, while as for her daughter-in-law, least said, or rather written, the better, as we hear 'Tom' [McGuirk] keeps a gun handy and can *shoot, even around corners.*

3 July 1902

James Bunn

A. Bunn   *Killegar*

The Bunn family of Killegar near Enniskerry, Co. Wicklow, were frequent visitors to McGuirk's. James Bunn travelled widely in North America and wrote a book about his experiences for his 'children, grandchildren and great-grandchildren' entitled *Go West Old Man*.

15 August 1902

Alfred A. Bruncker	*18 Grosvenor Place*
Miss K. O'Sullivan	*26 Highfield Road*

Alfred Arthur Bruncker (1875–1946) was, briefly, an international rugby player, appearing in his first international against England in February 1895 (England won by three points) and in his last game against Wales six weeks later, in which Wales won by two points. We do not know what led to his abandonment of what seemed a promising amateur career.

17 September 1902

Grace Guinness	*Stillorgan*
Victor Guinness	*Blackrock*
S. Darley	*The Grange, Stillorgan*
Robert Guinness	*Blackrock*
Severine Guinness	
Evelyn A. Darley	*The Grange, Stillorgan, Ireland*
Mary K. Falls	*Burton Hall, Stillorgan*
G.G. Guinness	*Glenart Avenue, Blackrock*
H. Grace Tucker	*Trent College, Derbyshire*
Darley Tucker	*Trent College, Derbyshire*

Beatrice Grace Guinness (1869–1944) was a frequent visitor to McGuirk's. She married John Christopher Peter du Toit in South Africa in 1911.

Sarah Darley (*b.* 1877) was the daughter of George Johnstone Darley of Blackrock, a land agent and civil engineer who started his engineering career as an articled pupil of the famous civil engineer Isambard Kingdom Brunel. Darley worked on the radical design for the Great Exhibition Crystal Palace of 1851, for which he received a medal. He was also a land agent in the west of Ireland for his relatives Robert Guinness and John Mahon, founders of the Guinness Mahon merchant bank.

Evelyn Adams Darley (1867–1939) was another daughter of George Darley.

Mary K. Falls (1867–1923), née Guinness, was the wife of John Alexander Falls whom she married in Cairo in 1895. She was one of the twelve children of Henry Guinness and his wife, Emmelina, who lived at Burton Hall, Stillorgan.

The Crystal Palace, Hyde Park, London, 1851

1903

10 April 1903
Seághan Ua Raghallaigh
Eamonn Ó Tuathaill
Seághan Ua Raghallaigh ag ól tae. Lá an bhreagha agus siubhal an fhada ón teach buidhe go dti Coill Chuinn.

Bhí Eamonn Ó Tuathaill annseo indiu in eineacht le Mac Uí Raghallaigh agus dearbhuighim go bhfaca mé é ag ól tae le mo dhá shúil agus buidéal uisge beatha ag duine d'ár gcuideachtan. Ní fhaca mé riamh acht tá fios agaibh gur bhfuil seanfhocal maith ann: 'An té bíonn siubhalach bíonn sceaghalach.'

This translates as:

Seán O'Reilly drinking tea. A very fine day and a very long walk from The Yellow House to Killakee.

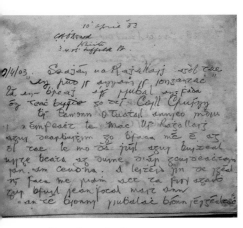

Entry for 10 April 1903

Eamonn O'Toole was here today in the company of the O'Reilly and I swear I saw him drink tea, with my own two eyes, even though one of our company had a bottle of whiskey. I never saw it before but you know there's a fine old saying: 'He who is travelled has a story.'

Entries in Irish were on the increase at this time as visitors proudly asserted their new-found cultural identities: many of the writers are practising their skill with the language, and the spelling and translation of English names into Irish varies. The reference to 'the O'Reilly' suggests that his companion was the clan chief of the Raghallaighs.

4 October 1903
Geo. Nesbitt   *Rathmines*
Nesbitt   *[illegible] of Berlin*

Rode from Roundwood to Lough Dan. Continued road till it stopped and then made straight across mountains (carrying or pushing our machines) till we reached the Military Rd. Thence we rode via Sally Gap here, and (half starved as we were when we arrived having eaten nothing since 9 o'c) did justice to some beautiful tea and bacon and eggs. Hope to get to Bray now.

This cycle tour was not an easy ride: after the long run to Roundwood and on to Lough Dan, going 'straight across mountains' meant carrying or pushing their machines over 4 km of trackless moorland, along the Inchavore River, to the Military Road. Seventy years later, J.B. Malone, the planner of the Wicklow Way, was not happy with the Way taking that route, because of how rough it was.

George J. Nesbitt (1871–*c*.1925) managed a mineral water production company on Dublin's Camden Street and was a founder member of the National Literary Society and the Irish National Theatre, later the Abbey Theatre. After the 1916 Rising, he was involved with the Irish National Aid Association and Volunteer Dependants' Fund, which not only assisted those affected by the rebellion but helped to shape the popular memory of it. It also contributed towards the radicalisation of Irish political life after the Rising, which led to the resumption of political life and the subsequent military campaign. In 1918, Nesbitt was appointed cotreasurer of Sinn Féin with the suffragist and nationalist Jennie Wyse Power, and was interned in Ballykinlar Camp during the War of Independence. He was an independent member of the Free State Senate from 1922.

The second signatory, another Nesbitt, was presumably a brother.

Jennie Wyse Power in the late nineteenth century

23 November 1903
Miss Gladys Grimshaw
Major Cecil T.W. Grimshaw

Gladys Grimshaw was a frequent visitor to McGuirk's with other members of the Grimshaw family, but this seems to be the first time she brought Cecil: he was probably her brother. This particular branch of the English Grimshaw family came to Belfast from Lancashire in the 1770s to introduce the cotton textile industry. Gladys's father, Thomas Grimshaw (1839–1900), was president of the Statistical and Social Inquiry Society of Ireland in 1888 and president of the Royal College of Physicians of Ireland in 1895, and was awarded the Commander of the Order of the British Empire (CBE) for his services to medicine in 1897. He lived on Molesworth Street with his wife, nine sons and three daughters, including Gladys and Cecil.

Major Cecil Thomas Wrigley Grimshaw (1875–1915) was another of Thomas Grimshaw's sons and, a couple of years before this visit, had fought in the Boer War with the Royal Dublin Fusiliers. He

Cecil Grimshaw raising the British flag following the liberation of the prisoner of war camp in Pretoria, 1900, in a contemporary illustration by Melton Prior

was captured during the Battle of Talana Hill and held in the same prisoner of war camp as Winston Churchill. His diary of his experience there comments that, when an escape was arranged for Churchill and a number of officers, Churchill slipped out alone, leaving his companions behind.

Grimshaw stayed in the British Army after the Boer War and served in operations in Aden in 1911. In WWI, he took part in the disastrous landing in the Dardanelles on 25 April 1915. When his colonel and other officers were killed before reaching shore, he assumed command of the regiment, but was killed himself the next day.

His grandson was Sir Nicholas Grimshaw, the distinguished architect who designed several outstanding buildings, including the Eden Project in Cornwall and Waterloo International Railway Station.

1904

7 February 1904
W.S. Gosset
G.C. Philpott

The visitors' books include the names of many Irish medical men and scientists who enjoyed their leisure time at McGuirk's, and who eventually emigrated and contributed significantly to the British Empire.

William Sealy Gosset (1876–1937) is an example of the opposite occurring. Born in England into an old Huguenot family, he was educated at Winchester School before obtaining first-class degrees in mathematical moderations and natural science at New College, Oxford. In October 1899, he joined the Guinness Brewery in Dublin, where, in 1907, he was appointed Brewer in charge of the newly established experimental brewery. He later established Guinness's statistical department, which he ran until 1936, when he transferred to the first Guinness Brewery to be established outside Dublin, at Park Royal in London.

8 May 1904

Frank Robbins   *15 Grosvenor Square*

John H. Gibbs   *49 Leinster Road, Dublin*

First Dublin Battalion Irish Association of Volunteer Training Corps on parade, *c.*1914

John Henry Gibbs (1861–1916) was born in Dublin and worked as a civil servant. He was a member of the Irish Association of Volunteer Training Corps, a kind of voluntary Home Guard formed during WWI. On Easter Monday 1916, Gibbs was among a group of 120 Volunteer Training Corps members returning from exercises at Ticknock, at the foothills of the Dublin Mountains, carrying rifles without ammunition or bayonets, when they heard about the Rising. Their commanding officer decided to march to Beggar's Bush Barracks in the city, unaware that Northumberland Road and Mount Street Bridge were guarded by a unit of rebels under Michael Malone. They had the misfortune to march straight into a fusillade of fire from Malone's men, which killed four, including John Gibbs. His name appears on the Memorial Wall at Glasnevin Cemetery.

24 May 1904

Taimid annseo go h-ocrach, tuirseach agus fuaireamar lán ár mbríste de ghach uile rud dá fheabhas. Bí úr agus bainne gabhar agus arán aráiste teacht. Annrath le fághail. Níl orm anois ach aon botúnas amháin. Níl aon biotáile le fághail. Is mór an truagh nach bhfuil focal gaedhilig le fághail annseo.

     Fear siubhail ó Āth Cliath

     Fear bocht ó Loch Riach

     Thaingimid annseo go h-ocrach.

Sketch left in May 1901

This translates as:

> We are here, hungry, tired and we got a trouser-full of everything of the best. Fresh food and goat's milk and orange [marmalade?] bread to follow. Soup available. All I need now is one mistake! No spirits to be had. Such a pity there is no word of Gaelic spoken.
>
> A tramp from Dublin
> [and] A beggar from Loughrea
> We came here hungry.
>
> **2 July 1904**
> *J.M. Synge*
> *F.J. Fay*

John Millington Synge (1871–1909) was a playwright, poet, writer and key figure in the early days of the Abbey Theatre and the Irish Literary Revival. He was born in Rathfarnham, Dublin, and went to Mr Harrick's Classical and English School on Leeson Street and Aravon School in Bray, Co. Wicklow. After leaving school, he studied at the Royal Academy of Music, followed by further studies in France, Germany and Italy. During his time on the continent, he changed the focus of his studies to literature and languages and, while studying at the Sorbonne in Paris, stayed in the Hotel Corneille, where he met and was inspired by W.B. Yeats. Yeats later remembered becoming friends with the 'poor Irishman at the top of the house'. On Yeats's advice, Synge spent time on the Aran Islands every year from 1898 until 1902, recording his impressions and gathering material for his writings. Synge's first play, *The Shadow of the Glen*, was performed in Dublin's Molesworth Hall in 1903. The audience hissed during the first performance at what Arthur Griffith felt was a slur on Irish womanhood, and many critics agreed.

The year of this visit to McGuirk's had not been good for Synge. His health had been deteriorating for some time: he had a frail constitution, having suffered from asthma in childhood, but by 1904 he was afraid that he might have tuberculosis. His second play to reach the stage, *Riders to the Sea*, opened at Molesworth Hall on 25 February 1904, four months before this visit to McGuirk's, but the performances had been marred by the audience reactions. *The Freeman's Journal* claimed in a review that the performance was 'a libel upon Irish peasant men, and worst still upon Irish peasant girlhood', and the *Irish Independent* felt the play was 'too dreadfully doleful to please the popular taste'. This visit to McGuirk's with his friend Frank Fay, however, happened at a time when things were looking up: his plays had been well received in London where he circulated in distinguished literary company and was introduced to English literary luminaries such as John Masefield and G.K. Chesterton.

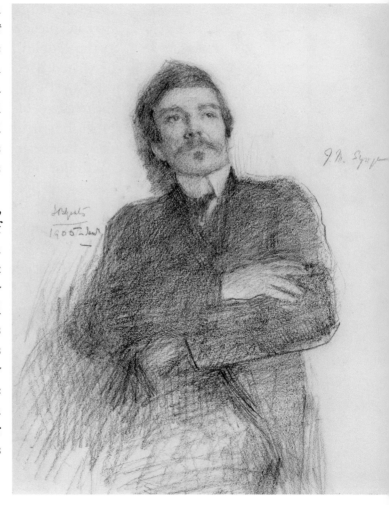

John Millington Synge by John Butler Yeats

Frank Fay (1870–1931) was an actor and, later, with his brother William, a founder member of the Abbey Theatre. The Abbey was an amalgam of the brothers' own Irish National Dramatic Company and the Irish Literary Theatre, and they were central in the evolution of the Abbey School of Acting. Unfortunately, due to disagreements with the other Abbey directors in 1908, the Fays left Dublin for the United States. William Fay moved to London, where he acted in theatre and in films: he played the bookseller in the film *Oliver Twist*. Frank settled in Dublin again after touring England with minor theatrical companies and made a living as a producer and teacher.

24 September 1904

G.H. Carpenter
E. Carpenter
G.C. Smith
E.W. Bateman
M.K. Bateman   *All of Rathgar, Dublin*

Rev. Dr George Herbert Carpenter (1865–1939) was born in London and, after studying at King's College London and the Royal College of Science for Ireland, became an assistant naturalist at the Dublin Museum of Natural History. In the same year as he visited McGuirk's, he was appointed Professor of Zoology at the Royal College of Science for Ireland, where he stayed until the change of government in 1922, after which, facilitated by provisions in the Anglo-Irish Treaty, he was able to transfer to the Manchester Museum as Keeper. He was editor of *The Irish Naturalist* for thirty years as well as being secretary of the Royal Zoological Society of Ireland and the Royal Irish Academy.

8 October 1904

H.G. Thompson	*Clonskeagh Castle*
E. Thompson	*ditto*
Frida K. Thompson	*ditto*
C. Eileen Galbraith	*Powerscourt Rectory*
A. Bowan	*County Kerry*
Ethel Georgina Hinde	*Co. Wicklow*
Stanley W. Kemp	*TCD [Trinity College Dublin]*
George P. Farran	*Templeogue*

The three Thompsons who give their address as Clonskeagh Castle are probably the children of Dublin solicitor George William Thompson.

Eileen Galbraith (1881–1946) was the daughter of the Venerable Archdeacon Galbraith, Rector of Powerscourt. She was a missionary in Africa and a teacher in Sudan before enrolling as a nurse with the Red Cross in France in 1916. After WWI, she married Dr Kenneth Fraser, and they set up a hospital and mission in Lui, Sudan. Eileen died in Nairobi in 1946.

Stanley W. Kemp (1882–1945) was a marine biologist and had attended Trinity College Dublin a few years after George P. Farran. The year before his visit to McGuirk's, he was hired as an assistant naturalist in the fisheries branch of the Department of Agriculture and Technical Instruction, in which capacity he probably met Farran. In 1910, he went to India, where he became the superintendent of the Zoological Survey in 1916. On his return to England in 1924, he was appointed Director of Research to the Discovery Committee, and over the next decades oversaw the collection by the *Discovery* (Robert Scott's ship) and other vessels of research results that filled thirty-eight volumes dedicated to oceanographic, biological and geographical data in the South Atlantic. He was acknowledged in his lifetime as Britain's foremost expert in marine biology.

George Philip Farran (1876–1949) studied natural science at Trinity College Dublin, graduating with a gold medal. His studies continued with a group of young scientists studying fisheries under Ernest Holt, who had brought, on behalf of the Royal Dublin Society, a mast-less brigantine named *Saturn* to the coast of Connemara to act as a floating laboratory. Farran became a greatly respected plankton scientist, widely published in the subject and consulted by scientists all over the world, eventually becoming Chief Inspector of Fisheries in Ireland. He died at his home in Templeogue.

Eileen and Kenneth Fraser in Lui, Sudan, with Sudanese people who had been injured by lions

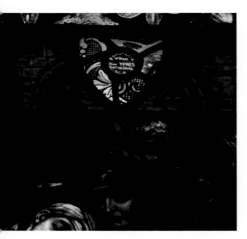

Detail of the French Family Window,
St Patrick's Cathedral, Dublin

20 November 1904

E.J. French   *St Anns, Donnybrook*
O.B. Daly   *23 Lr Hatch Street, Dublin*
Walked from Brittas by Kilbride Camp over Kippure.

We know more about E.J. French's sons than we do about him. In 1904, he had two sons, Claude, aged twenty-three, Charles, aged twelve, and a stepson, Bernard, who was ten. All three died during WWI. Charles was a lieutenant in the Royal Dublin Fusiliers when he was killed in action in Belgium in April 1915. Claude was a captain in the Royal Irish Regiment, and died from wounds received in action in June 1915. Bernard was in the Welsh Fusiliers when he died in action near Ypres in February 1916. The 'French Family Window' in St Patrick's Cathedral, Dublin, was erected by the young men's parents to commemorate them. Attributed to Joshua Clarke, father of the stained-glass artist Harry Clarke, the composition includes fragments of glass from the damaged Ypres Cathedral in Belgium, brought back to Dublin by one of the French sons while on leave.

1905

24 April 1905
Robert J. Rowlette
C.G. Clarke
C.E.R. Rice
W.E. O'Brien

Robert James Rowlette (1873–1944), born in Carncash, Co. Sligo, attended Sligo Grammar School and Trinity College Dublin, where he studied arts and medicine, receiving his medical degree in 1899. As a student, he excelled at long-distance running, and later became president of the Irish Amateur Athletic Association. He worked in the Rotunda, Dr Steevens', Jervis Street and Mercer's hospitals in

Dublin, and was King's Professor of Materia Medica and Pharmacy in Dublin University. He served in France during WWI, finishing the war as a lieutenant colonel. He was elected to Dáil Éireann in 1933, and was the first TD (*Teachta Dála*: Member of Parliament) to enter the Dáil without taking the Oath of Allegiance to the King, which had been abolished earlier in the year. With Oliver St. John Gogarty, he unsuccessfully opposed a Bill to prohibit the import and sale of contraceptives, arguing that it would lead to a rise in abortion, infanticide and venereal disease. In 1942, he got into a public controversy with Archbishop John Charles McQuaid about the provision of special treatment for tuberculosis sufferers. During WWII, he worked to prepare for the mass casualties that might happen in Ireland from air raids. He was a prolific writer and editor, author of *The Medical Press and Circular, 1839–1939*, and Dublin correspondent for *The Lancet*. An active member of many societies, he was elected president of the Royal College of Physicians of Ireland in 1940. A medical journal obituary suggested that his death in 1944 was due to overwork.

21 May 1905
William J. Mullin MB [Bachelor of Medicine]
Dunedin, New Zealand
William S. Haughton MD [Doctor of Medicine]
Dublin

William S. Haughton (1869–1951) was born in Dublin and, after attending Abbey School, Tipperary, and Portora Royal School, Co. Fermanagh, entered Trinity College Dublin, from where he graduated in medicine (with a gold medal) in 1894. When the German engineer and physicist Wilhelm Röntgen discovered X-rays in 1895, Haughton, a keen photographer, swiftly built his own X-ray machine, which produced films that compare well with modern examples. He became a pioneer in the science of X-rays

Wilhelm Röntgen and a patient in a nineteenth-century illustration

LA MÉDECINE

in Ireland and was president of the Radiological Society of Ireland since its foundation in 1932. In WWI, he joined the British Army and rose to the rank of major in the Royal Army Medical Corps. A Fellow of the British Orthopaedic Association and an honorary member of the International Society of Orthopaedic Surgeons, he kept himself fit with outdoor activities such as walking, cycling, yachting and rowing.

9 June 1905
Mr & Mrs W.P. Geoghegan
Carl Fuchs   *Manchester*

The Geoghegans of Rockfield House, Newtownpark Avenue, Blackrock, were collectors and keen patrons of the arts, and brought many distinguished musicians to Ireland to perform, including the German cellist Carl Fuchs.

William Purser Geoghegan (1843–1935) was Master Brewer at the Guinness Brewery, 1880–97, and, with others, was instrumental in bringing twenty-five 'modern' pictures to Dublin in 1906, forming the nucleus of what would become the Hugh Lane Gallery.

Carl Fuchs (1865–1951) was a German cellist. He had studied music under the celebrated cellist Bernhard Cossman, and through him came to know Clara and Robert Schuman. In 1886, in St Petersburg, he played in the orchestra under Anton Rubinstein, founder of the St Petersburg Conservatory, and met the composer Tchaikovsky. Invited to play in Manchester, he eventually settled down there, becoming Professor of Violoncello when the Royal Manchester College of Music was founded in 1893. He was interned on a visit to Germany in 1914 when the war broke out but returned to Manchester in 1919 and resumed his professorship, in which position he remained until his retirement in 1942.

7 July 1905
Cecil G. MacDowell

Greenfield,
Claremont Road,
Sandymount

Cecil Grange MacDowell (1880–1926) was born in Carlow. He worked as a draughtsman in Dublin Corporation but was also a skilled musician who played the organ at the church of Saint John the Evangelist in Sandymount. Around 1910, he became involved in the Irish nationalist movement and began to use the Irish version of his name, Cathal MacDubhghaill. He wrote a number of patriotic songs, and joined the local battalion when the Irish Volunteers was formed. At the beginning of WWI, his brothers, Robert, Donald and Raymond, enlisted in the British Army and his sister Florence served in the Voluntary Aid Detachment in France. Cathal decided upon a different course, however; he converted to Catholicism and during the 1916 Rising was part of the garrison at Bolands Mill, under Éamon de Valera. He was subsequently interned in Frongoch internment camp in Wales where he contracted tuberculosis, from which he never fully recovered.

After his release in 1917, he devised the musical arrangement for 'Amhrán na bhFiann' ('The Soldier's Song'), written by Peadar Kearney with music by Pádraig Ó hAonaigh. He toured the country accompanying baritone Edward O'Connor-Cox at nationalist gatherings. In 1921, he married Maeve Kavanagh, a republican poet who wrote, among other revolutionary works, poems to dissuade Irishmen from joining the British Army. Cathal set many of her poems to music. His health was poor, however, and Maeve took him to the south of France in 1926 seeking an improvement, but he fell from his hotel window and died.

A watercolour of Frongoch by Cathal MacDubhghaill

9 July 1905

W.J. Barden	*Ranelagh*
Winnie Barden	*ditto*
Joseph P. Hendeson	*21 Gardiner Place, Dublin*
J.B. Malone	*9 Barnsley Park, Ranelagh*

I must remark that I was treated very badly. I actually had to eat dry bread, a friend of mine having eaten all the butter.

James Bernard Malone was the father of the better-known J.B. (John Bernard) Malone, and he signed in (and left a humorous comment) with his Barden cousins, including Winnie, whom the young John Bernard had stayed with in Rathgar when he moved from England, aged eighteen. James Bernard's handwriting so resembles that of his son J.B. that it is uncanny. Twenty-eight years later, J.B., probably unaware that his father's signature was also in the book, signed himself as Jack Malone.

15 July 1905
Rev. Joseph Hartnett SJ [Society of Jesus]
Rev. W. Doyle SJ

Rev. Willie Doyle SJ

Rev. William Doyle (1873–1917) was born in Dalkey, Co. Dublin, and entered the Jesuit novitiate in Rathfarnham at the age of eighteen. The students and staff often walked in the nearby Dublin Mountains and he may have walked from Rathfarnham this day. On the outbreak of WWI, he was one of thirty-two Irish Jesuit chaplains to enlist in the British Army, and he was sent to France in 1915 with the Irish Fusiliers and other Irish regiments. He soon developed a reputation for fearlessness under fire, risking his life countless times giving solace to wounded and dying men on the battlefield. He served through a number of battles, including the Battle of the Somme, but was killed at Passchendaele in August 1917 while assisting wounded soldiers in no-man's-land. He was recommended for the Victoria Cross but did not receive it, due, it is said, to the 'triple disqualification of being Irish, a Catholic and a Jesuit'. He was, however, awarded the Military Cross for valour.

22 August 1905

The Misses Empsons	*Firmount, Kilternan*
Always glad to come here	
Mrs Arthur Allen	*Cheltenham*
Cadet C.H. Allen RN	*Royal Naval College*
	Osborne, I [Isle] of Wight

Scenery and Frockens [sic] ripping!

Fifteen-year-old Cadet C.H. Allen (*b.* 1890) was referring, in his comment, to fraughans, or wild blueberries, for which the surrounds of Lough Bray are still well known. Allen became an early submariner in the Royal Navy Submarine Service and was in command of submarine

E42 in April 1918 when it torpedoed the German battlecruiser SMS *Moltke*, for which he was awarded the Distinguished Service Order (DSO). He was promoted to commander in 1926, and was assistant to the King's Harbour Master, Portsmouth, in 1939. Relieved of duty in April 1940 for being 'incompetent in his job', he retired later that year, with the rank of captain.

26 December 1905
Miss Minnie Gamble
A.P. Hill
Fred. C. Gamble
W.B. Hill
Charles Gamble

Charles Gamble (*b.* 1868) was a solicitor and partner at Carruthers & Gamble of Fleet Street, Dublin. He was the author of *Solicitors in Ireland 1607–1901* (1921) and was, for a while, president of the Law Society. He married Gertrude King and they lived at various addresses in Rathgar and Killiney in Dublin. They had three children, but in 1894 Gertrude had an adulterous relationship, left Charles, and went to Canada. She applied for and was refused costs, custody of the youngest child and access to the others. In March of this year of his visit to McGuirk's, Gamble was granted a decree absolute and, knowing the law, also applied for damages for criminal conversation and was awarded £3,000. The following year, Gertrude kidnapped their son, Vyvian, from Woodtown Park School in Rathfarnham, but she was apprehended and arrested. Charles subsequently became engaged to a Miss Hill, daughter of Rev. Hill, the headmaster of Woodtown Park School, but instead married an English woman, Hephzibah Mary Prichard.

Frederick Charles Gamble was his brother. There seems little doubt that either A.P. or W.B. Hill was the Miss Hill to whom Charles was briefly engaged.

1906

8 April 1906

Alfred K. Moss　　　　*Dublin*
Don Piatt　　　　　　*Dublin*
A. O'Farrelly　　　　*Dublin*

2 June 1906

J. Hastings Otway
J.C. Dewhurst
W.G. Otway

James Hastings Otway (1879–1929) was educated at St Columba's College and Trinity College Dublin, where he studied civil engineering. After graduation, he worked as personal assistant to his father, also a civil engineer. Otway later worked in Egypt on the Egyptian State Railways. He married Mary Boileau in 1911 and they had two children. When WWI broke out, he joined the Ulster Division of Royal Engineers and saw action in France, where he was badly burned and gassed, severely affecting his health for the rest of his life. After the war, now a major, he was commandant of the Spike Island prison where Sinn Féin prisoners were held. Leaving the army in 1922, he worked on a number of major projects in England such as the Ford Motor Works in Dagenham and Wembley Stadium in London, but he eventually contracted tuberculosis as a result of his gassing and died aged fifty.

W.G. Otway may have been James Hastings's brother who joined the Royal Army Service Corps as a lieutenant in 1907.

29 June 1906
The King's Birthday
Amy L. Fox	*Brighton Square, Dublin*
Mabel Luke	*Grove Park, Rathmines*
Effie Luke	

14 August 1906
Alderman Cole
James Walker
Denis Carton
William Jones

Walter Leonard Cole (*d.* 1943) was a merchant, active Republican, and founding member of the Sinn Féin Printing & Publishing Company. He provided a meeting place at his Dublin home, 3 Mountjoy Square, for activists such as Tom Clarke, Patrick Pearse, James Connolly and Seán MacDermott (all of whom were executed after the 1916 Rising). He also hosted meetings of the early Dáil when it was driven underground in 1919. He was elected to Dáil Éireann in 1922 as a pro-Treaty candidate.

James Walker was a Dublin printer, owner of The Royal Colour Printing Works and the first in Ireland to operate a colour printing press. He was also one of the owners of the publishing house Sealy Bryers & Walker of Abbey Street, which also had a London branch.

April 1907

I gave her one kiss, one kiss one
I gave her one kiss, one kiss one
I gave her one kiss, and she said we have just
*   begun*
So we went kissing on, kissing on.

I gave her kisses two, kisses two
I gave her kisses two, kisses two
I gave her kisses two, and she said this will not do
So we went kissing on, kissing on.

I gave her kisses three, kisses three
I gave her kisses three, kisses three
I gave her kisses three, and she gave them back to
*   me*
So we went kissing on, kissing on.

I gave her kisses four, kisses four,
I gave her kisses four, kisses four,
I gave her kisses four, and she said I want some
*   more,*
So we went kissing on, kissing on.
Etc-etc-etc.

Magazine illustration by Fred Pegram, 1907

This flighty, anonymous entry suggests that times are changing and that the Victorian period is being left behind.

Regimental cap badge of the Royal
Inniskilling Fusiliers, *c.*1914

9 June 1907

| *Edward Read* | Foxrock |
| *Herbert St. G. Stewart* | Foxrock |

Herbert St George Stewart (1888–1932) was born in Kilkenny, where his father, Captain Hugh Stewart, formerly of the Cheshire Regiment, was Governor of Kilkenny Prison. At the time of his visit, Herbert was residing in the family home, 'Hatley', on Kerrymount Avenue in Foxrock, Co. Dublin. He joined the Royal Inniskilling Fusiliers at the outbreak of WWI and survived the war.

21 June 1907

J. Swift Joly

Signing with a flourish, the lone walking visitor, John Swift Joly (1876–1943), was born in Athlone, and is thought to have been a descendant of the famous Irish satirist Jonathan Swift's uncle, Godwin Swift. He attended The High School in Rathgar, followed by Trinity College Dublin, where he excelled in experimental science, chemistry, physics, botany and zoology, and in 1902 he graduated in medicine, obstetrics, and surgery. In 1904, he won a travelling scholarship that allowed him to work in the Kocher clinic in Berne. In this year of his visit to McGuirk's, he moved to London and became a distinguished urologist. During WWI, he joined the Royal Army Medical Corps and served in Egypt and Palestine. After the war, he took an active part in professional societies and wrote a number of learned papers. He was an expert photographer, and his favourite pastime was climbing in the Alps: he climbed Dent Blanche, one of the highest peaks in Switzerland, when he was sixty-one, and his alpine photographs are remarkable. His elder brother, Charles Jasper Joly, was the Royal Astronomer of Ireland, and his second cousin, John Joly, was Professor of Geology at Trinity College Dublin.

5 July 1907
F.G. Prideaux
R.E.L. Maunsell
Mrs R.E.L. Maunsell   *Inchicore, Dublin*

Richard Edward Lloyd Maunsell (1868–1944) was born in Raheny, Co. Dublin. He attended The Royal School in Armagh, followed by Trinity College Dublin, where he studied law. His main interest was railway engineering, however, and, when a student, he became an apprentice at the Inchicore Works in Dublin. Later he worked on the Lancashire and Yorkshire Railway, gaining experience as a draughtsman and as a locomotive foreman. He spent two years working for the East Indian Railway before returning to Inchicore in 1896 as works manager. Appointed locomotive superintendent in 1911, he created design teams to produce easy-to-maintain locomotives and was responsible for several important innovations and patents in locomotive design. He was awarded a CBE for his work during WWI.

Caricature of J.M. Synge by William Orpen, 1907

The McGuirks sometimes also took in lodgers. The playwright J.M. Synge is likely to have stayed with them for about four weeks in June and July 1907. In January 1905, seventeen-year-old Maire O'Neill, whose stage name was Molly Allgood, played a small part in his play *The Well of Saints*. She had worked as a shop girl in Switzers department store, but wanted to follow her sister, Abbey actor Sara Allgood, onto the stage. When Sara was selected for an important role in *The Well of Saints*, she managed to get an audition for her sister. As Synge coached her for a part in the revival of his play, *Riders to the Sea*, in 1906, he and Molly fell in love. He kept their relationship secret: it would not have been correct for a director of the Abbey to form a liaison with an actor, and his family would not have approved of the age difference and that Molly was a Catholic.

Molly Allgood, photographed *c.*1913

In June 1907, Molly and her sister boarded for a few weeks with the Dunne family in Glencree, near where Knockree Youth Hostel is today, a few kilometres down the valley from McGuirk's, where Synge was staying. In this way, Synge and Molly were able to spend time together, strolling and climbing the heathery hillsides.

It was to be their last summer together. A number of passages in Synge's book *In Wicklow and West Kerry* give glimpses of his time in McGuirk's that summer:

> a moan and rumble of thunder coming nearer, at times with a fierce and sudden crash. The bracken has a nearly painful green in the strangeness of the light … There is a strange depression about the cottage to-night. The woman of the house is taken ill and has got into bed beside her mother-in-law, who is over ninety, and is wandering in her mind. The man of the house has gone away ten miles for medicine, and I am left with the two children, who are playing silently about the door.
>
> The larches in the haggard are dripping heavily with damp, and the hens and geese, bewildered with the noise and gloom, are cackling with uneasy dread. All one's senses are disturbed. As I walk backwards and forwards, a few yards above and below the door, the little stream I do not see seems to roar out of the cloud. Every leaf and twig is heavy with drops, and a dog that has passed with a sad-eyed herd looked wet and draggled and afraid.

It's as if all the sadness, bewilderment and fear he sensed in the animals was his own. Tom McGuirk, Mary Jane McGuirk's grandson, told me that his grandmother hadn't got into bed beside her mother-in-law because she was ill, but because she was mortally afraid of the thunder and lightning storm that was raging. His father, Arthur, one of the two children, remembered Synge leaning out the open window to watch the storm, and his grandmother being terrified that 'the gintleman would be struck dead'.

Although he had often boarded in peasant cottages, this must have been an ascetic experience for Synge, as he slept on a 'press bed' that was kept in a cupboard (or 'press') and taken out at night. It can't have been comfortable, consisting of canvas stretched over a wooden frame, with no proper mattress; it is clear that Synge suffered for his love. The thunderstorms continued that July after Synge had left Glencree, as we see from the following entry.

24 July 1907

Caitlín Ní Dubhghaill   *Meirbhthe, Blath Cliath*

James Tallon
Seosamh Ua Cleirigh   *Páirc na Cabhraighe*
Proinnsias Ní Dubhghaill (a bhean)

A leithéid de thóirneach & teinntreach ní fhacathasagus a bhí ann indiú annso ag Loch Bhrí. Is baoghlach go gcaitheam go léir fanacht annso anocht. Más eadh, caithfidh seisear ná mór – seisear againn du lag codhladh i dtig na gcearc.

This translates roughly as:

Such thunder and lightning I have never seen or heard as that, here, today at Loch Bray. I fear we must all stay here tonight. If so, the six of us will have to go to sleep in the hen house!

The engines *Hibernia* and *Vauxhall*, which pulled the first recorded passenger trains on the Dublin and Kingstown Railway in 1834

12 September 1907
A.S. Pim

We arrived at Lough Bray (passed Pluck's Pub on the way)
And bathed in its cooling fountains
We intend to come back here some other fine day
And bask in the shade of its mountains.

A.S. Pim was a member of the Pim family, Quakers who originally settled in Mountmellick, Co. Laois, in 1659. They became associated with a variety of commercial enterprises in Ireland including brewing, soap-making, bacon and tobacco. One branch moved to Dublin in 1795, and James Pim was involved in building Ireland's first railway line, between Dublin and Kingstown (Dún Laoghaire), which was opened in 1834. Pim's Department Store opened on South Great George's Street in Dublin in the 1850s: it closed in the 1970s and a modern office block was built on the site.

Pluck's pub in Kilmacanogue, established in the early nineteenth century as a coaching inn, is still in business today.

1908

4 July 1908
Constance F. Alexander
Olive L. Alexander
Alfred Tahapan Alexander MD

The fourth day of a walking tour – from Rathgar via Lough Bray, Sally Gap, Lough Tay, Roundwood, Lough Dan, Laragh, Glendalough and Glenmacnass, arriving here yesterday at 7pm. Mrs McGuirk looked after us in the best possible manner and made us most comfortable. The male member being accommodated in the wooden shanty where he slept like a top. We regret having now to return to Dublin.

3 August 1908
Robt. Leask
J.J. Haydock
Harold G. Leask

From Curragh Camp to summit Kippure thence via Eagles Crag to Lough Bray. Slaked a £5 thirst at Mrs McGuirk's.

Sheep shearing at McGuirk's

Robert Heddle Leask (1838–1924) was a Scottish architect and engineer who came to Ireland to spend two years working for Bindon Blood Stoney's groundbreaking engineering firm before opening his own civil engineering practice in Dublin in 1874. The Stoney family was a fascinating one. Bindon's brother, George Johnstone Stoney, was the physicist who coined the term 'electron' and his nieces were Edith Anne Stoney, a pioneering medical physicist, and Florence Stoney, the first female radiologist in Britain or Ireland.

Harold Graham Leask (1882–1964) was Robert's son, an architect, antiquarian and author who became better known than his father. In 1909, he took up employment in the Office of Public Works as a temporary assistant surveyor, and went on to be involved in the creation of many well-known Dublin buildings, including the Custom House (after the fire of 1921) and the Land Registry Office. Promoted in 1920 to the rank of assistant architect, he became Inspector of Ancient Monuments in 1923. He was widely published in learned journals, as well as writing *Irish Castles and Castellated Houses* (1944) and *Irish Churches and Monastic Buildings* (1955), which remain the standard works on the subjects.

The Leask party left this sketch in August 1908

The mention of the Curragh Camp in the walkers' comment is puzzling: while Harold Leask was twenty-five in 1908, his father was close to seventy, and while he would, no doubt, have been capable of climbing the nearby Kippure peak, starting from the Curragh seems doubtful. It is more likely that they walked from Kilbride Camp, west of Kippure.

12 August 1908
Peadar UaBanáin

Molaim go h-ard an teach so & bean an tighe. Tá a teach ar fheabhas & a cuid tae & arán isailr é ná rud dá leithéid sin a chonnaiceas arriamh. Tiucfaidh mé thar nais tapa féin mar is fíor gaedhal bean a tighe & cuirfeadh sí áthas ar aoinne bheith ag caint léithi. Bail ó Dhia uirthi.

Peadar UaBanáin's note translates as:

Peter Bannon
High praise for this house and the landlady. Her house is perfect and her tea and bread better than I've ever tasted. I'll be back here soon because this woman is a true Gael and it's a pleasure for anyone to chat with her. God bless her.

31 August 1908
Robert C. Morrison Lieut. 1st Kingstown BB
Frank Godkin Snow Lieut. B Company Batt. 2, London

The Boys' Brigade ('BB') is a Christian Youth organisation founded in Glasgow in 1883 by Sir William Alexander Smith. While it was intended to be interdenominational, it is usually regarded in Ireland as a Protestant organisation.

30 January 1909

*Richard Brew Joyce, G.S. Rly [Great Southern
Railways], Dublin*

*Hurrah for the turf fire – Reminds me of Banagher, King's
Co. [now Co. Offaly]*

There is a tendency to judge, from the assured flamboyance of the handwriting, that the writer had a high status in society, but I frequently found that this was not necessarily true. This entry was written in beautiful copper-plate handwriting but Richard Brew Joyce was not a physician or a judge, but a railway clerk with Great Southern Railways. He did, however, manage to leave £201-10s.-8d. (about £24,000 today) in his will to his friend Arthur V. Chandler, a salesman.

17 March 1909

Edward J. Garland TCD
Samuel A. Ryder

Edward Joseph Garland (1886–1960) was a rare example of a Roman Catholic Belvedere College student attending Trinity College Dublin (TCD) at this time. Between 1870 and 1970, Catholics were banned by their Church from attending Trinity without a special dispensation, which usually had to be granted by the Archbishop of Dublin. Garland qualified as a teacher and spent a few years teaching in Ireland before emigrating to Canada in 1909, the year of his visit to McGuirk's. He settled in Alberta and took up farming, becoming politically prominent as a founder member of the United Farmers of Alberta movement. He later joined the Canadian Department of External Affairs. In 1946, he was Canada's Acting

Belvedere College, Dublin, around the turn of the twentieth century

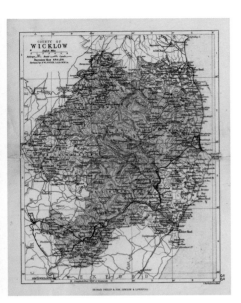

Map of Wicklow from *Irish Topographical Botany* by Dublin Naturalists' Field Club member Robert Lloyd Praeger

High Commissioner to Ireland and, by 1949, was the Canadian Ambassador to Ireland.

1 August 1909
Dublin Naturalists' Field Club
Mrs Harford
J. Harford
Miss Garner
W.F. Gunn
Roycroft
J. de W. Hinch

The Dublin Naturalists' Field Club were frequent visitors to McGuirk's; John de Witt Hinch (1875–1931) was an assistant in the National Library of Ireland at the time of this visit, but his geological studies led to his appointment as Superintendent of Maps and Collections in 1919, and as a geologist in the Geological Survey of Ireland in 1921. He contributed a number of learned papers to *The Irish Naturalist*. In 1909, the club counted among its members Nathaniel Colgan, author of *Flora of the County Dublin: Flowering Plants, Higher Cryptogams, and Characeae* (1904), and Robert Lloyd Praeger.

2 August 1909
Rev. F.M. Browne SJ	*Dublin*
H. Aquinas Flannery	*Dublin*

Francis Patrick Mary Browne (1880–1960) was a Jesuit priest who became posthumously famous for his photographic work. His visit to McGuirk's was three years before he sailed aboard RMS *Titanic* on her maiden voyage from Southampton, but had the good fortune to disembark at Cobh. At the age of nine he was orphaned and brought up by an uncle, Robert Browne, who was Bishop of Cloyne, and while the bishop's influence must have led Francis towards the priesthood, it was a gift from the bishop of a camera that began his interest in photography. He attended the Royal University of Ireland, where he was a classmate of James Joyce: Joyce wrote him into *Finnegans Wake* as Mr Browne the Jesuit. He went on to study theology at Milltown Institute of Theology and Philosophy. In the year that he took tea at McGuirk's, he visited Rome with his uncle, and they had a private audience with Pope Pius X, who allowed Browne to take his photograph.

His uncle gave him a present of a ticket for the maiden voyage of the *Titanic*, from Southampton to Cobh in Cork, during which he photographed many parts of the ship and took the last pictures of the captain, Edward Smith, and various members of the crew. An American couple he met on the short voyage were so impressed with him that they offered to pay for the rest of the voyage to New York but, when Browne telegraphed his superior for permission, he received the swift reply ordering him to 'get off that ship'!

While serving during WWI as a chaplain to the Irish Guards, Browne was wounded five times and awarded the Military Cross and Bar, and the Croix de Guerre for his courage tending to casualties under fire. After the war, he continued with his priestly duties but found time to take photographs all over Ireland, as well as Australia and every port between there and Europe. When he died in 1960, his photographic work comprising more than 42,000 photographs lay forgotten in a metal trunk until discovered twenty-five years later. Since then, they have illustrated numerous publications. Unfortunately, although he visited McGuirk's on a number of occasions, he did not take any photographs there.

Rev. F.M. Browne, photographed by Fr Michael Garahy in 1939

The original Mrs McGuirk (Mary) died in 1910 and, during the summer of that year, with her daughter-in-law Mary Jane continuing her good work, the numbers of tourists from Britain calling at McGuirk's increased to comprise one-third of all the visitors.

14 May 1910

Harold G. Leask   *Dundalk*
Edwin Bradbury   *Dublin*

By 1910, Harold Graham Leask had evidently moved to Dundalk.

Edwin Bradbury (1875–1948), a frequent visitor to McGuirk's, was an English architect and engineer who came to Dublin in 1895 and set up his own practice there in 1905. He was a founder member of the Architectural Association of Ireland and its president in 1908. He lectured widely on architecture, and his drawings were often published in *The Irish Builder*. Apart from his architectural work, he is also known for inventing a new patented junction interceptor for drains, known as the Bradbury. He was an enthusiastic cyclist and that is probably how he arrived at McGuirk's on this day. In May 1910, he would have been working on designs for the Church of the Blessed Virgin in Ballyheigue, Co. Kerry.

23 May 1910

T.W. Lyster   *10 Harcourt Terrace, Dublin*

Drawing of Thomas William Lyster
by John Butler Yeats

Thomas William Lyster (1855–1922) was the director of the National Library of Ireland from 1895 until 1920, when Robert Lloyd Praeger took over. He was editor of the *Intermediate School Anthology*, in which the works of Goldsmith and Ferguson inspired the schoolboy James Joyce, who later used Lyster as a model for the 'quaker librarian' in *Ulysses*. Oliver St. John Gogarty described Lyster in *As I was Going Down Sackville Street* as 'a lovable man, and I felt grateful when he beckoned us to his Librarian's office. His brown beard moved a little as he smiled, with cheeks as fresh as a child's, while his whispering, diffident, feminine voice invited us.'

6 June 1910
Mrs Standish O'Grady

Mrs Standish O'Grady (*b.* 1850), née Margaret Allen Fisher, was the wife of Standish James O'Grady, author, journalist and historian, who is often referred to as the 'Father of the Irish Literary Renaissance'. She claimed to have psychic powers and is said to have conducted séances in their Dublin home. She had three sons with O'Grady, one of whom, Hugh Art O'Grady, wrote a biography of his father, *Standish James O'Grady: The Man and the Writer* (1929).

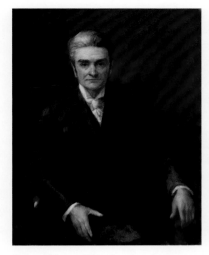

Standish James O'Grady, painted in 1904 by John Butler Yeats

23 July 1910
C.B. Gotch
Phyllis April Gotch   *Newlyn, Cornwall*

Caroline Burland Gotch (1854–1945), née Yates, was born in Liverpool and studied at the Slade School of Art in London and the Académie Julian in Paris. She married painter and book illustrator Thomas Cooper Gotch in 1881, and their daughter Phyllis was born in 1882. They travelled extensively, including a trip to Australia, but settled in Newlyn in Cornwall, where they were founding members of the St Ives Art Club. Caroline painted and exhibited regularly at the Royal Academy of Arts in London and with the Royal Society of British Artists and was awarded medals at the Paris Salon in 1897 and 1898. She probably came to know Ireland when she exhibited at the Royal Hibernian Academy in 1879.

Phyllis April Gotch (1882–1963), Caroline's daughter, was born in France and brought up in Newlyn. She wrote and illustrated two children's books and studied singing under the accomplished opera singer Charles Santley, concentrating on classical works and traditional songs. In the year of her visit to McGuirk's, she had put together a stage show and adopted a stage name, changing from Phyllis Marian Gotch to Phyllis April Gotch. She was married three times, marrying her third husband, barrister Jocelyn Bodilly, in 1935: he was thirty years her junior. He became Chief Justice of the Western Pacific, and she died in Hong Kong in 1963.

Motherhood by Caroline Gotch, *c.*1895

1911

6 June 1911

Annie Foster	*8 Charleton Terrace, Antrim Road, Belfast*
Edith Best	*35 Vesey Place, Dublin*
Mr & Mrs Lumus Jones	*Alderley Edge, Cheshire*

Edith Best (1865–1950), née Oldham, was born in Dublin, the youngest of fourteen children. Her sister Alice was the first woman to graduate with a university degree in either Great Britain or Ireland, and her brother was the first Professor of National Economics at University College Dublin. Edith studied at the Royal Irish Academy of Music (RIAM) in Dublin and the Royal College of Music in London, and after graduation in 1887 joined the RIAM as a piano teacher. She was a founding member of Feis Ceoil, an annual competitive festival of Irish music, working with Eoin MacNeill and the Gaelic League to promote it. She was vice-president of the Feis Ceoil Association from 1905 until her death.

16 July 1911

Julia O'Sullivan, 2 Mount Pleasant Terrace,
Rathmines, gave an unexpected visit to Lough
Bray Cottage, Glencree and got a real Irish
welcome from the owner, Mrs McGuirk.

There is a story that Glencree
Is nothing but hard labour,
But seeing is believing
And all visitors should encourage their
Friends to call at Glencree
And if they do not wish to be entertained
At the Reformatory
They are certain to be well catered
At Lough Bray Cottage.

Edith Best by Sarah Cecilia Harrison, 1924

The reference to 'hard labour' presumably relates to the nearby Glencree Reformatory that was housed in the former military barracks and run by the Missionary Oblates of Mary Immaculate. Here juvenile offenders were sentenced to spend time being trained in a variety of trades and occupations so that, when released, they would have the possibility of earning a living, rather than continue in crime – that was the ostensible objective.

1912

14 April 1912

J. Hearne	Waterford
D. Jennings	Dublin
R. Jennings	Waterford

Came in the motor.

To which some later visitor added 'Swank!'

The J. Hearne here was probably John Hearne of John Hearne, Building Contractors. The firm was founded in Waterford by his father, also John Hearne, around 1860, and from modest beginnings it grew to be one of the region's largest building firms. Among the major works carried out by the company were Mount Sion School in Waterford and the spire and nave of the Pugin-designed St. Mary's Cathedral in Killarney, which was completed in 1907.

7 June 1912
Henry Seymour
C.S. Downey
E.M. Murphy
J. Shelly

All of University College Dublin completed their Bathymetric Survey of Lower Lough Bray.

Theodolite manufactured before 1915

This may have only been a preliminary survey, because Henry Joseph Seymour (*b.* 1873) did not publish his results until 1939, when he gives the dates of the survey as 1915 and 1916, rather than 1912. He also noted that the survey required the undivided attention of a team of four: a skilled oarsman, a sounder to manipulate the sounding line, a note-taker, and someone to attend to the theodolite, presumably onshore. He warned, strangely, of the inaccessibility of the lakes due to their remoteness from roads and high elevation. The team he listed were engineering students attending UCD at the time.

20 August 1912
Joyce Collis
Bob Collis
Jack Collis　　　　　　　　　*Killiney, Co. Dublin*

These three names are written in the same hand, most likely that of Joyce Collis. Although only twelve years old at the time, Bob Collis is Robert Collis (1900–1975) of Kilmore House, Killiney, here with his twin brother Jack (John Stewart Collis) and one of their two sisters, Joyce. Although Lough Bray is over 20 km from their home in Killiney, they often undertook long family cycles into the Wicklow Mountains for picnics. Robert was educated at Rugby School and, while back in Dublin on Easter holidays some years later, during the 1916 Rising, he wore a Red Cross armband and worked in the streets and the Meath Hospital, tending to wounded civilians. He joined the British Army in 1918 as an officer cadet, but resigned in 1919 to study medicine at Cambridge and, later, at King's College Hospital in London. Returning to Ireland in the late 1920s, he worked in the National Children's Hospital in Harcourt Street and for Bethel Solomons, Master of the Rotunda Hospital, where he worked on the development of a special incubator for premature babies, and a special neonatal unit that was built in the hospital grounds.

Constance Markievicz seated on the right in a Red Cross ambulance during the 1916 Rising

At the end of WWII, he entered Bergen-Belsen concentration camp with the Red Cross, after the camp's liberation. He adopted two children from the camp. He founded Cerebral Palsy Ireland and encouraged Christy Brown in his writing, helping to get Brown's first book, *My Left Foot*, published in 1954. He wrote many influential papers on paediatrics and child health, as well as an autobiography, *The Silver Fleece* (1941), and a play about poverty in Dublin called *Marrowbone Lane* (1943). Living in Nigeria from 1957 to 1971, he wrote two books about his experiences there. He died after a fall from a horse in Co. Wicklow.

John Stewart Collis (1900–1985), Robert's twin ('Jack'), was a highly successful author and biographer and a pioneer of the ecology movement. He was also educated at Rugby but went on to Oxford. His biographical studies included works on George Bernard Shaw, Leo Tolstoy and Christopher Columbus. His most memorable works were on the subject of country life, based on his experience as a farm labourer in the Land Army during WWII, and his autobiography of 1971, *Bound upon a Course*, established his reputation as an ecologist, earning acclaim from the British writer and academic Robert Macfarlane.

21 August 1912
Nannie Griffin and Frances Jackson & party,
Ballybawn Camp, Kilmacanoge, Dublin

Tommy McGuirk gave us a splendid tea having lunched outside the fishing lodge and having seen some very nice motors.

All we know of Frances Jackson is her sketch of Tommy McGuirk.

Left: Frances Jackson's sketch of Tommy McGuirk, August 1912; right: sketch (subject unknown), September 1912

8 September 1912
Leonard Strong

McGuirk's was decidedly a teetotal establishment, a fact that was occasionally commented upon, as with the character in this sketch, depicting a thirsty Leonard Strong. I was tempted to believe that this was the prolific English novelist, critic and poet L.A.G. Strong, who often visited Dalkey and had an Irish mother, but the person depicted does not look like the more famous Englishman.

1913

16 June 1913
Mr & Mrs S. W. Le Bas   *S. C. Rd.*
[South Circular Road], Dublin

Samuel William Le Bas was a silversmith and a great-grandson of James Le Bas, an English silversmith who came to Ireland around 1800 and set up his workshop at Little Strand Street in Dublin. His firm became particularly known for their chasing of foliage, birds and flowers.

23 June 1913
Pierce Purcell
Thos Dillon   *per shanks with care*

Pierce Purcell (1881–1968) was born in Kilkenny and educated at Castleknock College, Dublin, and the School of Engineering at Trinity College Dublin, where he graduated with first-class honours, receiving the gold medal in experimental physics and chemistry in 1903 and a master's degree in engineering in 1908. After a period in London, he was appointed Professor of Civil Engineering at University College Dublin in 1910, a post he held for forty-one years. He also had a private practice and was involved in the design of bridges and drainage schemes.

Thomas Dillon (1884–1971) was born in Enniscrone, Co. Sligo. He studied at Clongowes Wood College, Co. Kildare, where he received a scholarship to study medicine at Queen's College, Cork. He instead studied chemistry and physics, and was awarded an MA in chemistry in 1908 from the Royal College of Science for Ireland.

Sketch of the Military Road in the rain left by Ernest Corr in June 1913

23 June 1913
Effie & Ernest Corr, Dublin

From Lough Dan, via Laragh the Military Road and Sally Gap. After the thunder and rain of the Military Road the shelter and good cheer of Lough Bray cottage were refreshing.

James Ernest Corr attended the Metropolitan School of Art in Dublin and, after marrying Effie, settled down at Mountshannon Road in Kilmainham, where three years later their son Rodney was born. Ernest was an artist and studied metalwork under Percy Oswald Reeves, a skilled artist who taught enamelling and metalwork in the Metropolitan School of Art (which later became the National College of Art and Design) and whose designs for panels, jewellery, albums, war memorials, tabernacles and trophies were sought after by private collectors.

Unfortunately, more information is available on Rodney than on his parents: he died as a trainee pilot officer in the Royal Air Force (RAF) in 1942, when the pilot of the Bristol Blenheim light bomber he was in lost control on a practice bombing run and crashed. Of Ernest and his career, only a bronze plaque he produced in 1906 is mentioned in sources – which is a shame when we consider the accomplished sketch he left in the visitors' book on the day of his visit to McGuirk's – and, of his wife Effie, as is usual with wives in the visitors' books, nothing is recorded.

28 June 1913
S. Johnson   *Dublin*

There is no tea left to pass remarks about!

A day later, the same visitor left this, unusually for the time, somewhat risqué doggerel:

> *Mary had a little bear,*
> *To which she was very kind.*
> *And every place that Mary went*
> *You could see her bear behind.*

20 August 1913

J. T. Lemass   *Dublin*
Noel Lemass   *ditto*

This sketch of a typical Edwardian scene was left in the visitors' book on 5 July 1913

John Timothy Lemass (*d.* 1947), a draper, of Capel Street, Dublin, was the father of Noel Lemass and Seán Lemass, Taoiseach, 1959–66.

Noel Lemass (1897–1923) was sixteen at the time of this visit to McGuirk's: two years later, he joined the Irish Volunteers and was wounded during the 1916 Rising. He was promoted to captain in 1919, and spent time in Mountjoy, Derry, Kilkenny and Kilmainham gaols. With his younger brother, Seán, he took the anti-Treaty side in the Irish Civil War, acting as an intelligence officer for the IRA. He was captured by Free Staters and escaped on two occasions, but in July 1923, two months after the Civil War had ended, he was arrested again, tortured and murdered. It was not until October that his mutilated body was found hidden on the Featherbeds, a mile from McGuirk's.

2 September 1913

Judge Todd, Recorder of Londonderry
Miss Eileen Todd
Mrs Andrew Todd
Mr Drew Todd

Andrew Todd (*d.* 1920) was a native of Castlederg, Co. Tyrone, who practised at the Irish Bar before becoming a county court judge and later Recorder for Londonderry. His son, also called Andrew, was a distinguished physician and was capped three times playing rugby for Ireland. For 'great gallantry under fire' during WWI, he was awarded the Military Cross. Judge Andrew Todd's grandson, Richard Andrew Palethorpe Todd, was a captain in the Parachute Regiment, one of the first British soldiers, and perhaps the first Irishman, to land in Normandy on D-Day, 6 June 1944. After the war, as Richard Todd, he became a highly successful film star, starring in numerous films, including *The Dam Busters* in 1955 and *The Longest Day* in 1962, which was about the D-Day landings he had taken part in eighteen years before.

17 September 1913

Eileen Galbraith	*Africa*
Mabel Law	*Howth*
Hugh Lane	*London*
Ella Fry	*London*
Neenie Gogarty	*Dublin*
Oliver Gogarty	*Dublin*
Kathleen E. Stokes	*Dublin*
Helen Duncan	*Dublin*

Lower Lough Bray and Eagles Crag, Co. Wicklow

Oliver St. John Gogarty and a coterie of artistic and literary friends used to picnic, on occasion, beside Lower Lough Bray, close to McGuirk's, from where they obtained boiling water for making tea. Hampers of fine foods and wine were brought and a picnic laid out beside the lake. Gogarty gave an account of one of these picnics in his book *As I Was Going Down Sackville Street* (1937):

> By the granite outcrops the feast was spread. One of the rocks made a natural table with its flat top. Hampers

were unpacked. Hard by, a cottage provided hot water for those who cared for tea. The sun shone on the lead-bright water … The lake by which we lolled was a crater once. Our very table, tricked out with mica, was of igneous rock that told of old incredible cataclysms before men narrowed Time to be a measure of his years and superimposed his squabbles on the silver-shining granite that had reached eternal rest.

A hundred yards from the road by a path that borders a rivulet the edge of the lake is reached. An ancient crater makes three-quarters of an amphitheatre which opens to the south and the east. The lake lies deep within. Beyond, the semi-circular cup is dark green like the colour that invests Eternity. Pine-woods lie in a level to the right and hem a crescent of white sand.

Sir Hugh Lane by Sarah Cecilia Harrison

On this particular occasion, when poor weather prevented the party from picnicking in the open, they retired to McGuirk's for refreshments, where, crowded together in the small tea room, they signed their names in the visitors' book.

Eileen Galbraith must have been back in Ireland on holiday from her missionary work in Africa at the time of this visit.

Hugh Percy Lane (1875–1915), born in Cork, was an art dealer and collector. In 1908, he established the Dublin Municipal Gallery of Modern Art (now Dublin City Gallery The Hugh Lane), the first such gallery, it is said, in the world, and he was knighted in 1909 for his services to art. Just one month before his visit to McGuirk's, he had donated five paintings to the National Gallery of Ireland, of which he was elected director in February 1914; two months later, he donated works by El Greco, Veronese and Piazzetta. He drowned two years after this visit to Glencree, when RMS *Lusitania* was sunk by a U-boat off the coast of Cork in May 1915: his body was never recovered.

Neenie (Margaret/Martha) Gogarty, née Duane, was Oliver St. John Gogarty's wife, and they lived at 17 Earlsfort Terrace in Dublin, which Gogarty referred to as a 'kind of flophouse'. It was there that their first son, Oliver Duane Odysseus, was born in 1907.

Oliver St. John Gogarty (1878–1957) was an Irish author, poet, otolaryngologist, politician and conversationalist. He was educated at Mungret College, Limerick, which he didn't like, and then Stonyhurst College in England, still widely considered the United Kingdom's leading Catholic independent school: Gogarty described it as 'a religious jail'. Failing admission to the Royal University of Ireland due to his carousing, he was accepted by Trinity College Dublin and, while studying medicine there, became part of the Dublin literary set, winning the coveted Vice-Chancellor's prize for verse three times. James Joyce, W.B. Yeats and George Moore were among the writers and poets he mixed with. He married Margaret (Martha) Duane ('Neenie') in 1906, and qualified as a doctor in 1907. He spent a year in Vienna studying otolaryngology and, returning to Dublin, set up what was to become a successful practice. He treated rich and poor patients; the poor for free. He was close friends with Arthur Griffith and, aligning himself with the pro-Treaty government, was made a senator in 1922. He carried out the autopsy on Arthur Griffith, followed shortly after by that on Michael Collins, with whom he had also been friendly. He narrowly escaped assassination during the Civil War, after which his literary output, including three plays put on by the Abbey Theatre, increased. Suffering financial setbacks, however, and becoming disenchanted with Ireland, he moved to London in 1938, and then to the United States in 1939, where he died in 1957.

Ellen Duncan we have met before.

Ella Fry was a friend of Hugh Lane's from London, and bought one of Monet's paintings of Waterloo Bridge from the Parisian dealer Paul Durand-Ruel for the Dublin Municipal Gallery of Modern Art. She came to Lough Bray again with Gogarty in 1915.

Waterloo Bridge (1900) by Claude Monet

In common with many of the female visitors, I could find no trace of Mabel Law or Kathleen E. Stokes.

While Gogarty's group picnicked at Lough Bray, the largest industrial dispute in Ireland's history was going on only a few kilometres away: the 1913 Dublin Lockout. As many as 20,000 workers and their families were affected, suffering hunger and hardship until the Lockout ended in January 1914. The 1913 Dublin Lockout is not mentioned anywhere in the visitors' books.

1 November 1913
John W. Healy
Cecil B. McWeeney
John Dunn

Tea at Lough Bray cottage 'maketh a full man as doth reading' (Bacon up-to-date).

Mont Blanc by Félix Vallotton

John Healy (1895–1975) started walking in the Dublin and Wicklow mountains when he was seventeen. He studied medicine at University College Dublin, interning in St Vincent's Hospital, and graduated in October 1918. He went to England in November of that year and took up a temporary commission with the RAF, which allowed him to progress from hill walking to more serious climbing in the mountains of Wales and Cumberland. Healy never married, and his annual holidays were devoted almost exclusively to mountaineering and travel, particularly in Europe. He climbed the Matterhorn in 1924 and Mont Blanc in 1925. He was a member of the exclusive Alpine Club in London, and a founder member of the Irish Mountaineering Club.

Cecil Brazil McWeeney (*b.* 1896) was the second son of Edmond Joseph McWeeney, who was the first Professor of Pathology in Ireland at the Catholic University. Cecil's grandfather was Theophilus McWeeney, a highly regarded journalist and chief

Cecil McWeeney and John Healy on
Mullaghcleevaun, Co. Wicklow

reporter of *The Freeman's Journal*, and whose funeral procession was said to be the longest Dublin had ever seen at that time. Cecil McWeeney joined the British Army and fought in France, as did his brothers Theo and Desmond: all survived the war, and Cecil went on to a successful career as a journalist and editor.

John Healy kept diaries of all his excursions into the mountains, and his diary for this day described taking, with his two companions, the 8 am steam tram to Blessington from Terenure, and walking east via Moanbane to reach Mullaghcleevaun, Wicklow's second-highest mountain, at 1.30 pm. From there, they went north along the undulating summits of Duff Hill and Gravale to reach the Military Road at the Sally Gap, and continued north to Lough Bray. After their refreshments at McGuirk's, they returned to Terenure via the Featherbeds, completing a not inconsiderable mountain trek of around 56 km.

On another occasion, the companions came across a strange scene near McGuirk's, which John Healy described in his diary:

> It was close under the trees but when we emerged on to the Featherbed it became cool. The upper part of Seechon was covered with mist and when we saw the whole Kippure chain in the throes of black clouds, we began to suspect that Kippure would slip out of our reach again. A very definite line demarcated the region of the mist from the valley below. The latter looked very clear and sharp in details. The Military Road was in very bad condition. When approaching the top of the pass we were surprised to hear the sound of a brass band. Soon we came in sight of it on a bend of the road beyond and below us, and it was accompanied by a long line of dark figures behind. Such an appearance in the mountain solitudes, together with the unearthly sounds of the band that were interrupted and modified by the gust of wind, might well have been

regarded as a supernatural visitation. It was like a bit of one of Poe's tales of the Rugged Mountain. On passing this awe-inspiring battalion we found that it consisted of the young criminals of Glencree Reformatory.

Glencree Reformatory today, now the Glencree Centre for Peace & Reconciliation

1914

26 February 1914

Lilian M. Slade	*Sanderstead (Croydon, South London)*
Bethel Solomons	*Dublin*
Barbara Donovan	*Dublin*

Motto for the day 'Don't worry'.

Bethel Solomons (1885–1965) was a frequent caller to McGuirk's. Born into a prominent Jewish family in Dublin, his father was Maurice Solomons, an optician whose practice at 19 Nassau Street also served as his base as honorary consul of the Austro-Hungarian Empire. Maurice is described in Joyce's *Ulysses as* 'Striding past Finn's hotel Cashel Boyle O'Connor Fitzmaurice Tisdall Farrell stared through a fierce eyeglass across the carriages at the head of Mr M. E. Solomons in the window of the Austro-Hungarian viceconsulate.' Joyce must have had a particular interest in the Solomons family, because Bethel also got a mention, this time in *Finnegans Wake*: 'in my bethel of Solyman's I accouched their rotundaties and I turnkeyed most insultantly over raped lutetias in a lock'.

Solomons attended St Andrew's College (then located at St Stephen's Green, now located in Booterstown), and Trinity College Dublin, where he studied medicine. He was an accomplished rugby player: he played with Robert Collis and earned ten international

The young Bethel Solomons

caps for Ireland between 1908 and 1910. At the time of this visit to McGuirk's, Bethel Solomons was beginning a distinguished career specialising in obstetrics and gynaecology: he was Master of the Rotunda Hospital, 1926–33. He counted Arthur Griffith, founder of Sinn Féin, as a friend. His son Dr Michael Solomons was also a gynaecologist and pioneer of family planning in Ireland. Bethel's sister Estella Solomons was an accomplished painter and a member of Cumann na mBan during the 1916 Rising. In the early 1940s, when Mona McGuirk was pregnant with her son Tom, Bethel Solomons brought her into the Rotunda in order to look after her for the birth.

17 March 1914

E. Keith Eason	Dalkey
Patrick	Kingstown
Ella Webb MD	20 Hatch Street, Dublin
Laura Stephens	Dublin
Marian G. Valentine	Ranelagh, Dublin
George R. Webb	20 Hatch Street, Dublin

Edward Keith Eason (d. 1960) was a director of Eason & Son (now Easons), an Irish wholesale and retail supplier of books, magazines, newspapers, stationery and cards that was originally founded in 1819. Fifteen months after this visit to McGuirk's, he graduated from the Officer Training Corps of the British Army as a second lieutenant in the 3rd Battalion of the Royal Dublin Fusiliers, a reserve battalion that spent WWI in Queenstown (now Cobh), Gateshead and Grimsby. The 4th, 5th and 10th Battalions were involved in suppressing the Easter Rising in 1916.

Dr Ella Webb (1877–1946), née Isabella Ovenden, received a science degree from the Royal University of Ireland and went on to the Catholic University School of Medicine, which began accepting women only in 1895. She graduated in 1904 with first place in the final examinations and, after further study in Vienna, was awarded a doctorate in medicine in 1906. She married philosopher and mathematician George Webb in 1907. Although working in a male world (even by 1918, fewer than 100 female students had qualified as doctors), Ella Webb had a spectacularly busy and distinguished career, combining clinical and teaching roles, and she was active in organisations such as the Women's National Health Association and the St John Ambulance Brigade. She received an MBE (Member of the Order of the British Empire) for her command of the St John Ambulance Brigade during the 1916 Rising. The first woman to be appointed to the medical staff of the Adelaide Hospital in Dublin, she was also involved in the foundation of St Ultan's Hospital for Infants in 1919 and the Children's Sunshine Home in 1924, but perhaps her most far-reaching achievement was the trail she blazed for women in the Irish medical profession.

George Randolph Webb (*d.* 1929) was a philosopher, mathematician and Fellow of Trinity College Dublin. He and Ella were the parents of George Allardice Webb, who would become a significant botanist and marine biologist.

April 1914
C. Poole
A. Alfred Dickie

Christopher Poole, second from left, on the roof of Liberty Hall, 1916

C. Poole is likely to be Christopher Poole (1875–1965), born in Dublin into a working-class nationalist family: his older brother Joseph was a Fenian who was executed in 1883 for a murder he didn't commit. In spite of this, Christopher joined the British Army in 1894 and fought in the Second Boer War. Back in Ireland, he was on the founding committee of the Irish Citizen Army with Jim Larkin and Countess Markievicz. He was second-in-command, under Michael Mallin, in the Royal College of Surgeons during the 1916 Rising, in which two of his brothers also fought.

Alexander Alfred Dickie (1868–1933) was born in Barronstown, Co. Louth, and qualified as a barrister in 1893, but despite enjoying a distinguished legal career, it was his wife, Marie Louise (1871–1947), née Coyle, who had the greater impact on Irish public life. She was the first woman to be employed by the Local Government Board for Ireland, the British government supervisory body created in 1882 that oversaw and controlled funding to Irish local authorities. Although she held a senior administrative position, her salary of £200 a year was less than one-third of what equivalent males received. Her work involved inspecting the conditions of foster or 'pauper' children in Ireland. In spite of widespread objections to 'a protestant lady' dealing with predominantly Catholic children, she gave valuable service before being appointed an Irish Insurance Commissioner in 1911 and a member of the Irish Public Health Council in 1919. She was the first married woman civil servant to achieve permanent and pensionable status, despite the introduction of the 'Marriage Bar' in 1924, and by the early 1920s she was perhaps the highest paid woman in Ireland.

Constantia Maxwell

12 April 1914
Constantia Maxwell
T. Maxwell
Isobel Gordon   *London*
Euphan Maxwell
A. Reeves

Constantia Elizabeth Maxwell (1886–1962) was the daughter of Patrick W. Maxwell, a Scottish ophthalmic surgeon at the Royal Victoria Eye and Ear Hospital in Dublin. She was educated in Scotland, and was among the first women to be admitted to Trinity College Dublin in 1904, where she studied history. A brilliant student, she was the first woman appointed to the academic staff at Trinity, as a lecturer in modern history, in 1909. She was made

Professor of Economic History in 1939, and Lecky Professor of Modern History in 1946. She wrote a number of groundbreaking books, including the influential *Irish History from Contemporary Sources: 1509–1610* (1923) and *Dublin Under the Georges, 1714–1830* (1936).

T. Maxwell was Constantia's brother, who was killed in WWI.

Euphan Maxwell (1887–1964) was Constantia's sister, and she also played an important role in shattering the glass ceiling. After studying medicine at the University of Dublin, she became Ireland's first female ophthalmic surgeon and a Fellow of the Royal College of Surgeons in Ireland. She was Assistant Surgeon and Pathologist at the Royal Victoria Eye and Ear Hospital in Dublin by the age of twenty-five. After working in a temporary hospital in Merrion Square attending wounded rebels and soldiers during the 1916 Rising, she briefly joined the Royal Army Medical Corps before returning to the Royal Victoria.

Alice Reeves (1874–1955) trained as a nurse at the Adelaide Hospital in Dublin and at the time of her visit to McGuirk's was Matron of the Royal Victoria Eye and Ear Hospital. In 1918, she was appointed Matron and Lady Superintendent of Dr Steevens' Hospital, a post she held for thirty years. Her great contribution to Irish medicine was her effort to improve professionalism and standardisation in nurses' training, and her assistance in the establishment of the Nurses Registration (Ireland) Act of 1919.

Eighteenth-century engraving of Dr Steevens' Hospital, Kilmainham. The building is now the administrative headquarters of the Health Service Executive

8 June 1914
J. Bayley Butler and party of students *University College Dublin*

James Bayley Butler (1884–1964) was born in India of Irish parents and educated at Clongowes Wood College, Co. Kildare; St Mary's College, Rathmines; and the Catholic University of Ireland School of Medicine in the 1920s. He graduated with a BA in science in

1905 and an MB in 1909. Concentrating on applied biology, he became an international expert on *Serpula lacrymans*, or dry rot, which, although representing a serious problem in buildings, was little understood at the time. He spent several years building a house called 'Glenlion' in Howth, Co. Dublin, which was based on a Roman villa and utilised stone salvaged from Butt Bridge, the Four Courts and the Custom House, in addition to fragments from the Roman Forum and the Baths of Caracalla. He served in the Royal Army Medical Corps during WWI, retiring afterwards as a major. He lectured on biology in University College Dublin, organising field trips to the Burren and the Dublin and Wicklow mountains.

22 June 1914

A. O'Morchoe	*Kilternan Rectory*
H.G. O'Morchoe	
Arthur O'Morchoe	*Kilternan*
Nial O'Morchoe	

O'Morchoe, or Murphy, is one of the few Gaelic clan names to survive the turbulence of Irish history, which involved tactfully adapting to the prevailing political and religious climate of the time: in this case, like their distant relatives the Kavanaghs of Borris, the O'Morchoes bowed to the wind and became Protestants. Dorothy O'Morchoe, Honor O'Morchoe, Arthur Donel MacMurrough O'Morchoe and Nial Creagh O'Morchoe are four of the seven children of the clan chieftain of the time, The O'Morchoe, otherwise known as the Rev. Thomas Arthur MacMurrough Murphy O'Morchoe (1865–1921). He studied at Trinity College Dublin and graduated with an MA. He was Church of Ireland rector of Kilternan Parish in Dublin, 1894–1921, and was a member of the Royal Dublin Society, the Royal Society of Antiquaries of Ireland, and the General Synod of the Church of Ireland. He wrote an authoritative history of

The O'Morchoe party's entry in the visitors' book, June 1914

Kilternan and its neighbouring parish, Kilgobbin. His grandson and then clan chief, Major General David Nial Creagh, showed Queen Elizabeth II around the National War Memorial Gardens in Islandbridge during her visit to Ireland in 2011.

1 July 1914
Rev. John P. Manly   *Newcastle-upon-Tyne*
Kevin O'Duffy Jn [Junior]   *Harcourt Street Dublin and*
                     TCD

Kevin O'Duffy

Kevin Emmet O'Duffy (1895–1915) was the son of Kevin and Pauline O'Duffy of 85 Harcourt Street, Dublin. He was educated at Belvedere College in Dublin and Stonyhurst College, a leading Catholic independent school in England, where he won four gold medals and one silver. He entered Trinity College Dublin in 1914 and joined the Officer Training Corps. After the outbreak of WWI, he joined the 7th Munster Regiment and was a lieutenant when he was killed in action in the Dardanelles in August 1915, a little over a year after this visit to McGuirk's.

Two days before this last entry, Archduke Franz Ferdinand, heir to Emperor Franz Joseph of the Austrian Empire, and his wife, Sophie, were shot dead by a member of the revolutionary movement Young Bosnia while on a visit to Sarajevo. The Archduke's assassination led directly to the outbreak of WWI, with Germany declaring war on Russia on 1 August and on France on 3 August, followed by the invasion of Belgium. The United Kingdom of Britain and Ireland declared war on Germany on 4 August. Although at this stage of the conflict it might have been thought that it would end quickly, there is no mention whatever in the visitors' books of the outbreak of what was to become the Great War or World War I. Before it ended, over 200,000 Irishmen would have fought in the war and as many as 45,000, almost 25 per cent, had died.

9 August 1914
W.P. Hackett
H. O'Neill
J. Gubbins SJ

William P. Hackett (1878–1954) was educated at Clongowes Wood College, Co. Kildare, and entered the Society of Jesus ('SJ') in 1895. After studying philosophy at Le Puy, France, he was ordained in 1912 and returned to Clongowes to teach. He explored the Dublin and Wicklow mountains over the next few years and wrote a series of articles in *The Irish Monthly* in praise of walking as a pastime. After WWI, he went to Australia where he had a distinguished career as a college rector; he also founded the Melbourne Central Catholic Library, modelled on that in Merrion Square in Dublin. He became a close friend of the Archbishop of Melbourne, Daniel Mannix, and they frequently holidayed together: after William's death in a motor accident, the archbishop gave the sermon at his funeral.

20 December 1914
Maurice Wilkins
Cormac MacTomáis
Seán Ó Conaire
John Palmer
(Na Sléibhteágaigh)

A contemporary illustration of hen grouse

From Rathmines over Kilmashoge to Fairy Castle, then over Boranaraltry Bridge to Prince William's Seat and Cloghnagun to Lough Bray. Home by Featherbed Mountain. Day clear calm and frosty – mountains lightly strewn with snow. Fine views of the Mourne Mountains, and Welsh Coast – Holyhead Mountain, Snowdon range,

and mountains further south, with Nant Francon and Llanberis Pass clearly distinguishable. Captured a hen grouse on Two Rock Mountain, with a broken wing. Snowstorm set in after arrival at Lough Bray, and held on during return march.

Douglas motorcycle (1913)

1915

8 March 1915

G. Lawton Moss, 7th Leinsters, Kilworth
Gerald M. Bagley 8th RIF [Royal Irish Fusiliers]

Royal Enfield motorcycle (1913)

Best motor run from Dublin on 'Douglas' and 'Enfield' we ever had. Never saw the roads so bad. Tea A1 as usual.

The 7th Battalion, Leinster Regiment, was raised at Fermoy, Co. Cork, in October 1914 as part of Kitchener's Second New Army. Geoffrey Lawton Moss was among 100 officer cadets based at Kilworth Camp, near Fermoy, between January and December 1915, when the battalion left for France. Moss survived WWI and WWII to write a popular and still much-sought-after book, *How to Build and Repair Your Own Fishing Rods* (1969).

Gerald M. Bagley was in the 8th Regiment of the Royal Irish Fusiliers, which was formed in Armagh and was also part of Kitchener's Second New Army. He fought at the Battle of Guillemont (1916) and the Battle of Ginchy (1916).

One of the two was riding a Douglas motorcycle, and the other, a Royal Enfield. Royal Enfield started making motorcycles in 1901, and the company supplied large numbers of them to the British War Department from 1914 onwards.

2 April 1915
Líam Ua Teannáim
Líam Ua Dubhthaigh
Mícheál Ua Teannáim
Victor Ryder

*Nice tea – Full up! Clonliffe Harriers flyers came from
Leeson Street in 3 hours, 10 minutes and 14 seconds. Climbed
to highest peak of Lough Bray.*

The Clonliffe Harriers cross-country running club was founded
in 1886. Three members of the club took part in the 1908 London
Olympics, one of whom, Joseph Deakin, came sixth in the 1,500
metres race. A few hours later, after attending a celebratory
champagne lunch, he took part in the five-mile race, but was
recorded as 'Did Not Finish'.

25 April 1915
Seán Ó Cogaire
Ambrose Paor
Seán MacEilthirigh
Cormac G. Mac Tomais

Initiation of a neophyte on Cleevaun.

*Blessington, Lackan, Kilmore, Whelps Rock, Brishy,
Mullacleevaun, Stoney Top, Cnoc Dubh, Gravale Carraig Mor,
Sally Gap, Knocknafoala, Loc Bri, Featherbed, Rath Fearrgain.
Splendid day of sun and wind. Heavy going between Cleevaun
and Stoney Top and Gravale & Carraig Mor.*

The idea of initiating new members into walking clubs was
common as part of a tongue-in-cheek ceremony, usually on a

The Sally Gap, a few kilometres south of
McGuirk's, 1914

mountaintop. The Brotherhood of the Lug, another walking group, founded in 1903 and, like the Clonliffe Harriers, still in existence, initiated their 'lowly asps' (aspirants) on the summit of Lugnaquilla.

20 June 1915

Mr & Mrs A.R. Cruise	*St Ronan's, Orwell Road, Rathgar*
Mr & Miss H. Raleigh Cruise	*Four Courts*
AJS, 6hp (two)	

The impressively named William Alexander Raleigh Cruise (1878–1928) was born in Co. Monaghan, son of Richard Joseph Cruise, a distinguished geologist who was a colleague of the artist/surveyor George Victor Du Noyer. As was common at the time, his wife has not only taken his surname but also his initials: her Christian names were Elizabeth Francesca (which is the extent of our knowledge about her). At the time of their visit to McGuirk's, William was general manager and secretary of the Hibernian Fire and General Insurance Company, one of the few native insurance companies then in existence.

I failed to discover William's relationship with Mr & Miss Henry Raleigh Cruise. Henry was a barrister, based at this time in the Four Courts in Dublin. The 'Miss' is likely to have been Henry's daughter: it seems that daughters also sometimes lost their first names when out with their fathers. Henry's brother, Richard, was a Royal Irish Constabulary officer based in Bantry, Co. Cork.

These four came to McGuirk's on motorcycle and sidecars: the two 'AJS, 6hp' (6 horsepower) were motorbikes manufactured by A. J. Stevens & Company of Wolverhampton, and were one of the most popular sidecar tugs at the time.

BSA Model K motorcycle (1914) with sidecar

4 September 1915
Mr & Mrs A. Wilkes   *BSA & SC*
Mr & Mrs W. Long   *Sunbeam & SC*
Mr & Mrs R. Walshe   *13 SA & SC*

This group also travelled on motorcycles with sidecars ('SC'). The BSA was manufactured by the Birmingham Small Arms Company, which had been making motorcycles since 1910. Sunbeam motorcycles first appeared in 1912, but I have not been able to identify the 13 SA. Sidecars were becoming popular at this time, and, assuming that the women rode in them, they allowed men to combine their love of motorbikes with outings with their wives.

8 September 1915
Mr Goodbody and party from Clara

It is not clear which member of the Goodbody family is mentioned here, but it is likely to be a grandson of Robert James Goodbody, a Quaker who set up a milling business at Clara, Co. Offaly, in 1825. Robert James had five sons who went on to found their own businesses, and one grandson, also named Robert James, founded the Goodbody stockbroking firm in 1877, which is extant today. The milling business was enormously successful and, by 1890, was employing more than 800 people. At the time of this visit, the business climate was changing, as Goodbodys faced serious competition from large English mills such as Ranks. In 1918, their main steam mill was burnt down, a disaster from which their milling business never recovered. Their jute business continued to do well, however, and a new factory was opened in Waterford in the 1930s. J. & L.F. Goodbody Ltd became one of Ireland's largest public companies, but competition from the Far East and the development of plastics took its toll and the Waterford factory closed in 1974 with the loss of 520 jobs.

26 September 1915

Neenie Gogarty
Mary Murphy
Kathleen Fox
Ruth Lane-Poole   *Greystones, Co. Wicklow*
Vera Hone   *Killiney, Co. Dublin*
Eleanor Duane   *17 Earlsfort Terrace*
W.F. Bailey   *3 Earlsfort Terrace*
Joseph Hone   *Killiney, Dublin*

Signatures in the visitors' book, September 1915

Seemingly without her husband this time, Neenie (Margaret/Martha) Gogarty was back at Lough Bray in 1915, and once again, probably due to bad weather, her group sheltered in McGuirk's. She gave her address as 17 Earlsfort Terrace, where she and Oliver St. John Gogarty spent the first years of their marriage.

Of Mary Murphy, I could find no trace.

Kathleen Fox (1880–1963) signed her name in a large, confident script. Born into a Catholic family in Co. Dublin, she studied drawing and painting under William Orpen, working for a while as his assistant. She became interested in metal, enamels and stained glass, an art form in which few women were involved at that time, and won a number of prestigious awards. She left Dublin in 1911 to continue her studies in Paris and Bruges before returning to Dublin in 1915. She became known as the 'Artist of the Rising' because she travelled around the battlefields of the rebellion, sketching and painting. Her large canvas depicting the surrender of Countess Markievicz and Michael Mallin at the Royal College of Surgeons is now exhibited in the Sligo County Museum and art gallery. She later married in London, but her husband, Lieutenant Cyril Pym, was killed during WWI, leaving her with a daughter. After a painting sojourn in Nice, she returned to Dublin in the early 1920s and worked as a successful portrait painter until her death in 1963.

The Angler (*c.*1912) by William Orpen. Vera Hone is the model

Ruth Lane-Poole (1886–1974), née Pollexfen, signed in tiny letters and underlined her name. Born in Limerick, she was a cousin of the Yeats family and was involved in the Irish arts and crafts movement. She was married to Charles Edward Lane-Poole, a forestry expert, and in 1925 moved with him to Australia, where she established herself as a highly successful interior designer.

It appears that the bold signature of Vera Hone (1885–1971), née Brewster, was made with Kathleen's pen. Vera and her husband, Joseph Maunsel Hone, lived next door to William Orpen in Killiney, and she modelled for the artist. He became somewhat besotted and painted her many times, including a famous portrait called *The Blue Hat*. Born in New York, she was a noted beauty and had appeared in the chorus line of a number of Broadway productions before marrying Hone and moving to Dublin.

Eleanor Duane, Neenie's sister, was also living at 17 Earlsfort Terrace.

The oldest member of the party was fifty-six-year-old William F. Bailey, the well-known barrister and Dublin figure, whom we have met before.

Joseph Maunsel Hone (1882–1959) signed in tiny, spidery writing. He was a major figure in the Irish literary and theatre scene in the first half of the twentieth century and one of the founders of the publishing house Maunsels, which, for a while, was Ireland's leading publisher, producing over 500 titles. He travelled to Persia in 1909 with architect Page Dickinson, who co-wrote Hone's first book, *Persia in Revolution: With Notes of Travel in the Caucasus* (1910), describing their experiences. He was a friend of Yeats, and his book *William Butler Yeats: The Poet in Contemporary Ireland* was published during the year of this visit to Lough Bray. An accomplished linguist, he translated several major works into English, and also wrote important biographies of George Moore and Bishop Berkeley.

The conversation these interesting people enjoyed over their steaming cups of tea and homemade cake in McGuirk's is not recorded, but if you read Chapter 25 of Gogarty's *As I Was Going Down Sackville Street*, you may guess what it might have been like.

5 October 1915

Captain Eoghan O'Brien RE [Royal Engineers]
Mount Eagle, Killiney

Mrs Eoghan O'Brien

One of the Gaelic Murrough O'Brien clan, Captain Henry Eoghan O'Brien (1876–1967) was educated at Eton and received his engineering degree from the University of Leeds, after which he became Deputy Chief Mechanical Engineer of the Lancashire and Yorkshire Railway. He joined the Royal Engineers in October 1914 and served in France, Palestine and Italy. Awarded the Distinguished Service Order, he reached the rank of colonel by the end of the war, when he joined the London and North Western Railway. Working in England, and as a member of the Alpine Club, he can't have spent much time at his Killiney home, Mount Eagle, but he did keep bees there and it is where he eventually died.

6 October 1915

Lennox Robinson   *Ballymona, Ballinteer, Co. Dublin*
Edward Travers Smith   *61 Fitzwilliam Square, Dublin*

Esme Stuart Lennox Robinson (1886–1958) was a prolific dramatist and poet who made his career in the Abbey Theatre. Born in Cork, he was educated privately and at Bandon Grammar School. His second play, *The Crossroads*, was performed in the Abbey in 1909, and he became manager of the theatre later that year, when William Fay resigned. He wrote twenty-two plays, *The Whiteheaded Boy* (1921) being the most successful, and one novel, *A Young Man from the South* (1917). In 1931, he married Dorothy Travers Smith,

Lennox Robinson, photographed before 1913

Alexander Foster, touring South Africa with the British Isles rugby team in 1910

an artist and screen designer at the Abbey and the daughter of his companion on this day at McGuirk's.

Edward Travers Smith (*d.* 1945) was a fashionable Dublin physician. His wife, whom he married in 1896, was Hester Meredith Dowden, daughter of the literary scholar Edward Dowden. In the year of this visit to McGuirk's, Edward had an adulterous affair, following which he divorced and Hester moved to London, where she became one of the most famous spiritualists of the twentieth century.

27 December 1915

A.R. Foster	*Drumfad, Northland Road, Derry*
F.C. Purser	*Dublin*
Edwin Solomons	*Dublin*

These three visitors seem to be connected through rugby.

Alexander Roulston Foster (1890–1972) was born in Derry and studied at Queen's University Belfast to become a teacher. He played rugby for Queen's and, selected for Ireland in 1910, played in the first Five Nations championship. He must have excelled, because he was later picked to play on the British Isles team that toured South Africa in 1910. He would play his last international match, against Wales, in 1921. After teaching at Foyle College, he became headmaster of the Belfast Royal Academy. He was instrumental in founding the Northern Ireland Civil Rights Association in 1964. Other than his connections with Irish rugby, it is not clear how he came to be a walking companion to the other two.

Francis Carmichael Purser we have met before.

Edwin Solomons (1879–1964), a brother of Bethel Solomons, was a prominent international businessman and first member of the Dublin stock exchange. He was president of the Trinity Football Club, 1927–9.

1916

2 April 1916

Samuel Cunningham
Paul White
M. Ó Crethigean
J.N. Beaumont
E.R. Dodds
Cormac G. MacTomáis
Ambrose Paor

Na Sléibhteágaigh

Brittas, Ballyfolan, Seefin, Seefingan, Tullacaion, Kippure, Eagle's Cliff, Lough Bray Featherbed, Rathfarnham.

Splendid sunny day, rather warm at times. Mountains in very good order, even the large patches of snow which in places bridged the courses of the streams for a considerable distance.

Sketch of summer weather from June 1916

In one of the rare mentions in the visitors' books of the Great War that was raging only 800 km away, a comment was later added to this entry: 'You should have been in France/or Germany – your allies perhaps.' On another occasion, when other members of Na Sléibhteágaigh mentioned wet weather during their mountain walk, a later visitor wrote diagonally across their description the snide comment, 'Ever tried France – Boys!'

I was only able to track down one of the members of Na Sléibhteágaigh listed here. E.R. Dodds (1893–1979) was a classical scholar, born in Co. Down into a Presbyterian family. He was educated at St Andrew's College, Dublin, and Campbell College, Belfast, from where he was expelled, it is said, for 'gross, studied

Classicist E.R. Dodds

and sustained insolence'. He read classics at University College, Oxford, where his friends included Aldous Huxley and T.S. Eliot. He supported the 1916 Rising, which took place three weeks after his visit to McGuirk's. He was appointed a lecturer in classics at the University of Reading, where he married Annie Edwards Powell, a lecturer in English. In 1924, he was appointed Professor of Greek at the University of Birmingham, where he met poets W.H. Auden and Louis MacNeice.

He continued hill walking in England and was on the summit of Helvellyn in the Lake District in 1926 when the aviator Bert Hinkler landed his aircraft there; he helped turn the plane for it to take off again. In 1936, he became Regius Professor of Greek at Christ Church, Oxford, despite opposition resulting from his support for Irish nationalism.

Within weeks of this last-mentioned visit, the 1916 Rising broke out, resulting in over 1,500 people being killed or severely wounded, and more than 170 buildings in central Dublin, an area of nearly 13 acres, being destroyed by artillery and fire. While it was perhaps telling that few remarks in the visitors' books allude to WWI, it is remarkable that the Rising, with its large number of casualties and considerable destruction in Dublin, is not mentioned at all.

Over the longer term, however, there is a discernible increase, after April 1916, in the numbers of visitors signing the visitors' book in Gaelic script. Even the Jewish doctor Bethel Solomons, a frequent visitor to McGuirk's, signed in on one occasion as Bethel MacSolomon!

7 May 1916

Bessie O'Grady   *Grosvenor Road*
Mrs B.M. O'Grady   *ditto*
Nancy O'Grady
L.S. O'Grady, Capt, RAMC [Royal Army Medical Corps],
                5th Scottish Rifles, BEF, France

Memorial in Glasgow to the Cameronians who fell in World War I

Note how Captain O'Grady makes sure that readers know he is with the British Expeditionary Force ('BEF') in France, and not connected with the British Army in Ireland. A doctor, he was seconded as Medical Officer to the 5th Battalion of the Cameronians in August 1916. He survived the war and signed his name in McGuirk's again in May 1959.

7 July 1916

M.J. Roddy
Mrs J. O'Doherty
D.O.D. Esq
Eileen M. Doherty
Sheila Noonan

Many thanks to Mrs McGuirk for her kindness.

Sheila Noonan wanted to stray,
And right away she made for Lough Bray,
And with her she brought the O'Doherty Clan
And brave Mrs Roddy also ran.
They hadn't got far until a tire burst,
And Daniel O'Doherty smiled sweetly and C----
[presumably 'Cursed']
We had tea in the open and oh! Such a spread
With blackcurrant jam and butter with bread
Then Right Ho! For Dublin with full steam ahead.

The memorial at Arbour Hill Cemetery, Dublin, where the bodies of the executed 1916 leaders are buried

20 August 1916

C.R. Vandeleur

C. Harold Heathcote, Major, & Wife

Greystones

Richmond

Barracks

There was a Lieutenant Colonel D.R. Vandeleur Ormsby in Greystones in 1910: C.R. Vandeleur may have been his son.

Whoever he is, his companion was a little-known but key figure in Irish history, Major Charles Harold Heathcote (*b.* 1876), who, like many previous visitors, didn't feel it necessary to give his wife a name. Born in Sale, Cheshire, Charles Heathcote trained as an architect before joining his father's architectural practice in 1900. His first wife, Catherine Howards Holderness, died in 1907 after falling from the first-floor window of their home at Old Trafford. He later married Ismay Eleanor Mary (surname unknown) and it is this wife who was with him at McGuirk's.

I wonder how many of the visitors taking tea in McGuirk's that day realised that the British officer in the room was the man who, between 3 and 12 May, had been the officer in charge of executing Patrick Pearse, James Connolly, and a number of others who had been sentenced to death after the 1916 Rising.

During the rebellion, the Sherwood Foresters Regiment suffered the highest losses of any British regiment. They had just arrived from England to reinforce the British Army in Dublin, but most of the men were relatively untrained. It is said that they had to be shown how to load and fire their rifles on the pier in Kingstown (Dún Laoghaire) when they disembarked. They set off towards the centre of Dublin but, just before Mount Street Bridge, met a maelstrom of gunfire from a small group of determined Volunteers guarding the bridge. At least 4 of their officers and 216 other ranks were killed or injured in a few hours, amounting to nearly half the total British military casualties during the rebellion. Four of the rebels died, but they held the bridge for nine hours.

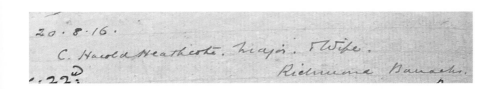

As a 'reward' for their gallantry under fire, the Foresters were chosen to form the firing squads to execute the condemned leaders of the Rising. The commander of the firing squads was Major Charles Harold Heathcote, second-in-command of the regiment. The firing squad consisted of twelve men: as was customary, the officer in charge loaded the rifles, eleven of which had live rounds and one a blank, so no soldier knew if his weapon had fired the fatal shot. The execution process was arranged as follows: when Heathcote waved his hand, the firing party came to the ready. The prisoners, blindfolded and with their hands tied behind their backs, were marched out, followed by a priest and a warder. When the prisoner had reached a point immediately opposite the firing party, the warder said, 'I am going to see that everything is ready.' The priest then gave absolution and moved away. Major Heathcote waved his hand and the firing party came to firing position. Heathcote yelled 'Fire' and the prisoner was shot.

James Connolly was brought to Kilmainham in an ambulance, seriously wounded and wearing pyjamas. Heathcote was of the opinion that he had been heavily drugged by the Medical Officer on the way from Dublin Castle. He was moved from the ambulance on a stretcher and lifted onto a chair where he sat in an extended position with his head falling backwards. Heathcote arranged with two of the firing party to aim at Connolly's head and he died without a movement.

After WWI, Heathcote returned to architecture, in London, and received a 'back-door' qualification, Licentiate of the Royal Institute of British Architects, in 1925.

James Connolly

Bullet holes from the Easter Rising can still be seen in the facade of the GPO, Dublin

Bullet holes from the Easter Rising can still be seen in the facade of the GPO, Dublin

15 October 1916
John Joly FRS [Fellow of the Royal Society]
Henry H. Dixon FRS
J.S. Franks

John Joly (1857–1933), born in Co. Offaly, was a second cousin of the astronomer Charles Jasper Joly. He graduated in engineering and modern literature from Trinity College Dublin and became Professor of Geology and Minerology in 1897. His finest achievements include developing radiotherapy in the treatment of cancer and techniques for accurately estimating the age of rocks based on the radioactive elements present in them. In 1973, a crater on Mars was named in his honour.

Henry Horatio Dixon (1869–1953) was born in Dublin, studied at Trinity and eventually became Professor of Botany there. In 1916, he was awarded the Boyle Medal of the Royal Dublin Society. He had a close friendship and working relationship with John Joly and with him developed a theory on the ascent of water and mineral sap in plants.

While the general population did not support the Easter Rising of 1916, the subsequent executions, together with the British Army's destruction of the centre of Ireland's capital, ignited a shift that began an inexorable move towards a wish for Irish independence.

6 May 1917
John L. Synge
E.E.M. Allen

John Lighton Synge (1897–1995), a nephew of J.M. Synge, was perhaps the finest Irish mathematician and theoretical physicist since William Rowan Hamilton. His father, Edward Synge, was land agent for Lord Gormanston, and his mother, Ellen, was the daughter of the civil engineer James Price. John entered Trinity College Dublin in 1915 and won a Foundation Scholarship in his first year, entitling him to free rooms and meals. After the 1916 Rising, he became a nationalist and joined the Gaelic League, spending two months in Co. Cork learning the Irish language. In Trinity he met Elizabeth Eleanor Mable Allen, a history student; they became engaged in the year they visited McGuirk's and were married the year after. John graduated in 1919 and was awarded, as an outstanding student, the Large Gold Medal (which he later sold when short of cash). He was appointed as a college lecturer in 1920, but later the same year became an assistant professor at the University of Toronto. He returned to Dublin in 1925 as Professor of Natural Philosophy and, over the next seven decades, worked again in Toronto, then Ireland and the United States. He is credited with introducing a new geometrical approach to the theory of relativity.

Elizabeth Eleanor Mabel Allen (1896–1985) was born in Co. Wicklow and, although she wanted to study mathematics, was persuaded by her brother to study history instead. She was forced, however, due to family financial circumstances, to leave Trinity before receiving her degree. She and John Lighton Synge had a clandestine marriage in a registry office, followed by a wedding feast of scrambled eggs in Synge's college rooms, and a cycling honeymoon in Donegal. They had three daughters, one of whom, Cathleen Synge Morawetz, became a distinguished mathematician and Professor of Mathematics at New York University.

7 May 1917

Nancy Campbell	*Kilmolin*
Gertrude Solomons	
Bethel Solomons	*42 Fitzwilliam Sq.*
Joseph Campbell	
Sophie E.R. Solomons	*Dublin*
Bethel L. Jacobs	*Hull*

St Enda's School in Rathfarnham, Dublin; today the Pearse Museum

Nancy Campbell (*b.* 1886), née Maude, was born in England, daughter of Colonel Aubrey Maude of the Cameronian Highlanders and granddaughter of Colonel Sir George Maude, who had been Crown Equerry to Queen Victoria. Her great-grandmother was a half-sister of Lord Edward FitzGerald, the nationalist hero of 1798. Nancy wrote poetry and was a devotee of George Bernard Shaw, rebelling against what she felt was the hypocrisy of upper-class Edwardian life. In 1910, against her family's wishes, she married the penniless Irish Catholic poet Joseph Campbell in London and moved with him to Wicklow. They separated in 1924.

Gertrude Solomons, née Levy, married Bethel Solomons in London the year before this visit to McGuirk's.

Joseph Campbell (1879–1944) was a poet, playwright, revolutionary and teacher, who was born into a Catholic nationalist family in Belfast. Moving to Dublin in 1902, he met many of the leading nationalists. During a stay in London, he married Nancy Maude and, back in Dublin, became friendly with Patrick Pearse and taught at his school, St Enda's. He was a founding member of the Irish Volunteers and had one of his plays, *Judgement*, put on by the Abbey in 1912: he admired Yeats, but was regarded by the poet as 'a poltroon'. He did reconnaissance work during the 1916 Rising, and took the anti-Treaty side during the Civil War, during which he was arrested and imprisoned. When he was released, his marriage broke up and, embittered by what he saw as the corruption and dishonour of the Free State, he moved to the United States in 1925, not returning until 1938 to live in Lackandarragh, Glencree, where he had bought a small farm in 1921. He died there in 1944. His several volumes of poems are mostly forgotten today, although his song 'My Lagan Love' has lived on.

7 July 1917

S.C. O'Grady   *RFC*
Mrs S.C. O'Grady
Mrs Standish O'Grady

Air Force Cross awarded during World War I

Standish Con O'Grady (1888–1968) was the youngest son of the writer Standish James O'Grady and his wife Margaret. He attended Trinity College Dublin and graduated in 1910 with a degree in engineering. He worked for the Congested Districts Board before emigrating to Canada, where he was employed by the Department of the Interior. He returned after the outbreak of WWI and joined the Royal Flying Corps ('RFC') in 1916. Joining No. 23 'Scout' Squadron in France in 1917, he had shot down his third German fighter just two weeks before this visit, while on leave, to McGuirk's with his wife and mother. He was awarded the Military Cross and the Airforce Cross for gallantry. After the war, he returned to engineering and became a lecturer in engineering in Durham University in 1931. During WWII, he was a flying instructor with the RAF, resigning in 1944 with the rank of squadron leader to return to Durham, where he lectured until his retirement in 1954.

We have met Mrs Standish O'Grady before: the year after this visit to McGuirk's, she moved to northern France with her husband.

6 August 1917

Seumas Ó Murgheasa IRA [Irish Republican Army]
Marcus Ua Ciomín IRA
Domnall T. Mac [undecipherable] IRA
V.A. Kelly
W. Maguire
Peadar Ó Brían IRA
Saegán Ua Gosnaigh IRA

The time is gone
To fawn and crouch
Like supplicants for our rights.

These lines are followed, in another hand, by the line:

Dear Land, Thou are not conquered yet!

This is slightly misquoted from a poem, 'Thou Art Not Conquered Yet, Dear Land', by the Republican and nationalist Michael Joseph O'Rahilly, better known as The O'Rahilly. These entries hints at the fact that, sixteen months after the 1916 Rising, Irish militant nationalism is simmering just below the surface.

6 September 1917
Austin Clarke

Plaque commemorating Austin Clarke in St Patrick's Park, Dublin

Austin Clarke (1896–1974) was a Dublin-born poet, playwright and novelist who loved the countryside. He studied at University College Dublin, and succeeded to the lectureship post made vacant by the execution of his one-time tutor, Thomas MacDonagh, after the 1916 Rising. Co-founder of the Lyric Theatre in Dublin, he also worked as a journalist and broadcaster. His marriage to Cornelia Cummins in 1920 lasted only days, after which he had a breakdown

Austin Clarke. Sept 1917

that hospitalised him for a number of months. His strict Catholic upbringing possibly made consummation of the marriage difficult, although his short poem 'Penal Law' is a sarcastic comment on attempts to suppress free thought and sexuality:

Burn Ovid with the rest. Lovers will find
A hedge-school for themselves and learn by heart
All that the clergy banish from the mind,
When hands are joined and head bows in the dark.

He subsequently met and fell in love with Norah Walker, with whom he lived in England from 1930 to 1937, marrying her in 1945 and having with her three sons. As well as a two-volume memoir and several plays, twenty volumes of his poetry were published, and his three novels were banned by the Irish Censorship Board. A bridge over the River Dodder, built in 1984, is named after him: his home, Bridge House, Templeogue, had been demolished after his death to make room for the bridge.

16 September 1917

H. McConnell
Miss A. Buckley — *Enniskerry*
Miss S. Buckley — *Enniskerry*
Miss G. McConnell
L/Cpl J.B. Sutcliffe — *Ballarat, Victoria, Australia, 3rd Pioneer Batt. AIF*

The young Australian lance corporal ('L/Cpl') was probably on leave from the Western Front in France, where the 3rd Pioneer Battalion of the Australian Imperial Force ('AIF') had arrived in late 1916 and remained until the end of the war. J.B. Sutcliffe does not appear in the list of 3rd Battalion casualties so, even though we have no further information on him, we can assume that he returned home safely.

Members of the Australian Imperial Force on the Western Front, 1916

30 November 1917
M. Kelly   *27 Charlemont Street*

Tis evening time, & the sun is setting. Herself and myself have come from hungry Dublin (of course owing to war) alass [sic] we come to a lovely homestead, The Grand McGuirk of Lock [sic] Bray. We were cold and dry, but the warm hand clasp, the sweet cup of tea, brown bread, nice fresh eggs, very very soon brought the fire to our eyes and a love in our hearts (again the sun rose). Herself and myself were hungry no longer Thank God Amen.

Thank Mrs McGuirk, not God
Socialism is the hope of the workers
The hard Martha and Mrs Nagle, angel face amen.

Whenever you feel tired or sick, in sorrow or in pain?
Remember one from [undecipherable] say fail who never failed and that was Thomas Ashe.
Also Remember Easter Week.

These three offerings suggest what people were thinking in Ireland in November 1917. The continuing Great War was generating serious inflation, and increasing exports of food from Ireland to feed the English were bringing hardship to the city's poor. In the winter of 1916, the Irish Labour Party leader Thomas Johnson compared the profiteering in selling food supplies to Britain with the exportation of grain from Ireland to England during the Great Famine in the

1840s. He advocated a 'New Protectionism', preventing any further exportation of food until the needs of the Irish people had been satisfied. At the beginning of 1918, the food crisis led to a herd of pigs, which were on their way to Kingstown (Dún Laoghaire) for shipping to England, being intercepted by twenty-four men armed with sticks, describing themselves as citizens of the Irish Republic. The pigs were taken to a Dublin Corporation yard in Portland Row and slaughtered, and the meat distributed to the residents of the inner city. A song called 'The Pig Push' became popular at the time:

> I met a friend the other day and this is what he said:
> Sinn Féiners they are out again, the streets are running red.
> The slaughter it was dreadful, thirty-four of them are killed.
> I never in my life, said he, saw blood so freely spilled.
> So, I says to him 'Your dreadful tale, it fills me with dismay,
> And have thirty-four Sinn Féiners bold in Dublin passed
>   away?'
> 'No, it's pigs, you fool, that's killed,' says he, 'myself I saw it
>   done,
> 'Twas Diarmuid Lynch that did the work, by the hokey there
>   was fun.'

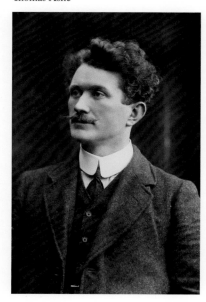

Thomas Ashe

Thomas Ashe (1885–1917), born in Kerry, studied to be a teacher in De La Salle College in Waterford and began teaching in Lusk, Co. Dublin, in 1905. He joined the Irish Volunteers in 1913 and was sentenced to death for his part in the 1916 Rising, which was commuted to penal servitude for life. He and thousands of other prisoners were released in June 1917 as part of the general amnesty, but he was imprisoned again on a charge of sedition in August of that year. He went on hunger strike, seeking prisoner-of-war status, and died on 25 September due to complications caused by force-feeding. His death and subsequent funeral had a significant effect on the attitude of Irish people in general to the British authorities.

The following two entries also refer to the food situation then pertaining in Ireland.

23 March 1918

R.J.M. Walker   *Bray*
Doreen Walker   *Bray*

Quite the best 'War Tea' I have yet had.

20 May 1918

Maximilian Kaplan   *TCD (Cape Town)*
B. Harris Cohen   *40 TCD (Sutherland, Cape Province, SA)*

Topping 'War' feed.

9 June 1918

Irish Road Club
P.G. Dardis
Edward P. Monks
M. Mac Donneada (M. Dunphy)
Risteard Mac Liubhaigh
Richard Walker
W.C. Rafter

The mountain dew was falling 'lightly' and a 'light' Westerly breeze wafted us from the city as we climbed Killakee and the Featherbed. As we reached Lough Bray, the weather was so fine that we decided it was too 'good' for an outdoor picnic, so we boiled our kettle in Lough Bray Cottage. The barographical readings at Mason's were Full Westerly gale accompanied by drenching rain. The heat of our language dried our clothes completely. A capital outing but slightly juicy.

28 July 1918

Pte [Private] Judd   *Royal Wilts Yeomanry*
                         Phoenix Park, Dublin
Pte F.W. Cook   *Royal Wilts Yeomanry*

*Proceeding to Newtown Mount Kennedy stopped for tea for
2 which was greatly enjoyed by both.*

British bicycle troops in the Somme, 1917

The Royal Wiltshire Yeomanry was stationed in Ireland in
early 1918. It was originally a mounted unit but converted to
being a cycling unit in 1916, so it is likely that these two were on
bicycles:

Cpl [Corporal] H.T. Hall   *Signals Oxford Yeomanry, Dublin*
Pte [Private] J. Allsop   *Signals Oxford Hussars*

Proceeding to Sallisgap [sic] stopped for tea.

19 August 1918

Alice D'Olier   *Knocklinn, Bray*
L.B. Wainwright   *Irish Batt., The King's*
Liverpool Regiment
Florence D'Olier
Betrand D'Olier

The Queen's Own Oxfordshire Hussars also converted to bicycles
in 1916 and were also stationed in Dublin in January 1918. These
entries showing a marked increase in the signatures of military
personnel are characteristic of many 1918 entries.

Alice Florence D'Olier (1864–1946), née Gore, was the wife of Edmund Guy D'Olier, who owned the Dublin firm Thompson, D'Olier & Co., Wine Merchants. She was the first secretary of the Mothers' Union branch established at Powerscourt (St Patrick's) Church, Enniskerry. She and Edmund lived at Knocklinn, Ballyman, Bray, and the Little Sugarloaf. She died at Fairy Hill, Bray, the childhood home, later demolished, of future Taoiseach Garret FitzGerald.

It is impossible at this remove to guess the British officer L.B. Wainwright's involvement with the D'Olier family; we have no other information on him. His regiment saw action in France at Ypres and Cambrai and was still in France on this date, so he was presumably on leave.

Florence Charlotte D'Olier (*b*. 1894) was one of Alice's three daughters. In 1922, she married Howard Cornewall Lewis in Bombay.

Bertrand Guy D'Olier (1902–1928) was one of Alice's two sons and was sixteen on this visit to McGuirk's. He went to Kenya with his brother Edmund in 1924, where three years later he married Beatrice Maura Massy of Stackallen, Co. Meath. He learned to fly in Kenya, but was killed in a flying accident at Digby aerodrome, Lincolnshire, aged twenty-six. He is buried in St Patrick's Church, Enniskerry, and his mother was later buried beside him.

Killakee House in the early nineteenth century

22 August 1918

Hon. Hamon Massy	*Kilakee [sic]*
R. Raby	*Federated Malay States*
Victor Irons	*9 Serpentine Tce, Ballsbridge, Dublin*

Hugh Hamon Charles Massy (1894–1958) succeeded to the peerage on the death of his father in 1926, but became known as the 'penniless peer'. He was born at Ardfinnan House, Co. Tipperary, into a world of privilege and grandeur. The Massys had been in Ireland since the days of Charles I and, by 1880, had landholdings in the country of over 30,000 acres, and houses in counties Limerick, Tipperary and Dublin. By the turn of the century, however, the extravagant lifestyle of the 6th Baron Massy, combined with changing land laws and poor investments, had left the family in serious debt.

Hamon suffered from poor health and did not enlist in the British Army during the war (unlike his brother, Tristram). In early 1918, he spent a period in Mercer's Hospital in Dublin, where he fell in love with nurse Margaret Moran and soon became engaged to her. At the time of his visit to McGuirk's, he was probably convalescing and taking a walk with companions from Killakee House, a few miles back along the road towards Dublin, while his parents were trying to get over the shock of their son's engagement to a Catholic with no significant dowry to alleviate their financial difficulties.

Beehive Cottage today

Hamon converted to Catholicism, married Margaret in 1919 at University Church, St Stephen's Green, and took up residence in Killakee House. To cover some debts, the family silver, jewellery and china were sold before the end of 1919, in addition to paintings by Giotto, Raphael and Osborne. Because of the unsettled political situation in Ireland at the time, these items realised only a fraction of their real value.

Hamon's mother left him out of her will when she died in 1923 and, with no source of income, the Munster and Leinster Bank foreclosed on him and took possession of Killakee House; he was ill at the time and refused to leave, so he was carried out in his bed and deposited on the public road, much to the horror of the locals. Many of them had earned good wages as servants, gardeners, coachmen, gamekeepers and stablehands at Killakee House in better times, so there was considerable sympathy for the young Hamon.

Later it was arranged that Hamon and Margaret could live in the pretty Killakee gatelodge, Beehive Cottage. In 1926, Hamon became Lord Massy, but with ill-health and no income, Margaret had to go out to work. The bank attempted but failed to sell Killakee House. It was eventually sold in 1941 for its salvage value and stripped of its slates, timber, joinery, flooring and cut stonework: what remained was demolished. After Hugh died in 1958, Margaret moved to England, where her daughter and son were living, and where she died in 1971.

1919

18 May 1919
Neans Ní Bhriain
Ruaidhrí Ó Concubair (7) [aged seven]
Pádraig Ó Brosnacháin
Micheál Ó Loinsigh
Próinshias Ó Rayla
Padraigh S. Ua Raghallaigh
Máire bean P. Ó Murcadha
Máireád Ághas
Muiris Ó Braonáin
Pádraig Mac Neasa
Tomás Breathnach
P. Ua Cathaláin
Frederick Bruder

This group were members of the Keating Branch of the Gaelic League from Gardiner Row in Dublin. The branch had been founded in 1901 and Cathal Brugha was its president in 1911. Other members included Piaras Béaslaí, Gearóid O'Sullivan, Thomas Ashe and Seán MacDermott. It was a recruiting ground for the Volunteers and Irish Republican Brotherhood, and soon became a hotbed of revolution. In 1914, most of the women members joined Cumann na mBan and, in 1916, members of the branch included Michael Collins, Con Colbert and Seán Heuston, the last two later executed for their part in the 1916 Rising.

Máireád Ághas (1890–1967) was born in Kinard, near Dingle, Co. Kerry, and went to school at the Presentation Secondary School, Thurles, Co. Tipperary. She met the future revolutionary, journalist and Abbey Theatre managing director Ernest Blythe in 1913 when he was working as a farm labourer in Kinard. She assisted him in forming a drama society in Dingle, despite the local parish priest's opposition, and she performed in a production of the Yeats and Lady Gregory play, *Cathleen ni Houlihan*. She spent two years working in a solicitor's office in Belfast and teaching Irish; returning to Dublin, she worked for the Irish National Teachers' Organisation and was active in Cumann na mBan during the War of Independence. Her brother Tomás was fatally wounded in the Lispole ambush in Kerry in March 1921. Ághas married a Limerick confectioner, Frank Geary; when he died in 1952, she became chairperson of his company.

Scene from an early production of *Cathleen ni Houlihan*

Muiris Ó Braonáin (*d.* 1972) was a member of B Company, 1st Battalion of the Irish Volunteers. He was part of the effort to block the advance of British forces into Dublin via the Navan Road during the 1916 Rising, when barricades were erected across roads in Cabra. Only 50 of the 150 men of B Company turned out, due to the countermanding order issued by Eoin MacNeill, and they had the misfortune to face artillery fire from the four eighteen-pounders brought into the city to quell the rebellion. The barricades were blasted away, and the Volunteers withdrew with one casualty, although eight civilians were killed. Ó Braonáin was imprisoned in Portland Prison in England after the Rising, rejoining his company after his release in 1917. During the Civil War he took the anti-Treaty side.

The Irish Constitution Committee in session, 1922. Edward Millington Stephens, secretary, is fifth from the left

6 July 1919
E.M. Stephens   Teach Beag, Killakee, Rathfarnham
L.M. Stephens
Denis Stephens
Doreen Synge

Edward Millington Stephens (1888–1955) was born in Dublin, the second child of Henry Stephens (a distant relative of the writer Lafcadio Hearn) and Annie Stephens, a sister of dramatist J.M. Synge, who gave his nephew a love of nature and took him walking, cycling and fishing in Wicklow. Edward studied law at Trinity College Dublin, and was called to the Bar in 1912. He later knew Michael Collins, who was probably instrumental in his becoming a director of Dáil Éireann's Land Bank, which redistributed land with the help of loans. He was with Collins in London for the fateful Anglo-Irish Treaty negotiations, and was a secretary to the committee that drafted the Irish Constitution in 1922. Between then and 1926, he was secretary of the Boundary Commission, which established the border between the Free State and Northern Ireland. Until his retirement, he was registrar for the Supreme Court and Appeals Court. He wrote a voluminous biography of his famous uncle, which, at 750,000 words, was unpublishable but was used as the basis for other biographies.

Lily M. Stephens was Edward's wife.

Doreen Hamilton Synge (1893–1988), probably a cousin of J.M. Synge, was born in Ashford, Co. Wicklow, and was a regular at McGuirk's for decades. She was an ambulance driver in the Voluntary Aid Detachment in France during WWI, and on her return to Ireland joined Cumann na mBan. She had a motorbike and sidecar that she used when she acted as chauffer to Countess Markievicz.

4 August 1919

Feast of St Dominic

Mrs Hampden Acton   *Knockeadar*

Captain E.L.L. Acton   *Leinster Regt*

Shig Weaver

R.M. Acton

B.J. Acton   *Particularly nice people!*

What did daddy do in the Great War?

Cap badge of the Leinster Regiment

Olivia Charlotte Hampden Acton, née May, was a daughter of the Right Hon. George Augustus Chichester May, Lord Chief Justice of Ireland.

Captain Edward Leslie Lowry Acton (1889–1965) attended the Royal Military College at Sandhurst and became a career soldier. He served in France and Belgium in the Prince of Wales's Leinster Regiment during WWI. At the Battle of Messines in July 1917, two years before this visit to McGuirk's, he received a serious head wound, causing some paralysis of his right leg and arm. He received the Military Cross for conspicuous gallantry in that action. In spite of his disability, he was able to remain in the army and served through WWII, retiring in 1946 as a lieutenant colonel.

Ruth Margaret Acton (*b.* 1894) was the daughter of Lieutenant Colonel James Lowry Cole Acton and Matilda Julia Milman. She married Edward Leslie Lowry Acton in 1920.

Bertha Joice Acton (*b.* 1896) was Ruth's sister.

1920

16 May 1920
Seosamh Mac Oireschtaigh
Mícheál Mac Giolla Críost

Ar lorg 'Laverney Spout', agus níl s'e fághta aca f'os agus ní bheidh mar bhuil sé ann le fághail.

This translates as: 'Searching for the "Laverney Spout", and it hasn't been found yet, and won't, because it doesn't exist.' The Laverney Spout is a spring on Duff Hill, south-west of the Sally Gap: it disappears from time to time and has a mysterious reputation, the meaning of which is lost in the past. It feeds the Laverney Brook, which was a very early east–west, cross-mountain route.

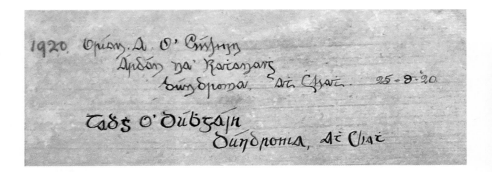

Susan Mitchell (1899) by John Butler Yeats

May 1920
Susan L. Mitchell
George Good
Eileen Good

Susan Langstaff Mitchell (1866–1926) was born in Carrick-on-Shannon, Co. Leitrim, but was brought up by three aunts on Wellington Road, Dublin, next door to the literary Purser family. In the Pursers' home she met the artist John Butler Yeats and his family, and became close to W.B.'s sister, Lily Yeats, the embroiderer and designer. Susan became subeditor of *The Irish Homestead* under George William Russell ('Æ'), and began to write poems and ballads that were celebrated in Dublin's social circles; she published two books of verse, *Aids to the Immortality of Certain Persons in Ireland: Charitably Administered* (1908) and *The Living Chalice, and Other Poems* (1913). In 1916, she published a biography of George Moore that received praise from George Bernard Shaw and James Joyce. Though quite ill with tuberculosis, she continued her output of verse and reviews, and her attendance at the Abbey Theatre, until her death.

George and Eileen Good may be the parents of George Fitzgerald Good, Bishop of Derry, 1967–84.

15 October 1920

Peadar Ua Dubhuidhe   *Cluaintairbh*
Proinsias T. Ó Raghallaigh   *Glas Mochonóg Nua*

Ní h-eól dam aon cúige nó dúnbhaile bréagh
Dá bhfacas im' shiubhaltaibh ba shúgaidhe le rádh.

This translates as:

I don't know a province or city as fair
As I've seen on my walks as this vista so rare.

1921

17 March 1921

Mr & Mrs Calvert Roberts   *Seapoint Villa, Monkstown,*
                                     Co. Dublin

And Miss Elizabeth Roberts

Calvert Roberts was the Dublin director of May, Roberts & Co., a London wholesale druggist and patent medicine company.

Three months after this visit to McGuirk's, Mrs Calvert Roberts was driving two of her daughters and 2nd Lieutenant Alfred Breeze of the British Army when they were stopped at a roadblock near Carrickmines set up by F Company of the Deansgrange IRA. Lt Breeze had only been in Dublin for ten days. There are a number of conflicting accounts of what transpired: the Irish Republican Army (IRA) maintained afterwards that the car would have been allowed to proceed, but it seems that the over-keen lieutenant drew his gun and was promptly shot, slightly wounded, disarmed and 'arrested' by one of the IRA men. Matters escalated after that. It was ascertained that Breeze was a British officer, possibly even an intelligence officer.

Lt Breeze's execution by the IRA as depicted in the *Illustrated London News*

His wound was roughly bandaged, the two daughters were taken out of the car, and Lt Breeze bundled into it with two IRA men. Mrs Roberts was ordered to drive on but, after a few miles, Breeze started to fight, and he was taken out of the car and shot dead.

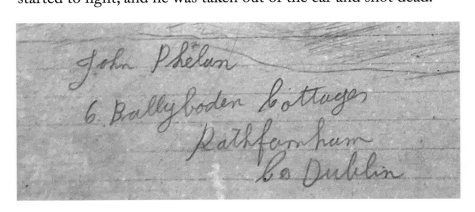

21 May 1921

John Phelan   6 Ballyboden Cottages, Rathfarnham, Co. Dublin

Wm Rodgers   Acrebrook, Rathfarnham, Co. Dublin

An increasing number of working-class visitors were now arriving at McGuirk's by bicycle. John Phelan lived in a terrace of simple cottages, now long demolished, in the village of Ballyboden. All we know of William Rodgers is that his brother George served in the 2nd Battalion, Leinster Regiment, and was killed in March 1918. Acrebrook has disappeared from Rathfarnham addresses.

19 June 1921

Hamar Greenwood Bart MP [Member of Parliament]
Denis Henry KC MP
Jemmie Craig Bart
M. Ó Coilean, Eamon de Valera, sorry we missed you.

Sir Hamar Greenwood, *c.1920*

This spurious entry featuring Hamar Greenwood, Chief Secretary for Ireland and closely identified with introducing the Black and Tans and the Auxiliaries into the War of Independence; Denis Henry, first Lord Chief Justice for the new state of Northern Ireland; and James Craig, who had been appointed the first Prime Minister of Northern Ireland less than two weeks before, includes a humorous reference to Michael Collins and Éamon de Valera: unlikely tea companions for this group!

Three days later, the new parliament of Northern Ireland was opened by George V at Belfast City Hall.

14 August 1921
Columba O'Carroll Heathcote
Dudley Heathcote

This was a honeymoon couple, but their marriage turned out to be short-lived. Columba O'Carroll (*d.* 1955) was the daughter of Dr Joseph O'Carroll, who became Professor of Medicine at University College Dublin in 1912 and, although nationalist in his politics, was appointed consulting physician to the British Army in Ireland at the outbreak of WWI. In 1920, he was awarded a CBE but refused it. The family suffered many misfortunes. In 1904, Columba's five-year-old brother was drowned; her brother Francis was killed after four days ashore at Gallipoli; and a third brother, Charles, died in action in France.

Columba met the poet and one of the leaders of the 1916 Rising, Joseph Mary Plunkett, in 1909. He wrote her lyrical love poetry, including *Sonnets to Columba* (1913), published by his Columba Press, which he named after her. She was not in love with him, however, and he finally turned to Grace Gifford, to whom he became engaged in December 1915 (and whom he married in his prison cell before his execution), about ten weeks after his last letter to Columba. Columba then fell in love with Dudley Heathcote but it is said that her father took such a dislike to him that he later beat her with a stick for seeing him. Nevertheless, the couple married two days before this visit to McGuirk's and, although the marriage was short, Columba bore him a son, Anthony Peregrine Dudley. Columba worked as a part-time actor with the Abbey Theatre and the Dublin Drama League, and briefly studied medicine at University College Dublin. In 1930, she moved to England, where she qualified as a doctor, getting married, again, in 1935, to Evan Guest, a botanist; they migrated to Malaya and later to Iraq.

Dudley Heathcote (*b.* 1877) was a journalist who wrote two successful travel books, *My Wanderings in the Balkans* (1925) and *Sweden* (1927). He married Ida Martheze in England in 1910, but the marriage ended in 1918. He married Jessie Dunbar in 1919 but the marriage did not last very long.

23 August 1921
William E. Hopkins

Director and Supervisor of trumpets and kettledrums attending the State in the Kingdom of Ireland. Organist, First Gentleman and Master of the Children of His Majesty's Chapel Royal in Ireland, sub-organist, St Patrick's Cathedral, Dublin.

Blinding mist and rain. Almost dark at 5.30. Very happy to renew my acquaintance with this charming spot and most excellent tea.

This visitor was anything but modest.

McGuirk's in 1922

28 May 1922

H. T. Flannery   Dublin
Terence K. Digby   Kerry

Tea very nice – very refreshing after long cycle ride. Only objection is that Mr McLaren wouldn't allow us to fish in Loch Bray. Easily seen he is a Scotchman and not an Irishman. Never mind, we will meet him again.

These two left a note including what may have been, with the times that were in it, an ominous and even threatening last sentence, referring to the gamekeeper overseeing Lough Bray. When the Guinness family had leased the shooting and fishing rights on Powerscourt Mountain, which included Lough Bray and the surrounding lands, around 1912, they brought over gamekeeper George McLaren from Pitlochry in Scotland to breed and protect their game. Tom McGuirk told me that McLaren always carried his shotgun with him, and had no mercy for peregrines or kestrels, which he believed stole his grouse. He also shot any herons he came across because he believed they took trout from the lake.

28 May 1922
Dr and Mrs V.M. Synge

Victor Millington Synge (1893–1976) was another nephew of the playwright J.M. Synge. He was educated at St Andrew's College and Trinity College Dublin. He loved to walk in the Dublin and Wicklow mountains and for many years climbed the Sugarloaf in Wicklow every Sunday. He served in the Royal Navy during WWI, after which he graduated with an MB (Bachelor of Medicine), MD (Doctor of Medicine) and DPH (Doctor of Public Health). He was appointed visiting physician to the Royal City of Dublin Hospital, on Baggot Street, and remained connected with this institution for fifty-seven years. He became King's Professor of Medical Practice at Trinity in 1934 and Regius Professor of Physic in 1960. He was an amateur botanist, and could converse in Norwegian and Russian. A true physician before 'holistic' medicine came into vogue, he aimed to treat the person rather than the disease: in spite of being a heavy smoker, he was eighty-three when he died.

1923

29 May 1923
Doreen Synge
Farrington

Doreen Hamilton Synge married her companion of this day, Anthony Farrington, in March 1924. After her marriage, she continued to come to McGuirk's, signing herself both as Synge and Farrington.

Anthony Farrington (1873–1973) studied engineering at University College Cork and became a major figure in the Irish geological world. He was a founder member of the Geographical Society of Ireland, assistant secretary of the Royal Irish Academy and sometime editor of the journal *Irish Geography*. He was a leading authority on Irish glaciology and published papers on the geology of the Ice Age in Ireland. After he married Doreen, they lived in Academy House on Dawson Street, Dublin (today the home of the Royal Irish Academy), until his retirement, when they moved to a house they had built themselves in Ticknock, Co. Dublin.

Academy House on Dawson Street, Dublin, now the home of the Royal Irish Academy

2 June 1923

P.S. Ó Raghallaigh
S. Mac Omeachtaigh
P. Ó Brosnacháin
O. MacBearnáird
Croinsíag MacBearnáird
Próinsias Ó Raghaillaigh
Seósamh Ó Tórna
Jack
Spot

This new walking club, Cumann na gCnoc, began to call at McGuirk's around this time and all of them, except their dogs Spot and Jack, signed the visitors' book in Irish.

5 October 1923

Proinseas M. Ó Flannagáin
Claud de Bhal   *Rath Ōmaíne, Āth Cliath,*
                                   Poblacht na hĒireann

Lá fuar fliuch dob'eadh indiu. Do shiubhaileamar ón gcathair go dtí Mám na tSáiligh nó 'Sally Gap' mar a dubhartar as Béarla é. Ag teacht ar ais do chuireamar stad fúinn ag dtig Mhic Uirc. Bhí tae an-mhaith againn ann [agus] taréis tamall do leanamar ar an t-slighe chun Rath Ō Maíne. Ag imtheacht dúinn anois tá an dorchadas tuithte ar na sléibhte. Go n-éirí an mbothar linn abhaile!

This translates as:

Today was a cold, wet day. We walked from the city to Mám na tSáiligh or 'The Sally Gap' as they say in English. On the way back we made a stop at McGuirk's house. We had a great tea there and after a while we followed the trail to Rathmines. On leaving now, darkness has fallen on the mountains. May the homeward road rise to us!

12 November 1923
Armistice Day 11/11/23
C.W. Brownlee

Armistice Day, commemorating the end of WWI, had been a low-key affair in the south of Ireland in 1921 and 1922. With the Civil War over and the Free State established, however, the national perspective broadened to accept that, for most, it was not a demonstration of loyalty to the British Empire but a commemoration of all the Irish who had died in the war. The following year, an estimated 50,000 people attended the ceremony at College Green in Dublin and wreaths were laid, including one from the Free State government, although there was no Minister present. *The Irish Times* went so far as to express the hope that the Irish ceremony would also commemorate those 'who died for the cause of freedom in the Irish Brigades of the 18th century, and of soldiers who died for the same cause of freedom in the Ireland of a few years ago'.

A Study of a Soldier (1917) by William Orpen

1924

The Irish Free State officially came into being in December 1922, six months after the beginning of a short but vicious civil war. Although the Civil War ended in May 1923, the resulting economic and infrastructural turmoil lasted years. McGuirk's continued to provide refreshment for excursionists, and visitors continued to praise the fare they received. The low volume of British visitors during the War of Independence continued through the Civil War but, by the mid-1920s, they were back in numbers again. Although

Iseult Stuart by an unknown photographer

the Anglo-Irish continued to frequent McGuirk's, their numbers were declining and a change is discernible in the increase in middle-class visitors, including artists, playwrights, writers and politicians.

25 May 1924
Iseult Stuart   *Robuck House, Clonskeagh*
H. Stuart

This couple had fascinating lives, ranging from strong connections with W.B. Yeats to imprisonment in Mountjoy Prison, and from winning a silver medal for prize-winning pullets to life in wartime Nazi Germany.

Iseult Stuart (1894–1954), née Gonne, was the daughter of Maud Gonne and her French lover, the journalist and politician Lucien Millevoye. She was educated in France and, when she came to Ireland, her mother passed her off as her niece. Iseult met the American poet Ezra Pound in France and, following in her mother's footsteps as a 'modern woman', was briefly his mistress. W.B. Yeats had long been in love with her mother but, in 1916, when he was in his fifties and Iseult was twenty-two, he proposed marriage to her but was turned down. She is the subject of two of his poems. She eloped with the eighteen-year-old Francis Stuart in 1920, and in 1928 Maud Gonne bought Laragh Castle, a disused Military Road barracks in Co. Wicklow, for them, where they went on to have two children. Iseult spent six months in custody in 1944 for assisting the German spy Hermann Görtz.

H. Stuart is Henry Francis Montgomery Stuart (1902–2000), whose life spanned almost the entire twentieth century. Born in Australia of Irish parents, he was brought up in Dublin and attended boarding school in England. From a young age, he frequented the literary and artistic scene in Dublin, meeting and marrying Iseult; through Maud Gonne, he became involved with the anti-Treaty side during the Civil War. Captured and jailed in Mountjoy and the Curragh, he read widely and wrote poetry. On his release, he published his first book of poetry, which drew praise from W.B. Yeats. A month before this visit to McGuirk's, Stuart produced a pamphlet, *Nationality and Culture*, in which he suggested that the Free State had no commitment to a national culture: Ireland should be more European and not model itself on England.

At Laragh, the couple's tempestuous relationship calmed down for a while and Stuart enjoyed a fruitful period of writing, publishing, between 1932 and 1939, eleven novels, a volume of autobiography, and a guide to horse-racing in Ireland. He got to know Helmut Clissmann, an Ireland-based German intelligence officer and Nazi party member, who invited him to Germany in 1939 to give a lecture tour. He was offered a post at the University of Berlin as a lecturer in English, where he remained for the rest of the war. During this time, he broadcast radio talks aimed at an Irish audience, in which he praised Hitler and said that Germany would help unite Ireland. When Iseult died in 1954, Stuart married his German mistress, Gertrude Meissner, and they returned to Ireland in 1958, where he had considerable literary success for the remainder of his long life, despite the controversy about his Nazi experience.

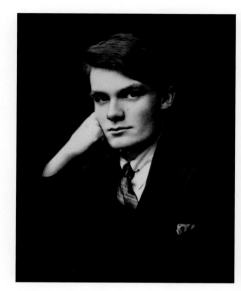

The young Francis Stuart

29 June 1924
Seán Mac Giolla Fhaoláin   Atha Cliath

This visitor adds a line from Brian Merriman's poem *Cúirt an Mheáin Oíche* ('The Midnight Court') to describe the mountains around Glencree:

> *na Sléibhte*
> *Ag bagairt a gcinn thar dhruim a céile.*

This translates as: 'the mountains rear their heads over each other's backs'.

7 December 1924

John B. Gregg   *TCD*

Cowper described Glencree when he said: 'Scenes must be beautiful which daily viewed please daily and whose novelty survives long knowledge and the scrutiny of years.'

1925

17 January 1925

T.J. Johnston   *TCD*

W.D.L. Greer   *TCD*

These two are Trinity College Dublin scholars. T.J. Johnston gave the Trinity Memorial Discourse in 1935 on the subject of Lord Chief Justice Henry Flood, the most talented patriot politician of his generation.

William Derrick Lindsay Greer (1902–1972) was born in Dungannon, Co. Tyrone, and educated at St Columba's College, Dublin, and Trinity College Dublin. He was Assistant Principal in the Ministry of Home Affairs in Northern Ireland, but joined the Anglican Church and was ordained in 1929. He was Bishop of Manchester at the time of his death, and Bishop Greer High School in Manchester is named after him.

The Brotherhood of the Lug in 1904

12 February 1925

E. Scanlan

E.A. Mooney

W. Connolly

M. Finn

Francis O'Meredith, The GM

Made the ascent of Kippure – much snow and stalagtites [sic] and other things.

Motif of the Brotherhood of the Lug from the visitors' book

Another walking club starting to sign in to McGuirk's in 1925 was the Brotherhood of the Lug, founded in 1903 and still in existence today. The club's activities, walks, daring climbs, dinners and songs over 120 years are contained in its written records. It is a rule that nothing is taken too seriously other than long walks in the hills, socialising with like-minded companions, and enjoying food and liquid libations. Indeed, it is not clear which activity they take more seriously.

A typical day's outing might involve a trek from Blessington via Ballysmuttan, the Coronation Plantation and the Sally Gap to Lough Bray, where they would have had 'dinner' in McGuirk's and, afterwards, their 'usual toddle' to Bray for the train back to Dublin, a round trip of about 35 km. When members of 'the Lugs' signed in, they sometimes included the Lugs' motif (derived from the Scots Gaelic for 'ear'), along with the founding date of 1903. 'GM' stands for Grand Master, the title of the club's president or leader.

19 July 1925
Lia Clarke
Marion Lavery
George Day

Lia Clarke (1889–1943) aka Margaret Lyster, née Cornelia Cummins, novelist, playwright, poet and psychic, grew up in Waterford but later lived in Dublin, where she came to know Maud Gonne, and where her experiments with automatic writing probably brought her into contact with W.B. Yeats and George Russell ('Æ'). Æ drew a pencil portrait of her that was sold in 2008 for €4,800. She was secretly married to the poet Austin Clarke in 1920, after he had spent a year in St Patrick's psychiatric hospital with severe depression. The marriage lasted just two weeks, but she refused to divorce him.

She later wrote for *The Irish Press* and, in the 1930s, became a Nazi sympathiser and wrote articles for German news agencies.

31 July 1925
Christabel Manning
Máire Ní Dubhthaig
Delle Chevenix Trench
Clare Chevenix Trench

Christabel Susan Manning (1910–1988) was the daughter of Susan Manning, née Bennett, and Fitzmaurice Manning. In about 1932, she married Robert Alden Childers, son of the nationalist Robert Erskine Childers, executed in 1922, and they had two children. They lived in England for most of their lives, until returning to Ireland in 1971 to live at Glendalough House, in Co. Wicklow. In 1934, she was awarded a short story prize by *Motley*, the Gate Theatre magazine, the editor of which was her sister, Mary Manning. Seán Ó Faoláin was the judge.

Clare Chevenix Trench, née Howard, was the wife of Major Reggie Chevenix Trench, who was killed on 21 March 1918, the day the final German offensive on the Western Front began. The casualties for that day alone, for both sides, amounted to around 78,000, the highest number for a single day's fighting in all of WWI. Clare was the sister-in-law of Cesca Chevenix Trench or Sadhbh Trinseach, the artist and nationalist activist, who died in the flu pandemic of 1918.

Delle was Clare and Reggie's daughter.

12 December 1925
William E. Hopkins
G. Trevor Lowry   *TCD*

George Trevor Lowry (1906–1941) was born in Kells, Co. Meath, educated at the Coleraine Academical Institute, and studied law

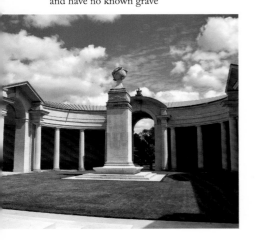

The Arras Memorial in France commemorates nearly 35,000 servicemen, including Reggie Chevenix Trench, who fell during the final months of World War I and have no known grave

at Trinity College Dublin; he was called to the Bar in 1933. He joined the British colonial service in Nigeria and was appointed Resident Magistrate in Hong Kong in 1940. When war loomed, he volunteered as a private in the Hong Kong Volunteer Defence Corps. Japanese forces attacked Hong Kong on 8 December 1941 and the British surrendered on Christmas Day. George was reported missing, presumed killed, during the fighting, and was one of more than 2,000 Commonwealth servicemen who died in the battle, or subsequently in captivity, who have no known grave.

1926

17 March 1926
O.S. Skeffington   *Rathmines, Dublin*

Owen Sheehy-Skeffington (1909–1970) was the son of Francis Skeffington and Hannah Sheehy. Francis, a socialist, pacifist and feminist, was picked up off the street during the 1916 Rising and summarily executed at Portobello Barracks two days later. Hannah was a suffragist and nationalist. Owen was seventeen at the time of this visit to McGuirk's and attending Sandford Park School; he later studied English and French at Trinity College Dublin. In 1933, he was on the teaching staff of the École Normale Supérieure in Paris, where he met James Joyce and Samuel Beckett. In 1935, he was awarded a PhD from TCD and became a lecturer in French there. He was elected a senator in 1954 and campaigned, among many issues, against censorship, corporal punishment and Apartheid; he also championed women's rights.

26 March 1926
Lady Alice Scott, and maids   London

McGuirk's tea room was still hosting the princes of the Church and the aristocracy: during 1926, two 'Ladys' and a bishop took tea there.

The young Owen Sheehy-Skeffington with his mother

The Duke and Duchess of Gloucester dressed for the coronation of King George VI and Queen Elizabeth in 1937

Lady Alice Christabel Montague Douglas Scott (1901–2004) was born in London, educated at St James's School for girls in Malvern, and continued her studies in Paris. She married Prince Henry, Duke of Gloucester, third son of King George V, in the Private Chapel of Buckingham Palace in 1935, two weeks after her father's death, and two months before her new husband's. During WWII, the Duchess worked with the Red Cross and the Order of St John and was head of the Women's Auxiliary Air Force (WAAF). After the war, she was colonel-in-chief of a dozen regiments of the British Army, and was promoted to Air Chief Marshal of the RAF in 1990. She published her memoirs at the age of eighty and her last public appearance was for her hundredth birthday in December 2001.

13 April 1926

✠ *Robert Browne*	*Bishop of Cloyne*
James Bury SJ	*Dublin*
M. Devitt SJ	*Milltown Park*
F.M. Browne SJ	*Dublin*

Milltown Park in Ranelagh in Dublin was a Jesuit novitiate, and the McGuirks, who were a religious family, were happy to host many priests and novices over the years. They must have been particularly proud to welcome a bishop. Signing with a cross before his name, Robert Browne (1844–1935) was born in Charleville, Co. Cork, and studied at St Colman's College, Fermoy, and St Patrick's College, Maynooth. He was ordained into the priesthood in 1869 and became Dean of Maynooth College in 1875. In 1894, he was appointed Bishop of Cloyne. Father F.M. Browne was his more well-known nephew.

30 December 1926

Lady McGrath   *11 Clyde Road, Dublin*
Miss L. McGrath

Eleanor Mary, Lady McGrath, née Alister, was the widow of Sir Joseph McGrath, who had died in 1923. Miss L. McGrath was one of their two daughters. Sir Joseph had been Registrar of the National University of Ireland and was created a knight in 1911 for his services in education. Their son Fergal was a Jesuit priest, a graduate of University College Dublin and Oxford University, a Newman scholar, and an author.

1927

30 May 1927

A.C.B. Neville   *Toronto, Canada*

Son of R.B.T. Neville, who formerly spent many pleasant & happy days at Loch Bray – a relative of Sir Philip Crampton – and was a son of Cannon [sic] Neville, Jubilee Hall, Bray. On a delightful visit to Ireland and England.

Sir Philip Crampton, Surgeon by Stephen Catterson Smith

Sir Philip Crampton (1777–1858), born in Dublin, was the original owner of Lough Bray Cottage, overlooking the lake, of which the McGuirks' cottage had been the gate lodge. He was a surgeon in the Meath Hospital and Surgeon General of the British Army in Ireland, and was made a baronet in 1839. His main home was 14 Merrion Square; a pear tree growing in the basement was referred to in James Joyce's *Finnegans Wake*. It is said that he could swim across Lough Bray, ride into town and amputate a limb – all before breakfast.

2 July 1927

W. Pakenham-Walsh London, England
E. Douglas Dublin

William Sandford Pakenham-Walsh (1868–1960), born in Dublin to an Irish clerical family, was a clergyman, educationalist and writer. In 1897, he went to China to work with the Dublin University Fukien Mission and act as chaplain to the British community in Fuzhou. Pakenham-Walsh remained in China until 1921, and from 1922 to 1956 was vicar of Sulgrave in West Northamptonshire, although he notes his address here as London. He spent many years researching the life of Anne Boleyn, and sought clairvoyants to help him connect with her. At the age of ninety, he completed *A Tudor Story: The Return of Anne Boleyn*, which was posthumously published in 1963.

10 July 1927

Muiread Trínseach
Diarmuid Ó Cobthaigh
Sorhy [?] Ó Doréin

Muiread Trinseach (*b.* 1889) was the sister of Sadhbh Trinseach, the artist and political activist.

Diarmuid Ó Cobhthaigh, or Diarmuid Coffey (1888–1964), born in Dublin, was the son of George Coffey, archaeologist, and Jane L'Estrange. They lived in Ely Place, Dublin, where W.B. Yeats and Douglas Hyde were frequent visitors, and Diarmuid attended Trinity College Dublin, graduating with a Bachelor of Law in 1910; he was later called to the Bar. He joined the Irish Volunteers and was on board the *Kelpie* with Conor O'Brien during the lesser-known August 1914 landing of guns for the Volunteers at Kilcoole, Co. Wexford. A follower of Douglas Hyde's policies, he was not in favour of the 1916 Rising and did not take part in it. He married Sadhbh Trinseach in 1918, but she died in the flu pandemic the same year.

Peugeot advertisement from 1927

23 August 1927
Sean Daly and James Pollard, having pushed a Peugeot car that should have carried them here, arrived exhausted. After having tea they departed in high spirits determined to push it back to Dublin.

In another hand:

Lucky it wasn't an Armstrong Siddley.

29 August 1927
H.E. Crook, Howth

Farewell, thou little nook of mountain ground
Thou rocky corner in the lowest stair
Of that magnificent temple which doth bound
One side of our whole vale with grandeur rare;
Farewell! – we leave thee to Heaven's peaceful care,
Thee and the Cottage which thou dost surround.

Quoting from William Wordsworth's poem 'A Farewell' to describe the cottage at Lough Bray, H.E. Crook, for some reason, omitted these two appropriate lines:

Sweet Garden-orchard, eminently fair,
The loveliest spot that man hath ever found.

Memorial for Captain Noel Lemass at Featherbed Mountain

As mentioned before, a notable characteristic of the entries in the visitors' books is that the outside world and what is happening there, even the most momentous events, are rarely mentioned. The following poetic entry is one of the exceptions. Just a mile from McGuirk's, on the Featherbeds, a Celtic cross marked the spot on the desolate moorland where the body of Noel Lemass was found after his murder by Free State 'supporters' in the summer of 1923, after the end of the Civil War. In October of that year, someone took pity on his mother and visited her in the family draper's shop in Capel Street to let her know where he was buried. His body was retrieved and the coroner at the inquest said that it bore signs of torture that would 'shame the most primitive savage'. The jury in the Coroner's Court found that the Free State Army was implicated in his death and called for a judicial enquiry, which the government refused. In the 1990s, the Celtic cross marking the spot was vandalised, and has since been replaced by a simple stone.

12 September 1927
Gladys Hynes, 41 Haverstock Hill, London

Lemass'es [sic] Cross
By the lonely mountain road stands a cross of stone
It marks where a bullet-pierced body lay, unknown,
While day followed night and night followed day,
And the quiet mountain folk passed by on their way,
And were long to learn
What horror lay hidden there under the fern.

But surely the Earth of Ireland was wiser and knew,
And bade the heather and fern bow down as they grew,
And hushed him in stillness there to peaceful rest,
While like a child he lay close to her breast.

Gladys Hynes (1888–1958) was born in India of Irish parents. She studied art in London and at the Forbes School of Painting in Newlyn, Cornwall. Proud of her Irish roots, Hynes was a strong supporter of Irish independence and also campaigned for women's rights. In the same year of this visit to McGuirk's, she was commissioned to illustrate a folio edition of Ezra Pound's *Cantos*. The horrors of the Civil War were still fresh in minds four years after it ended, inspiring the scribbled notes that follow this verse: 'They that live by the sword, die by the sword', and a later note, 'Cowardly'.

The stone bears the legend: 'In proud and loving memory of Captain Noel Lemass, 3rd Batt Dublin City Brigade IRA who died so that the republic might live. His murdered body was found on this spot 13th October 1923'.

7 September 1927
Catherine McGilligan
Gertie O'Connell
Koho
Ann Conolly
Kathleen McGilligan

Catherine McGilligan, Kathleen McGilligan and Gertie O'Connell, née McGilligan, are sisters of Patrick McGilligan, TD, academic and lawyer. He married Ann Conolly in 1929, built up his law practice and became Professor of Constitutional and International Law at University College Dublin. He subsequently became Minister for Finance and Attorney General, retiring from the Dáil in 1965 after serving as a TD for over forty years. His wife, Ann, gets very few mentions through his career, but does feature, however, in the files of Georg von Dehn-Schmidt, the German envoy to Ireland in 1930. He described McGilligan as 'a very able man, but completely dominated by his headstrong wife'.

Patrick McGilligan (centre) pictured with German politicians Julius Curtius, Wilhelm Cuno and Heinrich Brüning, Apostolic Nuncio Cesare Orsenigo and British Ambassador Horace Rumbold in Berlin, 1931

The explosion that destroyed the Four Courts complex on 30 June 1922

Gertie O'Connell married Lieutenant General J.J. O'Connell (known as 'Ginger') of the Free State Army, shortly after his release from the Four Courts following his kidnapping by the anti-Treaty Irish Republican Army (IRA) at the beginning of the Civil War. Having spent some time in the United States Army, he returned to Ireland and joined the Volunteers in 1914. He was interned in Frongoch internment camp after the Rising, and was IRA Director of Training during the War of Independence. He was Deputy Chief of Staff in the National Army under Michael Collins, and continued in the army until his death.

Koho, I presume, is a dog.

1928

5 August 1928
Dr Dorothy and Liam Price

Eleanor Dorothy Stopford Price (1890–1954), a frequent visitor to McGuirk's, was born in Dublin and studied medicine at Trinity College Dublin. During the 1916 Rising, she was a house guest of Sir Matthew Nathan, the British Under-Secretary in Ireland, and experienced the confusion the rebellion caused among the British administration at the time. She later espoused the nationalist cause. On qualifying as a doctor in 1920, she specialised in tuberculosis, particularly in children, and wrote well-received papers on the subject. A champion of the Bacillus Calmette–Guérin (BCG) vaccine for the disease, in 1949 she was appointed Chairman of the Consultative Council on Tuberculosis, and in that capacity opened the first BCG vaccination clinic in Ireland at Saint Ultan's Children's Hospital in Dublin. She contributed to saving the lives of thousands of young people and to ending the tuberculosis epidemic of the 1940s.

Her husband, George William 'Liam' Price (1891–1967), a barrister and district judge, is probably better known as an historian and president of the Royal Society of Antiquaries of Ireland, and for his papers and publications, particularly those related to historical topography and place names. He became engaged to Dorothy Stopford in 1924 and they married in spite of their political differences: she supported the anti-Treaty Republicans while Liam supported the Free State.

12 August 1928

H.B. Kennedy	*Dean of Christchurch, Dublin*
Wm Slader & Hilda A. Slader	*Lynton, Devonshire*

Herbert Brownlow Kennedy (1863–1939) was Dean of Christ Church Cathedral in Dublin and a clear-headed, independent thinker who wasn't slow to voice gentle opposition to the prevailing climate of moral opinion and censorship in the Irish Free State. He was a member of the Carrigan Commission, set up by W.T. Cosgrave in 1930 to determine whether new legislation was required to deal with juvenile prostitution. Among their conclusions in August 1931 was that the increasing sexual crime rate included a large number of cases of criminal interference with girls and children aged sixteen years and under, including many cases of children aged under ten: sometimes children were treated by the law as accomplices in a crime rather than its victims. They also recommended that the offence of solicitation should be applicable to the men buying sex as well as to the women selling it. The Department of Justice strongly advised against the report's publication and it was shelved because it was thought of as being 'too one-sided'.

Illustration by Herbert Cole for *The Rubáiyát of Omar Khayyám*

18 September 1928
Cercle Aphrodite D. Devlin
Mervyn Wall

Mihi terrarum ille praetor omnes Angelus ridet.

Cyril P. Crean, ibet iacere modo sub antiquo ilice modo in tenace gramine.
Claude Carroll, Eheu fugacis …

A book – a glass a milk and thou
Beside me singing in the wilderness
And old Lough Bray is paradise now.

This group of students from University College Dublin was clearly impressed by Lough Bray and McGuirk's, and some waxed lyrical with slightly misquoted lines from the Roman poet Horace and allusions to *The Rubáiyát of Omar Khayyám*. 'Cercle Aphrodite' is today a term that celebrates the concept of women enjoying their erotic powers: what connotations it had for this group in 1928 is not clear.

The first piece of Latin seems to misquote Horace; it should read *Ille terrarum mihi praeter omnes angulus ridet*, which roughly translates as 'This corner of the earth smiles for me more than any other'. The second piece also misquotes Horace, but Horace's version translates as 'It is pleasing at one time to lie under the ancient oak, at another time in the thick grass'. Claude Carroll also quotes a snippet of Horace; more fully, '*Eheu fugaces, Postume, Postume, Labuntur anni*' – 'Alas, Postumus [Horace's friend to whom the ode is addressed], the fleeting years slip by'.

Denis Devlin (1908–1959) would become a frequent visitor to McGuirk's around this time. Born to Irish parents in Scotland who had returned to Ireland in 1918, his father Liam was an intelligence officer with the IRA. Denis attended Belvedere College in Dublin, where he met Mervyn Wall, and Clonliffe College in 1926, to study for the priesthood. During his first year at Clonliffe, he also attended University College Dublin to study modern languages and, clearly finding UCD's student life preferable to Clonliffe's, enrolled in UCD in 1927. He graduated with first-class honours in English and French the year after this visit to McGuirk's and, following a period at the Sorbonne in Paris and teaching at UCD, joined the diplomatic service where he had a distinguished career that he combined with publishing his poetry. In his 1934 essay 'Recent Irish Poetry', Samuel Beckett named Denis Devlin and Brian Coffey as 'without question the most interesting of the youngest generation of Irish poets'.

Mervyn Wall (1908–1997) was a Dublin-born writer who published novels, short stories and plays, and wrote for a short-lived magazine called *Ireland Today*. He was educated at Belvedere College, Dublin, and University College Dublin, after which he worked as a civil servant until 1948, when he joined Raidió Éireann. He wrote two fantasy novels, *The Unfortunate Fursey* (1946) and *The Return of Fursey* (1948), about an Irish monk during the Dark Ages; these were highly successful in the United States and Canada, where they were described as landmarks in the history of fantasy literature. Both books are still in print. Wall was secretary of the Arts Council, 1957–75, and his wife, Frances Feehan, was a theatre and music critic.

Many years later, he wrote about J.M. Synge's connection with McGuirk's in a newspaper article:

> Young Dublin's great playground is the Dublin and Wicklow Mountains. We begin to discover them on foot or on bicycle from about the age of 15. For many years I walked those granite-grained white roads and climbed the hills, but after reading [Synge's] *In Wicklow,*

Prospectus for a 1904 performance by the Irish National Theatre Society noting the Wicklow setting of *In the Shadow of the Glen*

West Kerry and Connemara these solitudes are no longer empty, but had become peopled with phrases and lines of verse. One came to know 'the grey and wintry sides of many glens' [Synge] and no longer walked alone. While still in UCD I often led parties across the Featherbeds to Mrs Guirk's cottage by Lough Bray where *The Shadow of the Glen* was written. We would solemnly inspect Synge's signature in the visitors' book, look at his framed photograph and listen to Mrs McGuirk relating how she had brought in his shaving water each morning and how Mr Fay used to come up on a sidecar from Enniskerry to visit him.

It is unlikely that *In the Shadow of the Glen* was written at McGuirk's, however, as it was performed in 1903, several years before Synge stayed at the cottage.

Cyril P. Crean (*d.* 1973) was a Catholic priest before joining the British Army as a chaplain in 1941. The army was in his blood: his uncle, Major Dr Thomas Joseph Crean, was a British Army chaplain who won the Victoria Cross in the Boer War and the Distinguished Service Order (DSO) in WWI. On 6 June 1944, D-Day, Cyril waded ashore on Juno Beach at Bernières-sur-Mer with the 29th Armoured Division, and was with them as they advanced through France and Belgium; he was awarded an MBE. After the war, and back in Dublin, he was a curate in Donnybrook Parish and in 1955 was appointed Head Chaplain to the Irish Army. In 1960, he accompanied the 32nd Infantry Battalion of the Irish Army to the Congo on United Nations duty, during which mission nine soldiers were ambushed and killed by Baluba tribesmen at Niemba. He returned from the Congo in 1962 and was the parish priest of Donnybrook Parish until 1973.

27 September 1928
Shamrock Trench
Seán O'Sullivan
Harry Kernoff

Shamrock Trench sketched at McGuirk's by Seán O'Sullivan

Jean Martha Netta ('Shamrock') Trench (1908–1974) was one of two daughters of Wilbraham Trench, Professor of English Literature at Trinity College Dublin, and Mary Alicia Trench (née Cross), and was born at Ardmore, Co. Galway. Regarded as a wild child, Shamrock was sent to a series of schools, including Alexandra College, Dublin; Abbey College, Worcestershire; and St George's School, Hertfordshire, where she excelled at athletics and music. At the time of this visit to McGuirk's, she had spent a year in Germany studying music, where she met, in April 1928, Colonel James Fitzmaurice, the Commanding Officer of the Irish Air Corps, who had taken part in the first east–west flight across the Atlantic. She became interested in theatre and, on her return home, toured Ireland in stage plays with the English actor Anew McMaster and met his brother-in-law, actor and dramatist Micheál Mac Liammóir.

In 1931, inspired by James Fitzmaurice and encouraged by Oliver St. John Gogarty, Shamrock took up flying; Gogarty used to drive her to Baldonnel Aerodrome in his Rolls-Royce. She became the first woman to hold an Irish Free State Aviator's Certificate. She was married three times: through her second husband, she acquired the title Countess Metaxa. On the day of their visit to McGuirk's, Seán O'Sullivan drew a pencil portrait of her in the visitors' book. The sketch attracted admiration from later visitors, some of whom leave notes, such as 'belle gosse ["good-looking girl"]', 'There's a green little shamrock that grows in our isle' and 'Said Shamrock none too green!'

Seán O'Sullivan sketched at McGuirk's by
Herry Kernoff

Seán O'Sullivan (1906–1964) was a portrait and landscape painter, educated by the Christian Brothers at Synge Street before attending the Dublin Metropolitan School of Art in 1926, where one of his teachers was the painter Seán Keating. O'Sullivan studied lithography in London and painting in Paris. Having lived in London, he moved to Dublin in the early 1930s, where he soon earned a reputation for his work and became regarded as the best portrait painter of his time. He was very versatile and could turn his hand to any medium: his output included religious murals, Stations of the Cross and postage stamps. He painted portraits of Éamon de Valera, Douglas Hyde, James Joyce and W.B. Yeats. He was working on a portrait of the Abbot of Mount St Joseph in Co. Offaly in April 1964 when he had a stroke; he died a few weeks later. Harry Kernoff, his companion on the day of this visit, left a pencil portrait of him in the visitors' book.

Harry Kernoff (1900–1974) was born in London of Russian and Spanish parents. After the family moved to Dublin in 1914, he began to take night classes at the Dublin Metropolitan School of Art, where he met Seán O'Sullivan and was taught by Seán Keating, among others. He won the Taylor Scholarship in 1923 with his painting *At the Railway Station* and, like O'Sullivan, worked in a wide range of media and was extraordinarily prolific. He produced hundreds of miniature oil paintings, designed the settings for Seán O'Casey's play *The Shadow of a Gunman*, and produced numerous woodcuts and drawings for various publications, including *A Book of Dublin. Official Handbook* (1929). Although he represented Ireland in painting in the 1928 Olympics (Jack B. Yeats won Ireland's first ever Olympic medal in the 1924 Olympics with his painting *The Liffey Swim*) and exhibited in Italy, Paris, Canada and London, he was not fully appreciated until a few years before his death.

3 October 1928

Liam ua Féich   *St Michael's, Deilginis*
Brian Ó Brolcháin   *Dún Bríde, Beann Eadair*

Nach breagh an nidh, an t-slighe do chur uait
An gaoth it' aghaidh is tú gan streó
Gan cúram it' aigne nó trial faoi leith
Acht teacht fán deire don tigh maith seo.

Sult is suaimhneas, ar an t-sléibh amuigh
Cainnt is ciúnas sa tigh istigh
ailnach breá a rádh, a chara dhil
An teach chomh ghlan is na daoine fial.
Brian Ó Brolcháin

This translates as:

Isn't it grand to take to the road,
The wind in your face, all stress removed,
no care in the world, no worries at all,
Our destination, this fine house.

Calm and peace on the mountains outside,
Civil chat inside the walls,
What a fine feeling, my loyal friend,
Such a neat house and generous hosts.

Ó Brolcháin's companion, Liam ua Féich, also left a piece of poetry:

Bean Mhic Cuirc, blasta a béile
Ar a bhfuil de thighibh, féile
Ar chasas riamh in Inis Fáil
Dligheadh flaitheas do ghabháil.

This translates as:

> Mrs McGuirk, her food, such taste
> On all her houses, wealth be laced
> In all this isle, I never found
> Where such kind and generous souls abound.

9 October 1928
R. Gibbings (R. McGabhair)
Caoimhghin Ó Siadhail (Kevin O'Shiel)

Robert John Gibbings (1889–1958) was a Cork-born artist and writer. His early years were spent in Kinsale, Co. Cork, where his father was a Church of Ireland rector. After studying medicine at University College Cork, he changed direction and took up art, studying at the Slade School of Art in London. At London's Central School of Art and Crafts, founded by the influential architectural theorist and educator William Lethaby, he became strongly influenced by the Arts and Crafts movement. Joining the Royal Munster Fusiliers at the start of WWI, he was wounded in Gallipoli. After the war, he was a founder member of the Society of Wood Engravers. In 1924, he bought the Golden Cockerel Press and, with his wife, Moira, produced around seventy high-quality books in low print numbers between then and 1933, while continuing to illustrate other works. In the mid-1930s, suffering from depression and a broken marriage, his career as a successful author/illustrator was revived. During WWII, he began his series of river books with *Sweet Thames Run Softly* (1940). He married again, this time to Elizabeth Empson, with whom he had two children, but this marriage also failed and he eventually settled down in a cottage on the Thames with Elizabeth's sister, Patience.

Caoimhghín Ó Siadhail or Kevin O'Shiel (1891–1970) was a barrister and land commissioner. He was born in Omagh, Co. Tyrone, studied law at Trinity College Dublin and was called to the Bar in

Artist and typographer Eric Gill produced many fine engravings for the Golden Cockerel Press, including this cockerel motif for *The Four Gospels* (1931)

1913. He joined the Irish Volunteers but did not take part in the 1916 Rising because, as a devout Catholic, he didn't believe in taking secret oaths. He joined Sinn Féin in 1917 and was an unsuccessful candidate in the election of 1918, but in 1920 he was recruited by Arthur Griffith and became a judicial commissioner of the Irish Land Commission. He was assistant legal advisor to the Provisional Government in 1922, and was involved in drawing up the first Irish Constitution. From 1923 until his retirement, he was a commissioner on the Irish Land Commission. His first wife died young and he married Cecil Smiddy in 1929.

12 November 1928
Peg Fagan
C.R. White

The night was very parky
The car was rather done
But Peggy was so larky
We had a lot of fun.

26 December 1928
Seán Óg Ó Caomhánaigh
Harry Kernoff

Seán Kavanagh sketched at McGuirk's by Herry Kernoff

Harry Kernoff left a portrait of Seán Kavanagh on this St Stephen's Day. Kavanagh (Seán Óg Ó Caomhánaigh) signed the visitors' book in Irish, with a little quatrain:

Is truagh san, a leabhair bhig bháin
Do dtiocfaidh an lá 'gus gur fíor,
Go ndéarfaidh neach os cionn cláir
Ná maireann na lámha a scrígh.

This translates as:

> It's a pity, my little white book,
> That the day will come, and it's true,
> That someone will say, over a table
> That the hands of the writer are no more.

Under this, Kernoff wrote, also in Irish: '*An fear is mó óil in Éirinn!*' or 'Ireland's greatest drinking man!', to which Kavanagh replied:

> *A Éinrí, ar do láimh tréan*
> *A riomhaidh choin beacht an dréacht,*
> *Do neach ar bith ní misde*
> *Suide dod mhéir sárchlisde.*

This translates as:

> Harry, from your strong hand
> Comes the precise facial expression,
> Anyone would gladly sit, for
> Your gifted fingers.

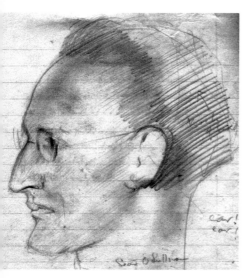

Herry Kernoff sketched at McGuirk's by Seán O'Sullivan

Seán Óg Ó Caomhánaigh (1885–1947), or Seán Kavanagh, also known as 'Seán an Chóta' (Seán of the coat), was born in Dunquin, Co. Kerry, and was a brother of Dr Séamus Caomhánach, Professor of Old Irish at University College Cork, and of the well-known Kerryman Muiris 'Kruger' Kavanagh. As a member of the Gaelic League and itinerant teacher of the Irish language, he travelled around the country organising Gaelic League branches and Irish classes. After a spell in the United States collecting money for Sinn Féin, he returned to Kerry in 1919 and became actively involved in the War of Independence; he took the anti-Treaty side and was interned by the Free State.

He translated classic stories such as *Aesop's Fables* and *The Arabian Nights* into Irish and he also wrote a number of novels, one of which was inspired by his brother Kruger's time in the States, when he associated with Samuel Goldwyn, May West and Al Jolson, worked for the Ziegfeld Follies, and was a bodyguard for Éamon de Valera during his American visits. Seán Óg taught Irish in the Masonic Boys' School and St Andrew's College, both Protestant establishments in Dublin, and was also a contributor to *The Irish Press*. The Department of Education commissioned him in 1935 to compile a gazetteer and dictionary of Kerry Irish, comprising in excess of two million words and phrases. This magnum opus was never published but is held in the National Library of Ireland. The Gaelic scholar Daithí Ó hUaithne has described him as 'not a scholar at all but a man who had acquired the full richness of his native Irish language and who always contributed to that wealth'.

Portrait of Éamon de Valera in America

1929

2 March 1929
Caoimhghin Ó Siadhail (Kevin O'Shiel)
Cecil Smiddy

On this day, Kevin O'Shiel (Caoimhghín Ó Siadhail) is with Cecil Smiddy, his second wife, daughter of Timothy Smiddy, an academic, diplomat and economist who was the Irish Free State's envoy extraordinary and minister plenipotentiary to the United States, 1924–9.

17 March 1929
J.W. Brownlee (alone and in search of the chaps of the Loraine Touring Club)

17 March 1929

W.H. Mowlds

Bertie Pemberton

F.W. Butterworth

T. Walsh

T. Abraham

G.S. Palmer

E. Watson

B.J. Kelly

F. Hoban

D.J. Hunter, all of the Loraine Cycling Club.

Sorry Mr B., we arrived about 10 minutes after you had gone.

This is one of many visits to McGuirk's made by the Loraine Cycling Club of Dublin. Founded in the early twentieth century, the club is said to be named after Robert Bilcliffe Loraine, who, apart from being an actor in London and on Broadway, was also an aviator who made the first aeroplane flight from England to Ireland. The flight almost came to grief when he had to land in the sea sixty metres short of the pier in Howth, Co. Dublin, but he swam ashore to be met by an admiring crowd, including members of an as yet unnamed cycling club. They were so impressed that they decided to name their club after him, and today the Loraine Cycling Club is one of the longest-lived cycling clubs in Ireland. Members were still visiting McGuirk's in the late 1950s, and Tom McGuirk told me that they always had a singsong after their tea.

10 April 1929

May and Felix Hackett of Rathgar

Actor Robert Loraine in a 1911 production of George Bernard Shaw's *Man and Superman*

Felix Edward Hackett (1882–1970), physicist, was born in Omagh, Co. Tyrone. At the time of his visit to McGuirk's, he was Professor of Physics at University College Dublin. As a Junior Fellow of the Royal University of Ireland, he had worked on the developing science of radioactivity with the Irish physicist J.A. McClelland. He was treasurer of the Royal Irish Academy, 1930–62, and honorary secretary of the Royal Dublin Society for twenty years, serving as its president, 1953–6. He retired from UCD in 1952.

Ballykinlar Internment Camp in 1920

7 May 1929
Maurice McGonigal
Patrick Bourke
The Wandering Gentiles:
Evaline Sibbald
Sheila M. O'Toole

Maurice McGonigal (1900–1979) was an Irish landscape and portrait painter who also designed sets for the Abbey Theatre and illustrated books and posters. He began his career as an apprentice in the stained-glass studio of his uncle, Joshua Clarke (father of the stained-glass artist Harry Clarke). He joined Na Fianna at the age of seventeen and was interned by the British in Ballykinlar Internment Camp, Co. Down, after the 1916 Rising. Following his release, he studied art at the Metropolitan School of Art in Dublin under the artists Seán Keating and Patrick Tuohy. At the time of this visit to McGuirk's, he had just returned from Holland where he had been studying painting. He was president of the Royal Hibernian Academy from 1962 to 1977.

2 June 1929

George Shackleton   *Lucan, Co. Dublin*
Rebecca Shackleton
Christine Shackleton
Janet Proctor   *York*

George Shackleton owned the Shackleton flour mills (also known as the Anna Liffey Mills) in Lucan. In 1913, he told his employees to resign from the Irish Transport and General Workers Union (ITGWU) or be given a week's notice. They refused so, on 26 August, Shackleton closed his business and 'locked out' his workers. On the same day, Dublin's trams, the life blood of the city's commerce, stopped running when the workers there went on strike, refusing a demand from their employer, W.M. Murphy, to leave their unions. Within a month, one-third of the population of Dublin was affected by the terrible hardships caused by the 1913 Dublin Lockout, which ended in short-term victory for the employers but which drew new attention to the plight of workers and, over time, led to improvements in housing, health and sanitary conditions generally. The unions, particularly the ITGWU, went from strength to strength.

22 July 1929

H.M.S. Catherwood's party, Belfast and Dublin, on a tour of Ireland

This is one of a number of Catherwood entries in the visitors' books. Harold Matthew Stuart Catherwood (1899–1973) established the H.M.S. Catherwood Ltd bus service in 1925. His first bus was a 32-seat Leyland that operated in Co. Antrim. He next opened a daily long-distance route between Belfast and Dublin and, by 1929, when he visited McGuirk's with a 'party', his fleet numbered 122 vehicles. It is very likely, at the time of his visit, that he was surveying

H.M.S. Catherwood timetable for 1930

JULY, 1930

H.M.S. CATHERWOOD LTD.
MOTOR SERVICE

OFFICIAL

TIME TABLE

Travel by Catherwood

H.M.S. CATHERWOOD LTD.
HEAD OFFICE - UPPER LIBRARY STREET BELFAST.
TELEPHONES
BELFAST 7452-3-4 LONDONDERRY 786 DUBLIN 43324
COLERAINE 452 PORTRUSH 95 BALLYMENA 214

THREE DUBLIN HOTELS
JURY'S, College Green (central position)
MOIRA, Trinity Street (opposite Jury's)
NORTH STAR, Amiens St. (Opposite G.N Railway)

TIME TABLE SUBJECT TO ALTERATIONS   NO SUNDAY SERVICE

additional routes in the Free State. He signs in again on 29 August, with a party of twenty-five. Innovative ideas for comfort, economy and timetabling of bus transport soon had his buses covering the whole of Ireland. His business in the Free State, however, was killed off following the 1932 Road Transport Act, which virtually wiped out private bus services. Two years later, the Northern Ireland government effectively nationalised all bus services, and this led to the end of the Catherwood bus service in 1939.

9 September 1929
Hilda Roberts   Dublin
Ena Dargan   Dublin

Hilda Roberts (1901–1982), like Maurice McGonigal, studied art under Patrick Tuohy at the Metropolitan School of Art in Dublin, graduating in 1924 and following up her education in London Polytechnic and the Académie de la Grande Chaumière in Paris. Returning to Dublin, she studied sculpture under Oliver Sheppard but soon became particularly known for her portraiture. She married Arnold Marsh, educationalist and headmaster of Newtown School, Waterford, and taught art there. With her husband, she was one of the initiators of the Waterford Art Exhibitions, which led directly to the establishment of the prestigious Waterford Municipal Art Collection and a permanent art gallery for the city. Her portrait of George Russell ('Æ') is considered one of the finest portraits of twentieth-century Ireland, and is now in the Ulster Museum, Belfast. In 1940, she and her husband bought Woodtown, a large house in Rathfarnham in South County Dublin, where they provided apartments for a community of like-minded artists and writers.

During the years after this visit to McGuirk's, Ena Dargan travelled extensively in South America, studying the customs, culture and architecture of the native peoples. She took particular interest in their traditional stories, music and dance, which recalled

The first Waterford Art Exhibition, Newtown School, Waterford, 1935

the hardships suffered under Spanish colonisation during the sixteenth century, and she wrote the seminal work *The Road to Cuzco: A Journey from Argentina to Peru* (1950), which is still in print. Unfortunately, like so many of the women whose names appear in the visitors' books, little information about Ena Dargan is readily available: she deserves to be better known.

1930

The early 1930s saw an increase in the numbers of visitors to McGuirk's, with as many as twenty guests being catered for in one afternoon. The cultivation of extensive coniferous plantations in the Dublin and Wicklow mountains did not begin until 1939, and vast areas of the mountains that are forested today were bare expanses of moorland bog then, crisscrossed by bog roads and easily accessible to a growing number of hill walkers. Private bus services ran frequent and reasonably priced routes between Dublin and Wicklow, providing transport into and out of the hills.

In 1930, the embryonic Irish Free State had a population of just under 3 million, an economy based on agriculture, and average unemployment at 50 per cent less than it had been in 1922: the Henry Ford factory in Cork alone employed over 7,000 people. Although the economic war with Britain would soon impose considerable economic hardship, it seems that more people had access to bicycles and motor cars than previously. Claude Wall, an experienced hill walker and author of *Mountaineering in Ireland* (1939), one of the first Irish-produced books about Irish mountains, wrote in his diary in 1930:

> Things have changed very much in the last few years. The 'Hiking' craze has taken the country by storm and large parties are now to be met on all roads within a radius of 10 or 12 miles of Dublin. Some hardy spirits penetrate further

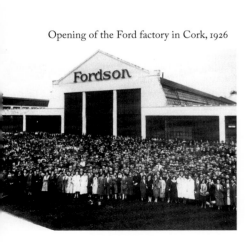

Opening of the Ford factory in Cork, 1926

than the roads but comparatively few seem to tackle the great moors. Cyclists and motorists seem to have multiplied wit' the 'hikers' so I am afraid Mrs McGuirk's can no longer be referred to as an oasis in the wilderness, even on a raw March day. It is all to the good I suppose, and we still have an immense wilderness to visit if we feel so inclined.

Between 1850 and 1913, more than 4.5 million men and women left Ireland for a new life abroad, most travelling to Britain or the United States but significant numbers ending up in Canada, Australia and New Zealand. It wasn't until the 1930s that the more prosperous Irish emigrants could afford to return to Ireland on holiday, and this is reflected in the visitors' books. In addition to the signatures of visitors from exotic locations, many pages for this period contain signatures of holidaying expatriates from places such as India, South Africa, the United States, China, Singapore, South Africa, Hong Kong and Japan. The tea room was popular among priests and those studying for the priesthood, and Jesuits from Milltown Park and Rathfarnham, as well as Holy Ghost Fathers from Blackrock College, were regular visitors on foot.

The growing influence of American popular culture is becoming apparent in the visitors' books; for example, a signature in August 1938 reads, 'Betty Boop, of Hollywood USA, remarks: Boop-boop a doop!' By the end of the 1930s, the incidence of women writing their own names, as opposed to their male companions signing for them, has increased, and more than 50 per cent of visitors are now female. It is clear that the current Mrs McGuirk also gives her guests a remarkable welcome and it must have been a wonderfully homely place, the praise is so consistently high over so many years.

Statue of Annie Moore by Jeanne Rynhart, Cobh, Co. Cork. In 1892, Annie was the first immigrant to the United States to arrive at the newly built federal immigration station on Ellis Island

Thomas McGuirk (third from left) with some visitors on the road outside the cottage about 1930

9 March 1930
Hector Hughes   *Dublin*
Isolde Hughes
Fionnuala Hughes

Hector Samuel James Hughes (1887–1970) grew up in Sandymount, Dublin, and attended University College Dublin, becoming, while there, a member of the Young Ireland branch of the United Irish League, which was founded by William O'Brien and which successfully fought for land reform in Ireland. Hughes lived an energetic life, being a founder member of the Irish Socialist Party, coming fifth in an Irish Grand National, and writing a number of legal commentaries. He married Isa Lawler, who was a suffragist as well as being involved in the founding of the Gate Theatre in 1928; she was the secretary and manager there for fifteen years.

Hector moved to England in this year of his visit to McGuirk's, and then to Scotland, where he fought for land rights, women's suffrage and the abolition of the death penalty. He published poetry and submitted an entry in the competition for a new national anthem for Ghana when it became independent in 1960. He became a Labour Member of Parliament (MP) for Aberdeen in 1945, and held his seat for the next six elections.

Isolde Hughes (1917–1989) (stage name Isolde Cazalet) was Hector's daughter. Educated in France and at Alexandra College in Dublin, she studied acting at the Royal Academy of Dramatic Art in London before returning to Dublin to work at the Gate Theatre. She was part of the Gate's successful tour in Egypt in 1936, and spent much of the 1940s and 1950s touring Ireland in repertory. Based in London since the 1960s, her last appearance on screen was in Neil Jordan's *High Spirits* (1988), starring Liam Neeson and Peter O'Toole.

Fionnuala Hughes was Hector's second daughter: she was a pharmacist and had her own chemist shop on Dawson Street, Dublin.

6 April 1930
Denis Devlin
Oscar O'Herlihy
Mervyn Wall
Joan O'Donovan
Michael Duignan
Mona [surname illegible]

Denis Devlin left this verse about one of his companions:

> *It would be much better if Mona*
> *And I were in this room alone-a*
> *For if we needed more jam*
> *Or more ham*

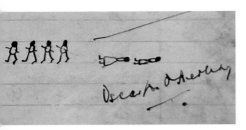

Sketch and signature in the visitors' book,
April 1930

It could be obtained through the telephone-a.
Her lips with too much jam if sudden red
Would find that hankies can be lost and then –
Oh then 'twere rapture her jammed lips to clean
And having been rebuffed, with groan and moan-a
To run all through the glen pursued by Mona.

Oscar O'Herlihy (1907–1978) also left a verse:

Four little college boys, all in a row,
[Then] two littler college girls, [one] fair, one tow!
I'd like to write further, but alas we must go
And leave Glencree valley – with the situation so.

11 May 1930
Mervyn Wall
Denis Devlin
Pierce Purcell
Lelia Sheridan
Niamh Fitzgerald

We have already met Mervyn Wall and Denis Devlin; on this
visit Wall writes verses in Latin about Lelia Sheridan and Niamh
Fitzgerald (it was not possible to find any information about these
two individuals). Devlin does the same in French, and Niamh writes
two verses in German about Pierce Purcell. Devlin adds:

Denis and Pierce are just charming
So Niav [sic] and Lelia think
Their smiling is simply disarming
Their pockets with sterling just clink.

To which Leila Sheridan replies:

> *There was a young fellow named Wall*
> *Who wasn't of that kind at all*
> *Said to him, a young woman*
> *'Come on, are you coming?*
> *It's private that side of the wall!!!'*

26 May 1930
Sheela Coughlan
Sean Coughlan

Tá átas an domhain orm bheit in Eireann arís agus
Cítig go bhuil an áit seo Chóm h áilinn is bhí sí riamh
Agus go bhuil an bhean a'tíghe comh slán is atá sí
Síle Ní Cocláin, Durban, Afric Theas [Durban, South Africa]

Sketches by the Coughlan party, May 1930

This verse and sketches were left by returned exiles Seán and Sheela Coughlan. The verse translates as:

> The delight of the world is on me to be in Ireland again
> and to see that this place is as beautiful as it was before,
> and that the woman of the house is as healthy as she is.

13 August 1930
Maurice J. Wigham and Barbara J. Wigham of Dublin

Maurice Wigham (1918–1998) was twelve years old when he visited McGuirk's with his sister, Barbara, probably on bicycles, given his age. Born in Dublin into a Quaker family, he attended Rathgar Junior School and Bootham School in York before studying agricultural science at Trinity College Dublin. On graduating, he taught at St Columba's College, Dublin, and then at Newtown School in Waterford, where he was appointed headmaster in 1961. His fine bicentenary *Newtown School, Waterford: A History, 1798–1998*, was launched after his death in 1998 by Professor Roy Foster.

5 October 1930
Brian Coffey
Mervyn Wall
Liam O Féich
Denis Devlin, all of UCD [University College Dublin]

We have met Mervyn Wall and Denis Devlin previously, but Brian Coffey (1905–1995) was another Dublin-born poet who had a brilliant career in a variety of arenas. He attended boarding schools Mount St Benedict in Gorey, Co. Wexford, and Clongowes Wood College, Co. Kildare, before studying classics at the Lycée St-Vincent in Senlis in France. Returning to Ireland in 1924, he gained advanced degrees in mathematics, physics and chemistry at University College Dublin, where he met Denis Devlin. They co-published a book of poems, entitled simply *Poems*, the same year they visited McGuirk's together. Moving to Paris in 1937, Coffey studied physical chemistry under Nobel Prize winner Jean Baptiste Perrin, and became friendly with Samuel Beckett and the Irish poet Thomas MacGreevy. During WWII, he taught at schools in London and Yorkshire, returning briefly to Paris after the war. After time spent teaching in the United States, McCarthyism encouraged his move to London in 1952. He published translations of French poems and his own work and, setting up his own publishing house, also produced the works of young Irish poets.

All we know about Liam Ó Féich is that he was, at this time, president of the Kevin Barry Memorial Committee, which was inaugurated in the early 1920s with the goal of erecting an appropriate memorial to Barry, a UCD medical student and Irish

Kevin Barry photographed in 1914

Volunteer who was executed in 1920 for his part in an ambush that resulted in the deaths of three British soldiers.

21 December 1930
William M. Glynn   *Waterford*
Sherwood Glynn   *Dublin*

William Mortimer Glynn (*b*. 1895), known as Willie or Liam, was born in Dublin into a Quaker family and educated at Great Ayton Friends' School in Yorkshire and Queen's University Belfast. He joined the Friends' Ambulance Unit at the outbreak of WWI and served in France and, on his return to Queen's, studied French and Celtic languages, developing a great interest in Irish. He taught in the Cork Grammar School and became acquainted with Cork writers such as Frank O'Connor, Daniel Corkery and Seán Ó Faoláin. He taught in Waterford until 1936, after which he became headmaster of Drogheda Grammar School. In 1949, he was appointed headmaster of Newtown School in Waterford, where he stayed until retiring in 1961.

Sherwood McClure Glynn (*b*. 1898) was William's brother.

1931

11 April 1931
Squadron Leader J.J. Lynch, RAF [Royal Air Force]

John Joseph Lynch (1896–1964) was born in Dublin and educated at Belvedere College and Trinity College Dublin. Early in WWI he was commissioned into the Royal Irish Regiment from the Royal Military College at Sandhurst; he learned to fly in 1915 and was attached to the Royal Flying Corps. After the war, he stayed in the RAF and, while serving in the Sudan three years after this visit to McGuirk's, was promoted to wing commander. In 1940, he was Air Officer Commanding No. 1 Group of Bomber Command, which

The Bomber Command Memorial in London

dropped a higher tonnage of bombs per aircraft than any other bombing group in WWII. After the war, as an air commodore, Lynch became head of the Postwar Planning Executive. He retired to Dublin with the rank of air marshal in 1946.

23 April 1931
It's a beautiful day in April
As we sit here with silent thoughts
Each thinking of days of yore
When O'Neill these same hills crossed
Not on a blissful day li'e this
With the sun's rays beaming down
But on a cold December day
With sleet and hail and frost
No Mrs McGuirk's
Wherein to get tea
And warm his weary limbs
But despite all this he trod along
Frozen, desperate and lost!
Anon

The thirteenth-century Bermingham Tower at Dublin Castle, where Red Hugh O'Donnell was incarcerated

This verse refers to the epic escape from Dublin Castle in 1592 by Art O'Neill, son of Shane O'Neill, Lord of Tyrone, and Red Hugh O'Donnell, son of the chief of the O'Donnell clan. They succeeded in travelling over miles of mountains in dreadful winter conditions but, only a few miles from salvation in Fiach McHugh O'Byrne's stronghold in Glenmalure, Co. Wicklow, Art O'Neill died of exposure. Red Hugh survived.

7 August 1931
Peter Cunningham-Gratten (The Roving Bard)
The Greatest gift from God to man
Is love for one another, o,

That man may share each joy and care
In the welfare of his brother, o.
Let every man give heart and hand
To help a 'lame dog' over, o.
Such heavenly seed on earth to breed,
Would make this world a lover, o.

Peter Cunningham-Gratten (*c.*1884–1956), 'The Roving Bard', was one of the last of the wandering troubadours. He travelled around Co. Wicklow from the 1920s to the 1950s, entertaining whomever would listen with his poems and songs. Thought to have been a veteran of WWI, he spent his winters in the Wicklow County Home and his summers travelling from village to village and from fair to fair, entertaining people. He wrote many songs and poems, such as 'Barry's Hotel' and 'The Banks of Avonmore', before dying of exposure in a ditch during a snowstorm in 1956. A booklet of his work was published in 2001 by Pádraig McCarthy.

The Great Depression is one of the few global events that gets a passing mention in the visitors' books. What was to become the worst economic downturn in the history of the Western world began after a stock market crash in October 1929. Ireland's economy, in difficulties since the foundation of the Free State, was already depressed when the crash occurred, but the situation deteriorated further when the economic war with Britain began in 1932. The following verse, left in September 1930 by a Terence Morton, alludes to the stock market crash:

The way was long the wind was cold
Our Singer was infernal old;

Crowds gather outside the New York Stock Exchange following the crash of 1929

Our last remaining shares were sold
And our doleful tale unfold,
But at the cottage at Lough Bray
A cheerful hour we whiled away.

'Our Singer' was probably the last Singer Ten roadster of 1919. Originally a bicycle manufacturer, Singer Motors produced a three-wheeled motor vehicle called the Tri-Voiturette in 1903, and their first four-wheeled car in 1905. By 1928, Singer was Britain's third-largest car manufacturer, after Austin and Morris; its reign had ended by 1970.

5 September 1931
Andrew Ganly   *Dublin*
Geoffrey Thompson
Alan Thompson

Andrew Ganly (1908–1982) had many careers, including being a dentist in Ireland and Malaya before becoming, briefly, a travel courier. Later, he became a playwright and novelist: his first play, *The Dear Queen*, was staged by the Abbey Theatre in 1938, and his best-known novel was *The Desolate Sky* (1966).

Arthur Geoffrey Thompson (1905–1976) was born of Quaker stock in Wexford and after attending Newtown School in Waterford and Portora Royal School in Enniskillen, Co. Fermanagh, he studied medicine at Trinity College Dublin. He was a Rockefeller Foundation Research Fellow in biochemistry and worked in London and Paris before returning to Dublin to work in the Royal City of Dublin Hospital, Baggot Street, the year before his visit to

McGuirk's. In 1934, he moved to London to train in psychoanalysis and, but for a period as a major in the Royal Army Medical Corps during WWII, worked in the Tavistock Clinic in London until his retirement in 1971.

Alan Thompson (1909–1974) was another medical student, later becoming Professor of Medicine at the Royal College of Surgeons in Ireland and president of the Royal College of Physicians of Ireland.

'Before tea; after tea.' Sketch left in the visitors' book, October 1931

11 October 1931
H. Horan   *Dublin*
Charles H. Rowe *Trinity College Dublin*

Charles Henry Rowe (1893–1943) was born in Cork and studied at University College Cork before taking his MA in mathematics and philosophy at Trinity College Dublin. In 1920, he travelled to Paris to study under the French mathematicians Jacques Hadamard, Henri Lebesgue and Édouard Goursat. He was appointed Erasmus Smith Professor of Mathematics at Trinity College Dublin in 1926 and, the year after his visit to McGuirk's, was invited to address the International Congress of Mathematics in Zurich.

22 November 1931
Jeff McGarry
In a corner in Glencree
With a swell kid on my knee
Nothing seems so sweet in life
As the prospect of a wife.

Some entries from the 1930s show the growing influence of American popular culture in Ireland, through films in particular: note the terms 'swell' and 'kid' in this entry.

Sketch of Lough Bray by a member of the Holiday Fellowship, December 1931

26 December 1931
Dublin H.F. Rambling Club
Phyllis B. Wood
Norah Kidd
Doreen Hall
Sheila Kidd
Sam Walkington
H.S. Wood
A.J. Wood
D. McIntyre

The Holiday Fellowship ('H.F.') had its origins in Lancashire, England. In 1891, as rambling began to become popular, Rev. T.A. Leonard starting taking young people walking in the hills, resulting in the Co-Operative Holidays Association; in 1913, it became the Holiday Fellowship, with an emphasis on healthy outdoor exercise and temperance (the latter has long since been abandoned!). The Dublin branch of Holiday Fellowship was founded in March 1930 and included many employees of the Guinness Brewery. The club grew, and today there are about 170 members. Among its membership in the early days were Owen Sheehy-Skeffington and Wilfred Bramble, part-time reporter for *The Irish Times* and occasional actor at the Abbey Theatre. He subsequently had a busy film career, starring in more than thirty productions, and in more recent times was known for his part in the television series *Steptoe and Son*.

1932

20 March 1932
W.J.E. Jessop
Kathleen Jessop
Samuel J. Suttle

John G. O'Keefe
Eugene F. Suttle (walking on my knees)
Brian Ó Brolcháin

We shink four loggish huckabees,
Flushing through the glire
With caumish glock and huggle hees
And glelly aiking chire.
But slock we slonk
And slooped the chonk
Within this wondrous blore
Till we could blog and sloop no more.
BÓB

A Node (or poem if you will)
Four lumpin gloits a lauming louthly
Did greetch and yammer stutteringly.
But gludding glay and buddly glug,
Did swoop their wharmish blee.
All staggerish with bapping flellies
They yarmed, the griffed, they glugged
And crunchingly with whoops of blee,
Did glump with goldy tea
They neeped and flizzed both had to go, barping blissfully.
Gazag! Gazag!

Sketch left by Samuel J. Suttle in March 1932

It is not clear which of these signatories wrote the second of these Lewis Carroll-inspired verses. William John Edward Jessop (1902–1980) was an academic, senator and medical practitioner. He was Professor of Social Medicine at Trinity College Dublin and had been appointed Professor of Physiology and Biochemistry at the Royal College of Surgeons in Ireland three years before this visit. After his retirement from Trinity, he became a visiting professor of chemical pathology at the University of Ife (now Obafemi Awolowo University) in Nigeria.

Eugene Francis Suttle (1909–1989) was Ireland's Comptroller and Auditor General, 1964–73, and an ex-officio member of the Dáil Committee of Public Accounts that inquired into the Arms Crisis of 1970.

Female graduates as depicted by *Punch* at the turn of the nineteenth century

20 March 1932

R. Flanagan BA	*Terenure*
Maura Flanagan	*Terenure*
Frances Ingram BA (H)	*Rathmines*
Bridie Lawlor BA (H)	*Rathgar*
Isolda Peterson BA (H)	*Rathgar*
Betty MacMahon 1st Arts	*Rathfarnham*
Mary Niall BA	*Rathfarnham*

(A very good tea)

This group of young women are proud to state the degrees, and, in some cases, the class of Bachelor's degree ('H' presumably means Honours) they have received.

24 April 1932

Ranelagh Branch   Cumann mBann [sic]
Louie Coughlan
Patty Coughlan
Eílbhán Ní Cochláin
Maille Ní Aoláin

Cumann na mBan Inghinidhe na h-Éirean [sic]
Bean Áine Ní Cléirigh

Cisner Ní Cléirigh
Sígle Ní Dubhgain
Eilís Ní Cúanaigh
Sighle Nic Ragh [illegible]
Sibéil Ni Feargháill

Columcille Branch
Kathleen Merrigan ex–Tribunal Prisoner 18.1.32
                                        Árd Craobh

Monica Devine

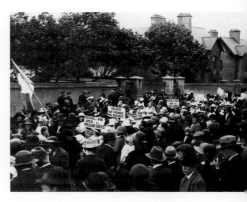

Members of Cumann na mBan protest outside Mountjoy Prison during the Irish War of Independence, 1921

Cumann na mBan or, in English, the Irishwomen's Council, was formed in April 1914, mainly from Inghinidhe na hÉireann (Daughters of Ireland), which had been founded in 1900 by a group of politically radical women that included Maud Gonne, Sinéad O'Flanagan (later wife of Éamon de Valera) and Kathleen Lynn, the doctor and Sinn Féin politician.

Cumann na mBan was initially formed as a Republican women's auxiliary force to the Irish Volunteers and its members were active during the War of Independence. They took the anti-Treaty side in the Civil War: pro-Treaty forces were very aware of Cumann na mBan's importance to the success of a guerrilla army and so they were declared an illegal organisation by the Free State government. This led to approximately four hundred women being detained: only fifty had been similarly detained by the British during the War of Independence.

When Fianna Fáil came to power in 1932, prisoners who had been sentenced under the Constitution (Special Powers) Tribunal, including Kathleen Merrigan, as is clear from how she signed herself, were released.

Tomás Ó Muircheartaigh's photograph of
Tomás Ó Criomhthain, 1932

16 May 1932
Tomás Ó Muircheartaigh
BÓB

Cincíse
Tagaithe ó Ghleann an Dá loch, agus
Gan de neart ionnam ach 'Té' do rádh.
Tar éis té d'fhághail, gan ag teastáil
Uaim a rádh ach 'Sásta'.
Tomás Ó Muircheartaigh

This verse translates as:

Pentecost
Having come from Glendalough, and
Without the strength to say anything but 'Tea'.
After getting tea, all I wanted to say was
'Satisfied'.

Tomás's companion, who signs himself 'BÓB' and could possibly be
Brian Ó Brolcháin, added these lines:

Ag druidim le deire an aistir
Ó Bóthar na Bruighne go Gleann Dá Loch
Is as san go Gleann Máigh Luighra
Loch dTáin is Loch Té [?] An Bearna is Loch Bré
NI raibh d'acfhainní i dTomás
Focal a chur as, idir Mám na Sailighe is Loch Bré
Go bfheodh [?] do mo chluasa idir seo is Áth Cliath!
BÓB

This translates as:

> Approaching the end of the trail
> From Bohernabreena to Glendalough,
> And from there to Glenmalure
> Lough Dan and Lough Tay, The Gap and Lough Bray.
> Tomás had no wish to mutter a word
> Between The Sally Gap and Lough Bray,
> But he withered my ears between here and Dublin!

Tomás Ó Muircheartaigh (1907–1967) was born in Dublin and joined the civil service after leaving school; he worked in the Department of Education, the Irish Placenames Commission and the Irish Land Commission. He became an important figure in Irish cultural life and, as a leading member of the Gaelic League, worked to promote the resurgence of native Irish culture through the language. In the 1930s, he spent holidays on the Dingle peninsula, where he knew and photographed Blasket islander Tomás Ó Criomhthain, and assisted in getting his classic book, *An tOileánach*, published in 1929. He was a keen photographer, and his studies of the lives of peasants in Kerry, held today in the National Folklore Collection, are an important record of the time. He was friends with many of the leading Irish literary and artistic figures of the early twentieth century, including painters Seán O'Sullivan and Seán Keating and the Cork sculptor Seamus Murphy.

Heading for the Blaskets, Tomás Ó Muircheartaigh, 1925

In the photo taken in the summer of 1925, Tomás Ó Muircheartaigh was twenty-five years old, just visible in a currach behind two girls heading for the Great Blasket Island. The girls do not seem like locals, and look slightly worried – you can just sense the excitement of an adventure, hear the slopping of the water against the hull and the creaking of the oars, and smell the salt Atlantic mixed with the sweat of the ragged, spare islander who is rowing.

30 May 1932

Sophie Jacobs *Rathfarnham and London*
Estella F. Starkey *Rathfarnham, Co. Dublin*

Estella F. Starkey (1882–1968), née Solomons, was Bethel Solomons's artist and political activist sister who, at the age of forty-three, married the poet, writer and publisher Seumas O'Sullivan, born James Sullivan Starkey, founder and editor of the influential *Dublin Magazine*. She attended the Dublin Metropolitan School of Art at the age of sixteen and was taught by the painters Walter Osborne and William Orpen. With her friends, the artists Beatrice Elvery and Samuel Beckett's aunt Cissie (Frances) Beckett, she went on to study at the Académie Colarossi in Paris.

Although she had been particularly interested in engraving early in her career, Estella produced some of the finest paintings, portraits and landscapes of early-twentieth-century Ireland and her subjects included Jack B. Yeats, Arthur Griffith and the writer James Stephens. Joining Cumann na mBan in 1918, she was active during the War of Independence and the Civil War, in which she took the anti-Treaty side. She later taught art in the Bolton Street Technical College.

SS *De Grasse* in the 1920s

12 June 1932

De Grasse
Mrs M.R.T. Foley *Que Street NW, Washington DC, USA*

Mrs Elizabeth Demsey Baylies *Bridgeport, Conn., USA*

With Patrick Cardinal Hayes *New York City*
John J. Foley (God bless all here) *59 Que Street, Washington DC*

Over five days in June 1932, the 31st International Eucharistic Congress took place in Dublin, representing a high point in Ireland's devotion to the Catholic Church. Nearly 800,000 people attended the inaugural Mass in the Phoenix Park, during which the famous Irish tenor John McCormack sang. Thousands came from abroad, including many Roman Catholic bishops and priests – some of whom visited McGuirk's.

SS *De Grasse* was one of thirteen ocean liners that brought pilgrims from around the world to the Eucharistic Congress, in this case from the United States. The *De Grasse* was launched in 1924 in Birkenhead, England; captured by the Germans early in WWII, it was used as a barracks ship for German soldiers and later as a base ship for Italian submariners. It was scuttled by retreating Germans in August 1944, but was refloated and refurbished, and resumed the New York–Le Havre route until 1953, when it was sold to the Canadian Pacific Steamship Company and renamed *Empress of Australia*. Sold again in 1956, it was renamed *Venezuela* but was wrecked off Cannes in 1962, and scrapped in La Spezia in the same year.

Patrick Joseph Cardinal Hayes (1867–1938) was born in New York of Irish parents and attended St Joseph's Provincial Seminary in Troy, New York. He was consecrated Auxiliary Bishop of New York in 1941 and, during WWI, as Bishop of the American Armed Forces, he helped to recruit hundreds of Catholic chaplains. In 1924, he was created a cardinal by Pope Pius XI. He strongly condemned birth control, abortion and divorce, opposed Prohibition, welcomed the election of Éamon de Valera as President of the Irish Republic, and contributed $1,000 to Sinn Féin.

Cardinal Hayes in the 1920s

20 June 1932
Charles Leech   *Blackrock*

At about 12 years old I visited this lovely spot, 76 years ago and find it as charming as ever. Even more charming now on account of seeing my old friend Mrs McGurk [sic]. G.M. Leech, wife of Charles Leech, aged 86.

An interesting entry, this: if Charles Leech's previous visit had been seventy-six years earlier, it suggests that McGuirk's was a teahouse in 1856, which is unlikely. The Mrs McGuirk running the tea room in 1932, however, was the daughter-in-law of the original Mrs McGuirk, who died in 1910.

1 July 1932
Barra Ó Briain
Anna Bean Uí Bhriain   *'Guagán Barra', Glenageary*

Barra Ó Briain (1901–1988), born in Dublin, joined the Free State Army and fought in the Civil War, and captained the guard of honour at Michael Collins's funeral. He later studied law at the Sorbonne in Paris, and was in the crowd at Paris-Le Bourget Airport when Charles Lindbergh landed after his solo flight across the Atlantic. On his return to Ireland, after working as a barrister on the western circuit, he became president of the Circuit Court. In the early 1960s, he was seconded to the United Nations as Chief Justice of Cyprus. After he retired, he was commissioned to investigate An Garda Síochána, resulting in the Ó Briain report, which recommended widespread improvements in civil liberties.

Anna Bean Uí Bhriain, née Flood, married Barra in December 1928 and had eleven children with him in nineteen years.

August 1932
Dorothy Macardle
Florence R. O'Byrne

Dorothy Macardle (1889–1958) was born in Dundalk into a wealthy brewing family. Although a Catholic, she was educated at Alexandra College in Dublin before attending University College Dublin, after which she worked as a teacher. She joined Cumann na mBan in 1917 and was arrested in 1918 for her activities. She sided with de Valera in the Republican split of 1921/22 and was imprisoned by the Free State government during the Civil War. After the Civil War, she worked as a journalist with the League of Nations and wrote plays under the pseudonym Margaret Callan. Her book, *The Irish Republic*, was published in 1937 and was a bestseller despite being clearly partisan: Éamon de Valera wrote the introduction. She bequeathed the royalties to him, although she was generally disillusioned with how women were treated in his constitution. She wrote four novels, three of which dealt with supernatural themes; her most successful, *Uneasy Freehold* (1941), was made into a 1944 horror film called *The Uninvited*.

28 August 1932
Lil Hackett   *Dublin*
John P. MacEnroe   *Virginia, County Cavan*

You do enjoy an egg and a cup of tea.

This John Patrick MacEnroe was the grand-uncle of the American tennis player John MacEnroe. John Patrick's brother, John Joseph MacEnroe, emigrated to New York from Ballyjamesduff, Co. Cavan, at the age of twelve. He was a musician and later had his own band, billed as 'Professor Sean MacEnroe and his orchestra'. He married a Westmeath girl in 1927, and their son, John Patrick McEnroe Junior, named after his uncle, was born in 1935. He joined the United States Air Force and, with his wife, Kay, was stationed in Germany, where John McEnroe, the international tennis player, was born in 1959.

T.H. McCalmont Barklie

8 November 1932

T. McCalmont Barklie

H. Rhys Davies

T.H. McCalmont Barklie was an Englishman who studied at Trinity College Dublin and who, although born into a Protestant family, had converted to Islam. He wrote extensively about the religion, which he believed was a simple logical faith that withstood the investigations of science and provided high ideals to live up to. He believed that Christianity was fast losing ground, with young people of the day finding little to interest them in the Church's pomp and ceremony that might have impressed their ancestors.

8 December 1932

Roibeárd Ó Faracháin

Fearghus Ó Cinnéide

Roibeárd Ó Faracháin (Robert Farran) (1909–1984) was born in Dublin and educated at St Patrick's College, Drumcondra. He worked as a teacher, holidaying in the Connemara Gaeltacht where he became fluent in Irish. He wrote short stories and published a book of his poems, *Thronging Feet*, in 1936. In spite of his youth, but probably because of his nationalism and knowledge of Irish, he was taken on by Raidió Éireann in 1939, where he remained for thirty-five years. By 1953, he was Controller of Radio Programmes and introduced many innovations. He was also on the board of the Abbey Theatre. His play *Assembly at Druim Ceat* was remade for radio in 1959 with a musical score by Seán Ó Riada. His best-known book is *The Course of Irish Verse* (1947).

Mara mbeadh an fuacht am'loma

B'é go bhéadfainn rann do chuanadh

Ach mo theanga dá reod in béal ó tá
Ní háil liom le rannta mé féin do chrádh.

The verse he left in the visitors' book that day roughly translates as:

> If the cold hadn't got to me
> I might have composed a poem
> But as my tongue has frozen to my pallet
> I'm afraid my verses may choke me.

Roibeárd's companion, Fearghus Ó Cinnéide, left the following riposte, also *as Gaeilge* ('in Irish').

> *Ins an aimsear aoibhinn Áluinn*
> *Sure it's then the muse is calling*
> *Ach, a Riobárd, ag loc Brí*
> *Bí i gconnuidhe dilis dí.*

The Abbey Theatre in 1953

This translates as:

> In this lovely, tranquil weather
> Sure it's then the muse is calling,
> But my Robert at Loch Bree
> Ever faithful to her be.

22 December 1932
Jean-Henry Morin, journaliste Français de Paris (France)
Maud H. Bluett   Kimmage, Co. Dublin

Jean-Henry Morin's French translation of Denis Gwynn's *The Life and Death of Roger Casement* was published in Paris in the same year as his visit to McGuirk's.

Maud Henrietta Bluett (1895–1963), née Cherry, was born in Dublin, the daughter of Richard Cherry, Lord Chief Justice of Ireland, 1914–16. She commemorated her father in *A short memoir of the Right Honourable Richard Robert Cherry Sometime Lord Chief Justice of Ireland* (1924), and also published *The Celtic Schools of Religious Learning* in the same year as this visit. She studied law and was called to the Bar; she married Rev. Augustus Sterling Bluett.

20 December 1932
Feast of the Holy Innocents
Raghnall MacSuibhlaigh CSSp
W.N. Summers CSSp
Séumas Ó Mucreadha CSSp
Éamonn Mac Tomáis CSSp
Séamua Ó Néill CSSp
Seamus Ó Tuathaibh CSSp
D. O'Leary CSSp (Up West Cork!!!)

The large percentage of visitors signing the book in Irish continued: this contingent are priests of the Holy Ghost Fathers, or the Congregation of the Holy Spirit, abbreviated from the Latin, *Congregatio Sancti Spiritus*, to 'CSSp'. The order was founded in France in the seventeenth century and has a number of schools in Ireland, including Blackrock College and St Mary's College, both in Dublin, the latter being the nearer establishment to Glencree. Archbishop of Dublin John Charles McQuaid was a member of this order. In recent times, it has been associated with a large number of child sexual abuse cases in Ireland.

1933

Thomas McGuirk, son of the original Mary McGuirk, died in 1933. He had been an employee of Lord Powerscourt and, on his death,

Sketch left in April 1933

the family had to begin to pay two shillings and sixpence rent per week for the cottage.

17 March 1933
St Patrick's Day
P. Fitzsimon
H. Kernoff   at home 7-10, No. 5 Duke St, Dublin
Dr McUisditiu

On the occasion of this visit, Harry Kernoff left a fascinating double-image study of a woman's face in profile, possibly one of his companions, and made sure that anyone interested is aware of when he holds soirées at his home in Duke Street.

22 March 1933
Seán O'Sullivan
Kevin O'Sullivan

The artist Seán O'Sullivan visited this time with his brother, Kevin (1906–1964).

19 April 1933
J.T. Paul
M.J. Walshe
Victor Gray
A.F. Kerrison

Old Wesley Rugby Football Club – Preparing for Southport

Old Wesley Rugby Football Club was founded in 1891. These four visitors, 'preparing for Southport', were clearly in training for the upcoming Wesley 1st XV tour to England at Easter, when they would play Liverpool and Southport.

Sketch left by Harry Kernoff in March 1933

30 April 1933
Radegonde Barden
Jack Malone

Radegonde Barden was probably named after St Radegund, the daughter of the sixth-century king Bertachar of Thuringia who founded the Abbey of the Holy Cross in Poitiers in 558 AD. Barden was a Loreto nun and cousin of J.B. Malone, the great Irish walker and author. She taught in the Loreto Convent School in Rathfarnham before going on the missions; she spent most of her life in Kenya, where she lived to be over 100 years of age.

John ('Jack') Bernard Malone (1913–1989) was Ireland's best-known hill walker and was at the vanguard of Irish hill walking becoming a hobby in the middle of the twentieth century. Born in England of Irish parents, he attended the Marist St Mary's College, a Catholic boarding school at Grove Ferry, near Canterbury. He had come to Ireland only eighteen months before this visit to McGuirk's, and became interested in exploring the Dublin and Wicklow mountains, something that was to become a lifelong passion. His companion on this day was his cousin Radegonde Barden. They undertook a long trek and, as he wrote in his journal later, sounding more like the explorer Henry Stanley in darkest Africa, 'for the first time I pushed on into the awful emptiness between Glencree and the Sally Gap'. Soon after turning left at the Sally Gap, they discovered Lough Tay and Luggala: 'Some things can be described: but Lough Tay, seen after marching through the high bogs of the Sally Gap, cannot be. If this is earth, then what is Heaven?'

Lough Tay, Co. Wicklow

11 May 1933

William P. Faye	*Dalkey*
Mervyn Wall	*The World*
George Morgan	*Co. Clare*

Charles Doran *Dublin*
D. O'Callaghan *Bray*

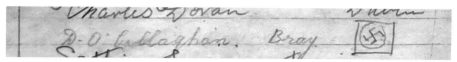

William Patrick Ignatius Faye (1909–1969), born in Co. Dublin, was a nephew of William and Frank Fay, who were closely associated with the early days of the Abbey Theatre. He was educated at Clongowes Wood College, Co. Kildare; the King's Inns; and University College Dublin, and had been called to the Bar a year before this visit. He spent much of his life working for the Department of External Affairs in Belgium and Sweden before becoming Irish Ambassador to France, Canada and the United States. He was married to Lillian Conolly, whose sister Violet, a Russian scholar, was head of the Soviet section of a research department at the Ministry of Foreign Affairs in London during WWII. Her brother was Thomas Conolly, an expert in Irish constitutional law, and another sister, Ann, was married to Patrick McGilligan, the politician, academic and lawyer.

Mervyn Wall we have met before.

A swastika was drawn after D. O'Callaghan's name, the first hint in the visitors' book of what was happening in Europe. Just over three months earlier, President of Germany Paul von Hindenburgh had offered Adolf Hitler the chancellorship of the country. On 27 February, the German parliament building, the Reichstag, was burned down. The cause of the fire remained unclear, but communists were blamed and, at the end of February, Hitler persuaded Hindenburgh to issue the Reichstag Fire Decree, which abolished many important civil liberties. In March, the Enabling Act, or 'Law to remedy the Distress of the People and the Reich', gave Hitler the power to issue laws and decrees without parliamentary consent. Within months, all non-Nazi political parties, organisations and unions had ceased to exist.

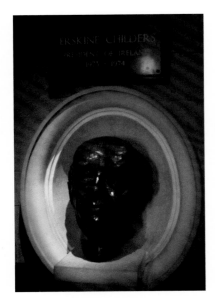

Memorial to Erskine H. Childers in
St Patrick's Cathdral, Dublin

11 July 1933
Erskine H. Childers
Mrs Fitzmaurice Manning
Mary Manning

Erskine Hamilton Childers (1905–1974) was born in London, one of two sons of Robert Erskine Childers, British naval officer, Irish Volunteers gun-runner, Republican activist, propagandist, and writer, who was executed during the Civil War, and the American Molly Osgood. He was educated at Gresham's School in England and Trinity College, Cambridge, returning to Dublin in 1932 to work as advertising manager for *The Irish Press*. He was elected as a Fianna Fáil TD in 1938, and remained a TD until 1973, when he resigned to become President of Ireland. He was a popular president who fought for a more open and involved presidency, but he died suddenly after a year and a half in office. Erskine's younger brother, Robert, married Christabel Susan Manning, one of Mrs Fitzmaurice Manning's daughters.

Mrs Fitzmaurice Manning (*b.* 1873), née Susan Bennett, was the daughter of a Dublin art dealer and sister of Louisa ('Louie') Bennett, the suffragist, trade unionist and writer. Susan's husband was a civil servant in the British colonial service and was rarely in Ireland: they had two daughters, Mary Manning and Christabel. He fought in WWI and was killed in West Africa in 1918. After the war, she ran a well-known teashop called The Sod of Turf on the corner of South Anne Street and Dawson Street, which was frequented by artists, writers and poets.

Mary Manning (1906–1999), Susan's daughter, was born in Dublin and educated at Park House school on Morehampton Road and at Alexandra College. She studied at the Abbey School of Acting, was friends with Samuel Beckett and editor of *Motley*, the Gate Theatre magazine, which published contributions from Francis Stuart, John Betjeman and Austin Clarke. Her first play, which was directed in the Gate by Hilton Edwards, featured Micheál Mac Liammóir. Two years after this visit to McGuirk's, Mary moved to Boston, Massachusetts, and married Mark de Wolfe Howe, a Harvard law professor. She became interested in avant-garde theatre, introducing Dylan Thomas and Samuel Beckett to American audiences, and writing novels. On her husband's death, she returned to Ireland, became the drama critic for *Hibernia* magazine and *The Irish Times*, and produced an adaptation of Frank O'Connor's book *The Saint and Mary Kate* for the Abbey Theatre.

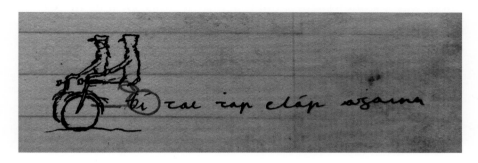

Sketch of cyclists from August 1933

1934

23 February 1934

Evelyn Barry	*S.C.R. [South Circular Road], Dublin*
Eva Earle	*Rathmines*
Dolly Culhane	*Clontarf*

En route for Dublin having walked from Lough Dan by Lough Tay, Sally Gap.

This entry suggests that women were now enjoying hiking in groups as well as cycling.

Sketch of Éamon de Valera, March 1934

30 March 1934

This cartoon of Éamon de Valera was left by a visitor in March 1934. In January 1933, de Valera's Fianna Fáil party had won an overall majority in Dáil Éireann: he became Taoiseach and remained in that role for the next fifteen years. Eighteen months before, the rotating office of president of the League of Nations based in Geneva had fallen to the Irish Free State and de Valera went to Geneva to open the plenary session. In his address, he lectured the League Assembly on their failures and, when he sat down, *The Irish Times* reported that 'there was a stoney silence, unbroken by a single note of applause'. In the year of this entry, he was Minister for External Affairs and supported the Soviet Union's admission to the League of Nations.

9 June 1934
U. White

The South of France is very nice
And Oranges are sweet –
I'd rather have an Irish fire
A fire of boggy peat.

The skies are always blue here
They are never dark and grey
I'd rather have an Irish sky
The sky above Lough Bray.

The people here are kindly
They smile at you and nod,
I'd rather have an Irish wife
Say 'Glory be to God!'

This visitor is clearly an exile living in France.

13 September 1934
R.M. Gordon
O. Exshaw
E.J. Holliday
Anne Butler Yeats
A.M. Gordon

Thoor Ballylee, Co. Galway, was home to
W.B. Yeats and his family in the 1920s

Of these visitors to McGuirk's, I could find only Anne Butler Yeats (1919–2001). The daughter of W.B. Yeats and Bertha ('Georgie') Hyde-Lees, she was born in Dublin and spent her early years between Thoor Ballylee in Co. Galway and her parents' other home in Oxford, until her father was appointed a senator in the Irish Free State in 1922 and they moved to Merrion Square in Dublin. She had a difficult childhood, spending three years in hospital before going to a boarding school in Switzerland at the age of nine. She studied painting at the Royal Hibernian Academy in Dublin, before a stint at the School of Theatrical Design (École des Arts Décoratifs) in Paris. She returned to work in the Abbey Theatre in 1938, becoming head of design there from 1939 until 1941, when she left to take up painting and book-cover design; she illustrated books by Denis Devlin, Thomas Kinsella and Louis MacNeice.

1935

From June 1935, a new volume was begun for the visitors' book, which, instead of providing a blank page, was now set out more formally, with columns for name, address, nationality and remarks. This format tended to discourage artwork and poetry and 'comments' are often reduced to short remarks such as 'Enjoyed my tea', 'Charming', and 'A lovely cup of tea'.

In 1935, the number of Irish visitors who signed their names in Irish fell to 29 per cent, less than the total number of English visitors this year, which increased to 37 per cent. Nationalistic sentiment, however, is still strong: in August 1935, when a H.G. Leech gives his address as 'Kingstown', it is crossed out in blue pencil and firmly corrected in another hand to 'Dún Laoghaire'.

7 July 1935
Peadar Ó Dubhuidhe
Próinsias Ó Raghalla
Lily Ryder   *Quo Vadis*
A. Cashman

Blessington 10.20, Ballynastockan Brook 11.50, Mullacleevaun Summit 2pm, Military Road (Inchavor) 4.45, Sally Gap 6.10, Lough Bray Cottage 7.30. Having previously done the same trip 2 June 1917.

Some visitors, particularly these energetic hill walkers, ignored the new format in describing their route through the hills.

9 July 1935
L. Fallon   *Dublin*

Old Friends are nice to see again.

This visitor left a caricature of Adolf Hitler, with, to its left, a ghostly sketch of Crown Prince Wilhelm, the last crown prince of the German Empire and Prussia. The year 1935 witnessed the German reoccupation of the Saar region, the establishment of the Luftwaffe, and the rearmament of Germany in violation of the Versailles Treaty.

Sketch of Adolf Hitler and Crown Prince Wilhelm, July 1935

17 August 1935

J.J. Hughes   *Dublin*

J.J. Hughes noted 'Exceedingly Irish' in the nationality column, and left the following verse:

> *O! little house among the hills,*
> *O! bean a tighe of kindly eye*
> *When full of age and many ills*
> *I will recall ye with a sigh.*
> *When on a stick I palsied lean,*
> *And think of scenes around Lough Bray,*
> *That which I'll cherish most, I ween*
> *Will be your glorious 'cup of tay'.*

4 September 1935

M.A. Keane   *Irish*
Ronald Mac Donnell   *American*
J.J. Walsh   *Yankee*

One of the three also left this verse:

> *We had chips for a start in Del Rio's*
> *Then in Bead Murray's Pub we had two*
> *Then the pier of Dun Laoghaire we sighted.*
> *Cait left when the 'Sarge' said 'How do.'*
> *We rested in Ashbrook till dawning,*
> *We grubbed well till 'Lee' came in view,*
> *Then 'Pat' suggested Lough Bray for a change,*
> *And the Rover groaned, I'm with you too.*
> *The sun was peeping thro' the clouds*
> *When your cottage came in view*

Sketch by M.A. Keane, September 1935

There were three packed tightly in a car
That was made to fit but two.
We fished a while, then climbed the rock
Then filled our 'tums' with tea.
Then into the old bus once again,
Ronnie, the Maestro and me.

8 September 1935

Vena Preston Ball	*Dublin*
Edward Preston Ball	*ditto*
Mary T. Cassin	*Waterford*

Vena ('Lavena') Preston Ball, née Weatherill, was married to Charles Preston Ball, a Dublin medical doctor from whom she separated in 1927. Six months after this visit to McGuirk's, she was murdered by her son, Edward Preston Ball.

Edward Preston Ball (1916–1987) was born in Dublin and educated at Shrewsbury School in England. After leaving school in 1934, he took unpaid walk-on parts in the Gate Theatre. When the Gate was embarking on a foreign tour in 1936, he asked his mother for £60 to join it; when she refused, he killed her with a hatchet and deposited her body in the sea at Shankhill. It was never found. He was, however, tried in May 1936, and found guilty but insane.

1 December 1935

Joy Mowbray-Green	*London SW7*
John Hunt	*Calcutta, India*
Hugh Hunt	*Abbey Theatre, Dublin*

Joy Mowbray-Green (1913–2006) was born and brought up in Wimbledon, London, and became an accomplished tennis player. While competing on the tennis circuit at Eastbourne, a few months before this visit to McGuirk's, she met John Hunt, home on extended army leave from India. Their signatures suggest that they came to Ireland during their courtship to meet with his brother Hugh. They married in September 1936 and, although she had never climbed a mountain, they spent their honeymoon rock climbing in the Lake District before sailing for their new home in Rangoon, Burma. She combined having four daughters with becoming an accomplished climber, and travelled the world with John on many expeditions. Aged eighty-seven, after his death, she climbed with her grandson to the highest roof point of Sydney Opera House.

John Hunt (centre) visiting the Caucasus in 1958

Brigadier Sir Henry Cecil John Hunt, Baron Hunt (1910–1998), was born in India and was a great-great-nephew of the explorer Sir Richard Burton. He was educated in England at Marlborough College and the Royal Military College at Sandhurst, and was posted as a second lieutenant to India in 1931. He climbed extensively in the Himalayas, reaching 24,500 feet on Saltoro Kangri in 1935 before returning to England, where he met his future wife. In WWII, he fought in Italy and Greece. In 1953, he was selected to lead the expedition to Mount Everest during which Edmund Hillary and Tenzing Norgay reached the summit. He himself had climbed to 27,350 feet – 1,678 feet short of the summit – in support of the final assault on the mountain.

Hugh Hunt (1911–1993) was born in Surrey and, after time spent at the Sorbonne in Paris, and in Heidelberg in Germany, studied modern languages at Oxford, and was president of the Oxford University Dramatic Society in 1933. He moved to Dublin three months before this visit to McGuirk's, as artistic director of the Abbey Theatre: he had been recommended to W.B. Yeats by the English poet John Masefield. At the Abbey, he directed plays by Teresa Deevy and George Sheils, and produced Yeats's *Purgatory* and dramatisations of Frank O'Connor's work. He also directed on Broadway and the West End and, after WWII, became artistic director of the Old Vic theatre in London. He retired as Professor of Drama at Manchester University in 1973.

1 January 1936

John Wilkinson	*Glenalbyn, Stillorgan, Co. Dublin*
E.D. Wilkinson (Mrs)	
F. Wm Lamb	*Rotunda*
R. Stewart Sasson	*Rotunda*
Edward Solomons	*Rotunda*

John Samuel Wilkinson (1871–1946) was from a wealthy Meath family of cattle dealers. He was an auctioneer and livestock dealer with premises at Prussia Street, Dublin, which is today the location of the Park Shopping Centre.

Evelyn Doris Wilkinson (*b.* 1884), née Warner, was John's wife. Glenalbyn House, their home in Stillorgan, is now the Glenalbyn Sports Club and Conference Centre.

Francis William John Alexander Lamb (1874–1959) was from Co. Offaly. After studying medicine at Trinity College Dublin, he became a gynaecologist. He worked for some years in the Rotunda Hospital where he took a particular interest in childhood cardiac conditions. He went on to lecture in pathology at the University of Birmingham before being appointed Professor of Forensic Medicine at Cairo University.

Edward Solomons was another brother of the famous gynaecologist and Master of the Rotunda Hospital, Bethel Solomons. Edward also was a gynaecologist and wrote a number of scholarly papers, including one entitled 'The treatment of Varicose veins in pregnancy'.

31 March 1936

G. Kohlmann	*Aix-la-Chapelle,*
	Nordic – Heil Hitler!!!

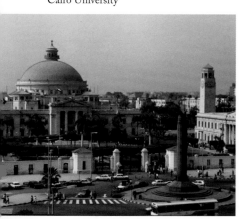

Cairo University

There is no doubt where G. Kohlmann's loyalties lie: Aachen in Germany, formerly Aix-la-Chapelle, was occupied by the Allies after WWI until 1930. The city was heavily damaged during WWII, and was the first German city to be captured by the Allies, after a long siege in 1944.

The first American tank enters Aachen, October 1944

1 August 1936

Professor Robert Dwyer Joyce	*Dublin*	*Cosmopolitan*
Mrs Mary Dwyer Joyce	*ditto*	*Compot [sic]*
W.R.D. Joyce, Junior	*ditto*	*Abysinnian [sic]*

Under the heading 'Nationality' in the visitors' book, this family left these playful descriptions.

Robert Dwyer Joyce (1874–1959) was an ophthalmic and aural surgeon and son of Patrick Weston Joyce, educationalist, historian and collector of Irish traditional music. His uncle, also called Robert Dwyer Joyce, was a medical doctor and songwriter who wrote such songs as 'The Boys of Wexford' and 'The Wind that Shakes the Barley'. Our Robert Dwyer graduated in medicine in London in 1895 and became a Fellow of the Royal College of Surgeons in Ireland in 1899. He worked as an ophthalmic surgeon in the Mater and Richmond hospitals and, a year before this visit to McGuirk's, was appointed Professor of Ophthalmology in University College Dublin.

Mary Dwyer Joyce was his wife; W.R.D. Joyce was their son.

24 September 1936

D.C. Cruise O'Brien	*44 Leinster Road, Rathmines*
Flann C. Campbell	*Cabinteely, Co. Dublin*
Edgar M. Gillespie	*Dublin*

Conor Cruise O'Brien and Máire Mhac an
tSaoi, 1997

Nineteen-year-old Donal Conor David Dermot Donat Cruise
O'Brien (1917–2008), better known as the politician, writer, academic
and historian Conor Cruise O'Brien, was educated at Sandford
Park School and Trinity College Dublin, after which he joined
the civil service. His father, Francis ('Frank') Cruise O'Brien, was a
journalist, while his mother, Kathleen Cruise O'Brien, née Sheehy,
was a teacher, Irish-language advocate, and suffragist. Political and
cultural activists of the time comprised a relatively small group
and often had familial or inter-marital connections, irrespective of
political leanings. Conor Cruise O'Brien's aunt Hannah Sheehy was
married to the pacifist Francis Skeffington, who was murdered by
the British after the 1916 Rising. His marriage to Christine Foster
in 1939 ended in divorce after twenty years.

In 1961, he was attached to Ireland's United Nations delegation
in New York and became a special representative to the Secretary
General, Dag Hammarskjöld. After Hammarskjöld's death,
Cruise O'Brien resigned from the UN and the Irish diplomatic
service. He married the poet Máire Mhac an tSaoi, daughter of
Seán MacEntee, then Fianna Fáil Tánaiste, in 1962. After a period
as Vice-Chancellor of the University of Ghana, O'Brien was the
Albert Schweitzer Professor of Humanities in New York University,
1965–9, during which he was arrested for taking part in a protest
against the Vietnam War. He was elected to Dáil Éireann as a
Labour Party deputy in 1969, and became the Minister for Posts
and Telegraphs in the coalition government of 1973. Deeply hostile
to militant Irish republicanism, he enforced censorship on Raidió
Teilifís Éireann (RTÉ) with regard to broadcasting interviews with
members of Sinn Féin. He was editor of the *Observer* newspaper
in Britain, 1978–81, wrote a number of books and television scripts,
and held many visiting lectureships and professorships around the
world, particularly in the United States.

Flann C. Campbell (1919–1994), educationalist and historian,
was born in Glencree and was a son of the poet Joseph Campbell and

Nancy Maude Campbell, both of whom we have already met. Like Cruise O'Brien, he attended Sandford Park School and received a BA in economics and political science at Trinity College Dublin. In 1951, he received a PhD in sociology at the London School of Economics and from 1959 to 1980 was head of the Department of Education at the College of All Saints in London, which was to become the Middlesex Polytechnic. He returned to Dublin in 1988 and contributed to many newspapers and journals until his death.

2 October 1936
Frank Mitchell   *Dublin*

George Francis Mitchell (1912–1997) was born in Dublin and educated at The High School in Rathgar before attending Trinity College and graduating with a BA in natural sciences. In 1935, he received a Master of Science degree in geology and, at the time of his visit, was studying for an MA in the same subject, which he received in 1937. While his chosen field of study was the Quaternary period, he eventually enjoyed an international reputation as a geologist, botanist, archaeologist, ornithologist, geographer, social historian, and author. An early mentor was Arthur Wilson Stelfox, naturalist, architect, and father of Dawson Stelfox, the first Irishman to climb Everest, and he met Robert Lloyd Praeger through the Dublin Naturalists' Field Club. Mitchell's two best-known publications are *The Book of the Irish Countryside* (1987) and *The Way That I Followed: A Naturalist's Journey around Ireland* (1990), which set out to provide a contemporary companion to Praeger's *The Way That I Went*. He was Professor of Quaternary Studies at Trinity College Dublin and president of the Royal Irish Academy as well as of a number of other learned societies. He was also the recipient of many academic honours, including the Cunningham Medal of the Royal Irish Academy, which had not been awarded for the previous 104 years.

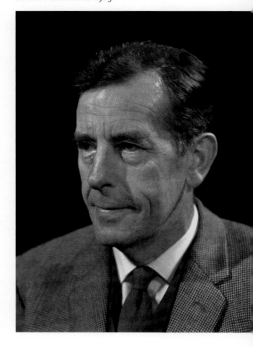

Frank Mitchell in 1965

Former An Óige Youth Hostel at Glencree, Co. Wicklow. The building, located near McGuirk's, became a youth hostel in 1950

1937

11 April 1937

Jack Sutton	*Dublin*
A.M. Colatin	*ditto*
H.S. Crone	*ditto*

An Óige: Mullacleevaun was tough: ten miles to go.

This group were members of An Óige, an organisation founded in 1931 to foster an appreciation of the Irish countryside and heritage in the youth of Ireland, and to encourage international co-operation. One of An Óige's founders, Chalmers ('Terry') Trench, had been inspired by the *Jugundherbergen* in Germany, and brought the idea back to Ireland: the first An Óige hostel, providing basic accommodation and cooking facilities for young hikers, was opened in Glendalough in 1931. Trench's sister was Jean 'Shamrock' Trench.

20 May 1937

Daniel Broad	*Drumcondra, Dublin*
Violet Wood	*Santry, Co. Dublin*

Half-way House, Dublin from Glendalough.

Daniel Broad met Violet Wood, from South Africa, in the same year they visited McGuirk's: they both shared a love of hiking and were later married. He became a stock controller in the Inchicore Railway Works and their son, Ian Frederick, followed in their hiking footsteps. Graduating from Trinity College Dublin in 1969, he taught in The High School, Rathgar, where he introduced field trips to Wicklow, Achill, Clare and Connemara. He took part in protests against the demolition of Georgian Dublin and helped establish the Dublin Arts Festival. He spent ten years teaching in China, Bhutan and South Africa before returning to Ireland where he taught for a time at Alexandra College. He died of COVID-19 in January 2021.

21 July 1937
A. O'Brien	*Dublin*
Máire O'Brien	*Áth Cliath*
Eleanor Butler	*Áth Cliath*

Eleanor Butler, Lady Wicklow (1914–1997), was born in Dublin and, after attending school at Tudor Hall in Kent and Alexandra College in Dublin, studied architecture at University College Dublin, where her father, R.M. Butler, was Professor of Architecture, 1924–42. She was a member of the Irish Labour Party and a Labour senator, 1948–51. Through the poet John Betjeman, then press attaché at the British Embassy, she met William Howard, who became the 8th Earl of Wicklow on the death of his father. They married in 1959. Later in life she converted to Catholicism and worked to secure a peaceful solution for Northern Ireland: she was instrumental in the establishment of twenty women's organisations in the North that lobbied for peace. Forty years after her visit to McGuirk's, she was a founder of the Glencree Centre for Peace & Reconciliation, based in the former Glencree Reformatory, near McGuirk's.

Alexandra College on Earlsfort Terrace, Dublin. The school continued to use these Victorian buildings until its relocation in the 1970s

30 August 1937

G.B. Warner   *Royal Air Force, Tern Hill, Market Drayton, Shropshire*

L.W. Warner   *Assam, India*

Gerald Bernard Warner (1917–1996) was born in Assam, India, and had joined the RAF just five months before this visit to McGuirk's. He was an exceptionally skilled bomber pilot during WII, and by 1942 had achieved the rank of wing commander. He was awarded the Distinguished Flying Cross and the Air Force Cross, and survived at a time when 55,500 out of 125,000 aircrew died.

25 December 1937

Midnight Mass

Edie Mitchell   *Stephen's Road, Inchicore*

Cathy Rochford   *15 Herbert Street*

Kevin Richardson   *77 Botanic Avenue*

Jimmie Geoghegan

John E. Maguire

Ella Banim

After Midnight Mass, a good solid feed went down well, and swelled Jimmie so that he wanted the whole lot to himself. I cannot be more complimentary than to say I'm coming here again.

It is likely that this group attended midnight Mass in the chapel in the Glencree Reformatory. As mentioned previously, McGuirk's seems to frequently have been open at all hours; this entry shows just how keen they were to do business.

St Kevin's Church, next to the former Glencree Reformatory

29 December 1937
Constitution Day, Lá an Bunreachta
T. Burke   Ballybunion, Co. Kerry
N. Byrne   Dublin

Postage stamp commemorating the Irish Constitution, 1937

The pair above saw fit to announce that the new Constitution of Ireland came into effect on this day, replacing that of the Irish Free State. Initially drafted by a legal advisor to the Department of External Affairs, John Hewwarne, the new constitution was personally supervised by Éamon de Valera and, amended many times, remains the longest continually operating constitution within the European Union.

1938

The handwriting of many of the signatures in the visitors' book for 1938 is illegible, making it difficult to identify visitors in this period.

11 March 1938
Peter E. Verdon
W. Warnock
F.J. Davys
V. Gough
S. Lacey

William Warnock (1911–1986) was born in Dublin and educated at The High School, Rathgar, and Trinity College Dublin, where he studied modern literature and Celtic studies. He was also a notable linguist and, after a year's teaching, joined the Department of External Affairs. Fluent in German, he was appointed secretary to the Irish Legation in Berlin in the same year as this visit to McGuirk's, and was acting chargé d'affaires there from autumn

William Warnock (right) during his time as Irish Ambassador to West Germany, 1961

1939 to March 1944, the sole Irish diplomat in Germany for most of WWII. He survived a bombing raid on Berlin in which the Irish Legation was burned down and, after being replaced in 1944 by Con Cremin, he subsequently served in Stockholm, Berne and Vienna before returning to Germany (then West Germany) in 1959. He was Ireland's first Ambassador to India in 1964, following which he served as Ambassador to Canada, the United States and Israel.

4 September 1938

*Louis O'Farrell, 14 Herbert Place, Dublin S, All Ireland
 Final, Up Waterford!*
*Bríghid Ní Fhinn, 111 Cuarbothar Theas, Áth Cliath, Buadh
 le Áth Cliath! [Victory for Dublin!]*
*Judy O'Farrell, 17 Ballybrickan, Waterford, Up Waterford
 every time!*

Sporting events are not often mentioned in the visitors' books, but these visitors refer to the All-Ireland Hurling Final that was taking place that day: Waterford was defeated by Dublin, 2-5 to 1-6. Waterford eventually won two hurling All-Irelands, in 1948 and 1959: Dublin has not repeated its 1938 victory.

5 November 1938

T.J. Johnston   St Catherine's Rectory, Dublin
John Johnston   St Catherine's Rectory, Dublin
Rev. R. Bird   St Kevin's Rectory, Dublin

Of these three visitors, we know that T.J. Johnston wrote pamphlets about St Columba and the expansion of the Celtic Church and, with co-authors J.L. Robinson and R.W. Jackson, *The History of the Church of Ireland* (1953).

1939

Although few pages from the visitors' books survive for late 1938 and 1939, it is clear that the number of visitors to McGuirk's began to drop off dramatically from September 1939. On 3 September 1939, when Britain declared war on Germany, the Emergency Powers Act was passed by the Dáil. Days later, a maximum price for foodstuffs was established and petrol was rationed, followed by coal in January 1941, but food rationing did not come into being until the end of May 1942. With the War of Independence and the atrocities of the Black and Tans fresh in people's memories, Ireland took a neutral stance in the war, but petrol rationing, together with the ban on private motoring, would have drastically reduced the number of motor-car tourists. Bicycles, however, increased in number: 90 per cent of Irish people now used them, and Flann O'Brien's novel *The Third Policeman* (1967) was inspired by their ubiquity at the time.

1940

The uncertainty that reigned in the early months of WWII had dissipated greatly by early 1940 as people got used to what became known as the Phoney War. Although Britain sent a large expeditionary force to reinforce France after Poland had been invaded, little happened on the Western Front. After six months of relative inactivity, however, the Phoney War came to a sudden and violent end on 9 April 1940 when German forces began to move west and in two months had defeated Denmark and Norway, followed by the routing of the combined French and British armies. The fact that the Germans trampled over the neutrality of Luxembourg, Belgium and the Netherlands along the way brought home to the Irish the fragility of neutrality. Many had joined the British forces at the beginning of the war, and the shock suffered at the British defeat was shared by many in Ireland. A swift invasion

Glencree in 1940

of Britain was expected, followed, perhaps, by an invasion of Ireland; as if only then becoming aware of the seriousness of the situation, the Irish authorities scrambled to organise a national defence. A major military recruitment campaign began and, on 24 May, the Local Security Force was established as an auxiliary to An Garda Síochána: within two weeks, over 44,000 men had enrolled in the new force.

The good weather in the summer of 1940, however, brought large numbers back into the mountains and to McGuirk's, and there is little mention of the war in the visitors' books.

During the 1926 disturbance at the Abbey, W.B. Yeats rose to praise *The Plough and the Stars* and to tell the audience that they had disgraced themselves again. This caricature by William Orpen shows the poet addressing the audience during the *Playboy* riots of 1907

12 May 1940

Ria Mooney	*Abbey Theatre, Dublin*
Elsie Jacob	*Dublin*
E.J. Jacob	*Dublin*

Ria Mooney (1903–1973), stage and screen actress, was the first female producer at the Abbey Theatre. Born in Dublin, she was in her teens when she sang on stage with the Rathmines & Rathgar Musical Society. She attended the Dublin Metropolitan School of Art but was invited to join the Abbey in 1924, an important time in the history of the Irish stage. She played Rosie Redmond in *The Plough and the Stars* in 1926, when the cast was attacked during rioting in the theatre. Playing prominent roles in many important plays, she worked with actors Cyril Cusack, F.J. McCormick and Molly Allgood (Maire O'Neill). Ria left the Abbey in 1944 to direct the Gaiety School of Acting, but returned in 1948 as resident producer. She directed most of the seventy-five new plays produced by the Abbey between 1948 and 1963.

11 August 1940
Dorothy Day   *2 Winsor Road*
Michael McAuliffe *Dublin*
Mr & Mrs Le Brocquy *51 Kenilworth Square, Dublin*

Albert le Brocquy (1898–1976) was the grandson of a Walloon who came to Ireland to buy horses for the Belgian army, married a woman from Kilkenny, and never left. In 1915, Albert married Sybil le Brocquy (1892–1973), née Staunton, a conservationist and patron of the arts who, under the nom de plume Helen Staunton, wrote plays and dramas staged by the Abbey Theatre and broadcast by Raidió Éireann. She wrote four books on the life and work of Jonathan Swift, was a trustee of the National Library of Ireland and initiated the Book of the Year award, now the Irish Book Awards. She had three children, including the painter Louis le Brocquy.

22 August 1940
Mr & Mrs James J Halpin

If Hitler comes, let's hope he samples Mrs McGuirk's tea, home-made bread and fresh egg as we did, to our complete satisfaction.

This couple left a note hinting what was on many people's minds, in Ireland as well as Britain, during August 1940, but also invoking Adolf Hitler in a way that in the years to come would seem strange. Four days later, German bombs killed three young women at Campile in Co. Wexford.

Memorial to the victims of the 1940 bombing in Campile, Co. Wexford

21 September 1940
Mrs Sean Lester
Mrs McGilligan
Miss Sheila Conolly

Mrs Seán Lester was the wife of Irish diplomat Seán Lester, and although she played an important if not essential part of his career as an Irish diplomat, this is rarely acknowledged. He was born in Co. Antrim in 1888; the son of a protestant grocer, he joined the Gaelic League as a youth, and later the Irish Republican Brotherhood. He was a journalist, and became news editor of *The Freeman's Journal* in 1919. In 1923, he joined the Department of External Affairs, and in 1929 became Ireland's permanent delegate to the League of Nations. He was the League's High Commissioner in Danzig, 1934–7, during which time he repeatedly protested to the German government over its persecution of Jews. In 1940, he became Secretary General of the League of Nations, and his wife must have been on a visit to Ireland from Geneva at the time of her trip to McGuirk's. Their granddaughter Susan Denham was Chief Justice of Ireland, 2011–17. Mrs McGilligan, née Ann Conolly, was married to Patrick McGilligan, Free State Minister for External Affairs at the time of their wedding in 1929.

By 1940, entries in the visitors' books are beginning to suggest that visitors with addresses in the well-off areas of Dublin are becoming less frequent, while addresses such as Home Farm Road, Iveragh Road, Mount Tallant Avenue and Cabra Road signal an increase in the numbers of lower- and middle-class excursionists in the mountains. Many of the visitors now leave a sketch of the triangular motif of the walking and outdoor organisation An Óige.

Sketches of the An Óige motif left in the 1940s

9 February 1941

Éamonn Ó Riain	*Óglac [sic]*	*Bearraic Portóbelló [sic]*
Seámus Ó Cathasaigh	*Óglach*	*Ceannasardheata, Aer Cosanta*

These are two members of the defence forces, which still had the tradition of its members giving themselves the title *Óglach* (young warrior) or Volunteer. Ó Cathasaigh jokingly claims, in Irish, to be Commander-in-Chief of the Irish Air Corps.

2 March 1941

Joe Groome   Bray

Ate 3 eggs, 6 rashers and drank 8 cups of tea.

7 August 1941

Joan Brown   Rotherham, Yorkshire and Dublin
Roy Brown

No rationing here!

A British ration book and two ration supplements

Rationing had been introduced in Britain in January 1940, with severe restrictions on foodstuffs like sugar, tea, eggs and meat. Although rationing in time of war had been first explored by the Irish government in 1935, with manufacturers and importers of essential goods being encouraged to lay in at least six months of reserve stocks by 1938, the measures weren't taken up. So, by 1941, food rationing had made no impact in Ireland, and certainly not in Glencree, as these two entries suggest.

Scene of the North Strand bombing, May 1941

7 September 1941
Arthur Fitzpatrick

On to Leningrad, Ein Volk, Ein Reich, Ein Fuhrer [sic]
[One People, One Realm, One Leader]

Despite the bombing by the Luftwaffe of Belfast in April and May, resulting in the deaths of almost one thousand civilians, and the bombing of the North Strand in Dublin in May, in which twenty-eight people were killed and three hundred houses destroyed or damaged, this entry suggests that at least some Irish people observed the advances of the German army with satisfaction. The deaths of civilians in Belfast might not have been significant for them. Germany had turned east against Russia in June 1941 and, a day after this pro-Nazi comment was left in the visitors' book, the Wehrmacht cut off the last road into Leningrad and laid siege to the city, a siege that lasted for 872 days. The destruction and loss of lives was without precedent: over 1.5 million civilians and soldiers perished. In the Ireland of the 1940s, and certainly among many Irish Catholics, however, Communist Russia was regarded as 'Godless', and I doubt there was widespread sympathy for the Russian people.

12 October 1941
Buck Greene
Fred Lynch   From the Bombed Area – That shook yeh!

A strange comment, suggesting that maybe Fred Lynch was from the North Strand in Dublin, where Luftwaffe bombs had fallen nearly six months before.

4 April 1942
Risteard Grenfell Morton

From over the mountain, far and away,
Came four lonely travellers one fine April day.
They admired the lake,
They admired the view;
But more so the tea so strong and true
That they found in the cottage by the wayside
When for a meal they called and cried
So they entered the cottage and had their tea
Then over the mountain and far away lea!

Richard Grenfell Morton was a writer, little chronicled – we do not even know his date of birth – who much later produced a range of works, including *Standard gauge railways in the North of Ireland* (1962), *Elizabethan Ireland* (1971) and *Home Rule and the Irish Question* (1980).

Tommy McGuirk died young, early in 1942. The then President of Ireland, Douglas Hyde, who had himself visited McGuirk's but omitted to sign the visitors' book, wrote a letter of sympathy to Mrs McGuirk, attaching an autographed photograph that was framed and prominently displayed.

Mary Jane McGuirk was sixty-eight years old when her son died. His older brother, Arthur, was forty-five, and in the summer of 1942 married Mary Gallagher, later known as Mona, probably to distinguish her from her mother-in-law. Mona was forty, the only girl in the Gallagher family, and the second-eldest of

Ireland's first president, Douglas Hyde, and the letter of sympathy sent to Mrs McGuirk

UACHTARÁN NA hÉIREANN
(PRESIDENT OF IRELAND)

BAILE ÁTHA CLIATH
(DUBLIN)

15th April, 1942

Dear Mrs McGurk,

You might perhaps like to have the enclosed autographed photograph of the President as a memento of his visit to your house some years ago.

I hope that you have now recovered from the great shock of your recent bereavement.

Yours sincerely,

SECRETARY TO THE PRESIDENT.

Turf drying, Co. Wicklow

eleven children, which suggests that she might have been glad to leave the job of looking after all her siblings, even if it meant moving in with her mother-in-law. Her considerable baking skills ensured that she was soon running the tea room, and providing accommodation and meals for men who worked cutting turf on the Featherbed bogs. These men slept in a timber prefab at the side of the house, which the McGuirks called The Little House, and there was also space to sleep in the turf shed across the road from the cottage. Making breakfasts, lunches and dinners for the turf cutters meant considerable extra work for Mona, in addition to baking bread and serving teas to the tourists and hikers. Bread became a rationed food item in 1942, but McGuirk women baked their own bread.

In the 1930s, approximately 2,500,000 tons of coal and 3,500,000 tons of turf were burned annually in Ireland. Two days after WWII broke out, the Dublin Coal Office was forced to close as a result of panic buying, and the cost of coal increased by 50 per cent. Although a small amount of coal was mined in Ireland, most of it was imported from Britain and now was not only increasing in price but reducing drastically in quality. The government turned to turf in an effort to solve the fuel problem, and the production of hand-won turf was encouraged. Turbary rights were granted to local authorities as well as to private producers, voluntary bodies, parish councils and families, in a national effort to become self-sufficient in fuel. Private turf production in the Dublin Mountains amounted to around 8,000 tons annually at that time, and the Featherbeds, half a mile from McGuirk's, was a hive of activity as large numbers of Dubliners from diverse backgrounds and occupations worked side by side to secure their fuel needs. Some of these were provided with bed, breakfast and an evening meal by Mrs McGuirk, as the following entry illustrates.

6 May 1942

Patrick Conniffe   15 Iveragh Road, Whitehall, Dublin

Spent a week here, cutting turf on the mountain, very, very tired, but well catered for at this cottage, never-the-less, I don't think I will try turf cutting again.

27 September 1942

O.O. Heeney
K.A.G. Heeney – Heil Hitler und die neue Ordnung
*   [Heil Hitler and the new Order]*

German troops in Stalingrad, winter 1942

Written underneath this entry, in another hand:

Nieder mit den Englandern [sic] – Gott sei Dank
(Down with the English – Thank God)

Here again, the outside world intrudes briefly into the visitors' book: although the tide of war was turning against Nazi Germany, it still had its Irish supporters. On this same day, 27 September 1942, the Manhattan Project to develop the atomic bomb was approved in the United States and given the highest level of priority for emergency procurement. Around the same time, Joseph Stalin ordered the Soviet nuclear research programme to be resumed after being delayed for a year, and the German forces began a new offensive with the Battle of Stalingrad.

18 October 1942

J.F. Corcoran
Col D. Neligan   Booterstown, Dublin

Good Welcome, tea and comfort.

Statue of Lady Justice on the gates of
Dublin Castle

Colonel David Neligan (1899–1983) was born in Co. Limerick, the
son of two teachers. He joined the Dublin Metropolitan Police
in 1917 and, along with Eamon Broy, who later became Garda
Commissioner, was an agent for Michael Collins, to whom he
passed much critical information. After being recruited by MI5, he
became the most important mole in Dublin Castle. He was active
with the National Army during the Civil War and was associated
with several atrocities in Kerry, before being promoted to colonel and
made Director of Intelligence. He later joined An Garda Síochána
and was involved in the establishment of the Special Branch, but
when Fianna Fáil came into power in 1932, he was moved to the
civil service. He had the unique experience of drawing pensions
from the Dublin Metropolitan Police, MI5, An Garda Síochána,
the Old IRA and the civil service.

1943

28 March 1943
E. Peard, inaugurated the fencing school
E.N. Roberts
Liam Miller
Dorian de Witt

E. Neville Roberts (*b.* 1882) was born in Dublin and worked as a
clerk until joining the Royal Irish Fusiliers in 1911 and serving in
France; he was wounded at the Battle of the Somme. On returning
to Ireland, he organised coach tours for H.M.S. Catherwood Ltd
and also worked as a journalist, illustrator and poet. He was friends
with the left-wing writer and trade unionist R.M. Fox, children's
author Patricia Lynch and painter Jack B. Yeats, but when someone
offered to introduce him to W.B. Yeats, he said, 'No thank you,

I have been introduced to him twice before and it was once too much.' He was an enthusiastic hill walker and a great supporter of An Óige: he celebrated his seventieth birthday by climbing Mount Brandon in Co. Kerry.

Liam Miller (1924–1987) was born in Mountrath, Co. Laois and, although he had studied architecture, he devoted his life to publishing. After spending time in London working on post-war reconstruction, he returned to Dublin in 1951 with his wife, Josephine, to found the Dolmen Press, through which he published the works of many Irish writers and poets, including Richard Murphy, Thomas Kinsella, Austin Clarke, John Montague and Padraic Colum. The finest Dolmen production is said to be Thomas Kinsella's *The Táin* (1969), illustrated by Louis le Brocquy, and Dolmen received many publishing and design awards. Miller also designed sets for the Abbey Theatre: for *The Plough and the Stars* in 1966 and *The Countess Cathleen* in 1969. Dolmen Press used equipment from the Dun Emer Press, which had been run by Lily and Lolly Yeats, sisters of W.B. and Jack B. Yeats.

Elizabeth Corbet 'Lolly' Yeats (right) with Esther Ryan and Beatrice Cassidy at the Dun Emer Press, *c.*1903

23 April 1943
Aoine an Chéasta, Mí na Aibreán 1943
Peadar Mac Giolla Bríghde

D'fhágas an cathair, ag trial ar sléibhte Baile Átha Cliath
chun móin do bhaint air.
Ar ndóig tháinig an fearthainn agus b'éigean dom an lá do
chaitheamh annso. Ní raibh aithne agama r aoinne annso
agus is cuma mar bhí na daoine godeas go linn an lae. Bhí
gach oiread le n–ithe is le n'ól ann agus dubhras liom féin go
dtiucfaidh mé thar nais uair éigin le cóngnamh Dé.
Go bhfágaidh Dia do shláinte chugat, a bhean bhig.

This translates as:

Good Friday, April 1943
Peter Gilbride

I left the city, making for the Dublin mountains to cut turf there.
As usual, it rained and I had to spend the day here. I knew no one but what matter, as the people here were pleasant. There was lots to eat and drink and I said to myself that I will return some time with God's help. May God spare you the health, little woman!

Baint na Móna
Is modh duine teacht ar Iarthar an Chláir.
Mar a bhfásann ubhla milse cubhradh
Ární dubh sa mbláth
Bíonn Luingeas ann is bád
Ag rodhuidheacht ann gach lá
Bíonn bric is éisc san doimheán go h-éinneach
's an eala gléigeal bán.

Cutting and footing turf, Co. Wicklow

These lines left by an unknown visitor on the same day as Peadar Mac Giolla Bríghde's entry translate as:

Cutting Turf
Many people come to West Clare
Where sweet-scented apples grow
Black sloes in flower
Fleets of ships and boats
Cycling each day
Trout and fish all over the deep
And the bright white swan.

22 April 1943
Annraoi Ó Liatháin
Dáithí MacOistín

Annraoi Ó Liatháin left a long poem in Irish, with the title *Tá Caidreamh againn leis an mBás, uch ochón* ('I fear that we flirt with Death'). It translates as:

When the dawn sun strikes Ireland
And the hills are immersed in mystic light
It's said that to go tramping is wonderful
Over the hills to Glendalough.
This is well known to Dáithí and I
We organised a trip for Good Friday
Through fairy glens and over rough mountains
To Glendalough, my pain, my torture!
As the clouds thickened over Mólann,
The sky darkened and torrents fell
Our coats and capes gave little shelter
We were drenched to the skin from head to toe.
Now we've arrived to partake of food,
Bread, eggs, jam and hot tea,
And a fire, food and hospitality.
Outside the storm is angrily howling.
Someone says it's time to leave,
We have no option but to spoil it all,
Colours of death, the end, the trident …
Fever of the bones, cold and weakness.
But what say Dáithí or myself?
Better to just sit by the fire
On Good Friday in Glendalough,
By the mountain stag! We'll not leave now!

Glendalough, Co. Wicklow

Annraoi Ó Liatháin (1917–1981) was born in Co. Galway and educated at the Patrician Brothers school in Tullow, Co. Carlow, and the Christian Brothers in Youghal, Co. Cork. He worked in the civil service and was a prominent member of the Gaelic League, editor for a time of its journal, *An Glór*, and president of the Gaelic League, 1950–2. He published more than one hundred short stories in Irish and *Cois Siúire*, his travelogue of the River Suir, won first prize in the Oireachtas literary competition in 1981. He had eight children with his wife, Margaret Fox.

9 June 1943
John Harrington
James O'Shea

Spent 10 days with the McGuirk family, had an excellent time, good food, great hospitality & looking forward (Deo Volente) to spending another 10 days in the year 1944.

There is no evidence that they returned in 1944.

1944

10 April 1944
Noel Hartnett	*Dublin*
Donal May	*Dublin*
M. Casey	*Dublin*

Noel Hartnett (1909–1960), born in Kenmare, Co. Kerry, was a barrister, political activist and broadcaster. His attendance at Trinity College Dublin was funded by scholarships, after which he joined

Raidió Éireann as an announcer, scriptwriter and commentator. He joined Fianna Fáil while at Trinity and was called to the Bar in 1937, assisting Seán MacBride on several cases. Disappointed at the lack of progress in Fianna Fáil, he left the party and became a founder member of Clann na Poblachta, working closely with Noel Browne on the Mother and Child Scheme. Dissatisfied with his new party's performance, he rejoined Fianna Fáil and was elected to Seanad Éireann (the Irish Senate) in 1951. He contested a by-election in 1958 as a candidate for the National Progressive Democrats but failed to win the seat; after this, he devoted himself to his legal work, always happy to work in defence of the less well off.

Aerial view of the D-Day landings, 1944

17 June 1944
Wilfred Brewer   *7 Anglesea Street*
Harry Thompson   *ditto*

After a week of 'turf' work we are fitter than ever thanks to Mrs McGuirk's nourishment of the first order. There's no fuel like the old fuel – turf!

There is no mention in the visitors' book of the D-Day landings in France, the largest seaborne invasion in history, which had taken place eleven days before this entry.

There were few entries in the visitors' book for August 1944 because Mona was in the Rotunda Hospital, giving birth to her son Tom, who was delivered by Bethel Solomons, a frequent visitor to the tea room. This entry suggests that she was quickly back in harness after giving birth.

30 August 1944
Stiophán Breathnach

Caitheas deich lá annseo go suimhneach sásta. Bhí an biadh go maith agus an freastal dá réir. Bhí flaitheamhalacht agus cairdeachas o mhaidin go h-oidhche. Bhí aoibhneas istigh agus amuigh. Bhí radharc áluinn le feiceál ins gach áit, agus go mór-mhór sa ngleann ar aghaidh an tighe. Beannacht Dé ar an mbothán agus ar na daoine a mhaireann ann.

This translates as:

Stephen Walsh

I spent ten days here, contented and happy. The food was good and the service equally. There was generosity and friendship from morning to night. A pleasant atmosphere inside and out. Wonderful views in every direction, particularly over the glen in front of the house. God Bless this cottage and the people who live here.

8 October 1944
Morgan McGelligott   *Marlboro Road, Donnybrook*
James T. Doyle   *Anglesea Rd, Ballsbridge*

Morgan McGelligot with the UCD Boat Club's men's senior eight team (1947)

Edmund Morgan McGelligott (1925–2016) was an Olympian oarsman and cardiologist. Aged nineteen, he was captain of the UCD Boat Club when he made this visit to McGuirk's and, four years later, at a time when it was a great achievement in Ireland simply to compete, he took part in the men's eight rowing event in the 1948 Olympic Games. He spent most of his career working in Portiuncula Hospital in Co. Galway, and he was joint master of the East Galway Foxhounds.

4 January 1945
Fr R. Ingram SJ
Fr M. Sweetman SJ

Father Richard Ingram (1916–1967) was born in Belfast. He entered the Jesuit order at St Mary's in Emo, Co. Laois, in 1933 and was ordained at Rathfarnham Castle in 1944, where he also took over managing the seismograph that had been constructed there. The Jesuits had become interested in seismography after the Japanese earthquake of 1889, and the facility at Rathfarnham was just one of a number they had established around the world. Ingram went on to study mathematics at Johns Hopkins University in the United States, receiving a PhD in 1948. He returned to Ireland as part of the teaching staff at University College Dublin and was instrumental in having a seismograph installed in the Meteorological Observatory at Valentia, Co. Kerry. He was later Visiting Professor of Mathematics at Georgetown University, Washington DC, and became Associate Professor of Mathematics at University College Dublin in 1966.

Father Michael Sweetman (1914–1996) was born in Dublin and educated at Mount St Benedict, Co. Wexford; Clongowes Wood College, Co. Kildare; and University College Dublin. He joined the Jesuits in 1931 and was ordained in 1945. His career was devoted to social reform, particularly the issue of public housing, and he lived for a number of years in Dublin's inner city in order to experience the conditions there. He was a member of the radical Dublin Housing Action Committee and a believer in the concept of 'a just society'.

Fr Michael Sweetman in 1974

American troops of the 1139th Engineer Combat Group drinking champagne on Victory in Europe (VE) Day, 8 May 1945

6 May 1945

Patrick Phelan   *74 Church Rd, Dublin*

Patrick Creagh   *4 Great Western Ave, Dublin*

These two Patricks, who are otherwise undocumented, visited McGuirk's just before WWII ended in Europe. No mention is made of this momentous event in the visitors' book.

1946

6 June 1946

G. Cullen   *Liverpool*
(By air from Liverpool)

Much of the 1945, 1946 and 1947 visitors' books are in very poor condition, but it is clear from what remains that a great return to the hills took place after the war ended. G. Cullen boasts in this entry that he has flown from England, which is all we know about him.

27 July 1946

Moll & George Clune

Delighted to meet Master Tom McGuirk (age 1 yr. 11 months) for the first time. Had a most enjoyable tea, no limit, no ration cards, no coupons.

1 August 1946

C.L. Thompson   *Bray*

Changeless in a world of chaos – McGuirk's, after nine years, still stands for quality and quantity in food and hospitality.

From 1946 onwards, there is a large increase in foreign visitors to McGuirk's, particularly from England but also from faraway places such as India, Hong Kong and West Africa. For a period after May 1947, English visitors outnumbered Irish. These visitors are fulsome in their compliments about the good fare provided: in Britain, rationing was still quite severe and remained that way for some years. Clothes rationing there did not end until 1949, sugar was still rationed until 1953 and it was not until 1954 that meat and other food rationing came to an end. Although rationing was still in place in Ireland at the time for items such as tea, sugar, butter and flour, meat and eggs were not rationed, and in the countryside it was possible to obtain 'country butter' and adequate flour. Rationing in Ireland finally came to an end in December 1951.

I came across only one reference in the visitors' books to the fare provided by Mrs McGuirk that was rather less than the usual high praise. In 1949, John Wood, an English travel writer, hiked through eighteen counties of Ireland for two months and wrote a book, *With Rucksack Round Ireland* (1950), describing his experiences. McGuirk's was the only 'tea-place' along his route south from Dublin to Glendalough, and it had been highly recommended. He was hungry and, as he recounted in *With Rucksack*, soon learned that

> a plain tea in Ireland is really plain. No buns or cakes are served, as is usual in Britain, and at some places not even jam, nor did I ever see cress. Generally, there are two kinds of bread, baker's and homemade, and English visitors sometimes call the latter soda bread, though I have not

Irish soda bread

heard the term used by anyone Irish. The price was then usually 1s. 9d., or even 2s., but occasionally (as at Lough Bray) only 1s. 3d.

Wood went on to suggest that the purpose of Mrs McGuirk's visitors' book was possibly to 'convince the food office that she was entitled to all the tea, sugar and butter that she claimed, but as two recent callers had signed themselves Dorothy and Lilian Gish of Hollywood, I am not sure of the book's value as evidence'. He was not aware that food supplies often ran out at McGuirk's, particularly if there was an unexpected flood of visitors, and sometimes the McGuirks themselves had to do with very little. As Wood mentioned, their prices were lower than elsewhere because, for some reason, Arthur McGuirk wouldn't let Mona increase them, and so they remained unchanged from the 1930s through to the 1950s.

German children at Glencree with the Save the German Children Society after WWII

From 1945 to 1950, the nearby Glencree Reformatory, which had closed in 1940, was busy catering for child refugees from war-torn Europe, including Germany, Poland and Austria. The Save the German Children Society was founded in October 1945 to find foster homes for German children in Ireland. It proposed housing Catholic and Protestant children but, strangely, did not take in Jewish children, the excuse being that they might not integrate. As far as I can ascertain, the Irish Jewish community was not consulted. While some of the children were orphans or had parents who had not been located after the war, many had parents who simply couldn't afford to house or feed them, and who had no choice but to send their children into temporary foster care. Over five years, around 1,000 children aged between five and fifteen, many of them malnourished and some near death, were nursed back to health in Glencree by the Sisters of Charity of Saint Vincent de Paul. Once recovered, they were taken into foster care by Irish families in response to a call by the Red Cross. Usually, after about three years, children were reunited with their own families where possible; however, some did not wish to return to Germany and remained with their foster families, later settling down in Ireland.

1947

Mary Jane McGuirk died on 7 January 1947. Mona later mused that they would have been unable to bury her if she had died a little later, because the early snows that year turned into a major climatic event in mid-January, when a period of severe anti-cyclonic weather from Siberia gripped Ireland in two months of blizzards and icy conditions. The temperatures dropped to -14°C (the lowest temperature ever recorded in Ireland is -18°C), icy east winds frequently reached 70 mph and snow and ice covered the entire country. In the Dublin and Wicklow mountains, farmhouses, hamlets and villages were cut off.

On 24 February, the *Irish Independent* published the good news that there were 'Hopes for a break in cold spell', and the *Evening Herald* predicted 'fine weather' for the next day. On 25 February, however, a blizzard began that lasted fifty hours, the longest continuous snowfall ever recorded in Ireland. In mountainous places like Glencree, six-metre snowdrifts were common, but one was reported in *The Irish Times* as being sixteen metres high. Arthur McGuirk and some neighbours had to battle their way through snow drifts to reach Enniskerry in order to get food; because rationing was still in place, they could only buy one week's supply at a time.

Arthur McGuirk had saved little turf in 1946 because of the wet weather, and the only firewood available to the McGuirks was the grove of rhododendrons at the back of the cottage: Arthur had to

Snow blocking a country lane during the blizzard of 1947

dig his way to them every day for what must have been a doubtful haul. He also had to use a sledgehammer to smash the ice in the nearby stream to get water. Young Tom McGuirk had to be dragged away from gazing at the snow from the cottage windows because his mother was afraid he would get frostbite.

Although the local breadman made it to the refugee centre at Glencree on foot, it was impossible to adequately supply the children and the nuns with food and fuel. When one of the children developed acute appendicitis, an ambulance could only make it to within about 3 km of Glencree, and the boy had to be carried by stretcher across the snow to the ambulance. Farm animals died in large numbers, and although sheep have been known to live under snow drifts for a fortnight or more, few survived.

Glencree was cut off until 7 March, when a bulldozer arrived to clear the road. No one had seen such a machine before, and there was great excitement in the glen. Young Tom McGuirk was so impressed by it that he remembers getting a Dinky toy bulldozer afterwards.

4 September 1947
Mr and Mrs Squire   *Dun Laoghaire*

God's handywork [sic] is marvellous on this glorious day, but we think of others hungry and not so fortunate in these days of stress and trouble.

It's not clear what 'stress and trouble' this visitor, presumably 'Mr Squire', is referring to, but he might be drawing attention to the subcontinent of India, which, under Lord Louis Mountbatten, had been partitioned into the states of India and Pakistan on 15 August of this year, leading almost immediately to the single largest migration in human history and the loss of hundreds of thousands of lives.

28 February 1948
Bonnie Redmond

Many thanks for a lovely evening. The Glencree Glamour Girls on their Annual night out from the Reformatory.

Bonnie Redmond was one of the Red Cross nurses working with the refugees in the former Glencree Reformatory.

6 March 1948
Sir G. Reginald
Mrs F. Banks
Jimmy

Many a moon has passed since we were here last – and many a change – but not here, where time allows no changes – just the same good tea and home-made bread. This time our company is different, the rattletrap is not with us – being absent on other business – we are still three in number but the third is a newly initiated member, the other being across the water. Enough said, I am told to go, so go I must – till next time – and thanks for everything.

> *Seoirse Mach Gabhann*
> *Is iongartach an áit*
> *Is iongartach an tae.*

This translates as:

> George McGowan
> The place is amazing
> The tea is amazing.

Sketch of McGuirk's left in April 1948

Sketch of a hiker left in 1948

29 March 1948

Muriel Wiley   *Worcester, England*
Patience Lipton   *London, England*

He makes good strong tea
Does Mr McGuirk
We enjoyed it, did we,
So now full of 'perk'
We're all off with a jerk.

During a rare period when Mona McGuirk was away, it seems that Arthur McGuirk was looking after the tea room, and so gets a rare mention in this entry.

13 July 1948

Micheline Renard-Boussit   *La Tour de Peilz (Suisse)*
                                [Swiss]

We have had a lovely tea: our Swiss friend is charmed with this lovely Irish setting but we miss our dear old friend Mrs McGurk [sic], who was still here to welcome us last time we were here. May her soul rest in peace. She made a wonderful hostess and a good friend.

This visitor was noting the death in the previous year of Mary Jane McGuirk, who had run the tea room since her mother-in-law's death in 1910.

7 August 1948

J. Rongally   *St Helens, Lancs*

From Enniskerry to Lough Bray
Stopping at the tea-house on the way

Though we arrived at near midnight
A cup of tea was a welcome sight
And in the morn at 9.30 past
We were obliged with a good breakfast!
Thanks a lot.

This entry shows that the McGuirks were used to providing last-minute accommodation for travellers.

1949

For a while in 1949, more than 50 per cent of the visitors to McGuirk's were from overseas, mainly England, and the English visitors greatly outnumbered the Irish.

27 March 1949
Sophie Jacobs   *London*
E.F. Starkey   *Dublin*
J.S. Starkey

Sophie Jacobs and Estella F. Starkey last came to McGuirk's on 30 May 1932, but this time they came with J.S. Starkey (1879–1958), also known as Seamus O'Sullivan, poet, and editor of the influential *Dublin Magazine*. He was a friend of many leading literary figures in Dublin, including James Stephens, George Russell ('Æ') and W.B. Yeats, who strangely omitted O'Sullivan from his anthology of Irish poets, *A Book of Irish Verse* (1900). Yeats once commented that 'the trouble with Seamus is that when he's not drunk, he's sober'.

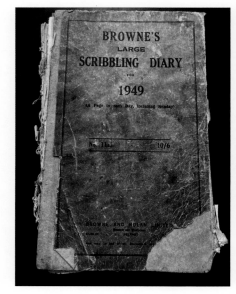

Cover of the visitors' book for 1949

Louie Bennett, c.1945

16 April 1949
Louie Bennett, Marie Allen, Mamdohas As Sayada
(Lebanon), ole Uncle Tom Cobbleigh and all!
Tea here on the day of Declaration of the Republic.

Louie Bennett (1870–1956), born Louisa Bennett in Dublin, was a pacifist, feminist and trade unionist. She was educated at Alexandra College in Dublin and an academy for young ladies in London. She studied singing in Bonn and wrote two romantic novels before getting involved in the suffragette movement, but distanced herself from violent action. Among a large number of activities at home and abroad related to women's rights and labour issues over her long lifetime, she reorganised the Irish Women Workers' Union, was the first woman elected president of the Irish Congress of Trade Unions, and served as a Labour Party councillor on Dún Laoghaire Borough Council.

Her note of celebration was two days premature. The Republic of Ireland Act 1948 had been signed into law on 21 December 1948, but did not come into force until 18 April 1949, the thirty-third anniversary of the 1916 Rising.

12 June 1949
Madeleine Murray   *33, St Anne's Road, Drumcondra*
Patrick Rocca   *41, Home Farm Park, Drumcondra*
Italian (P. Rocca)

Tante Grazie, per ogni coza era benissimo. [This loosely translates as 'Many thanks for everything – it was fine.']

Patrick Rocca (*d.* 1995) was the son of Egidio Rocca, an Italian marble mason who came to Dublin to work on the restoration of the Four Courts after their destruction in 1922. He stayed in Ireland and, with his son Patrick, went on to found the very successful firm

Rocca Tiles, which prospered through securing contracts for the new hospitals and sanatoria being built in Ireland in the 1950s and 1960s. Patrick's daughter, Michelle Rocca, was Miss Ireland in 1980.

6 July 1949

Walter Herron   *23 Roseleigh Street, Belfast*
D.J. Magee   *Ballybofey, Co. Donegal*
G. Lambert   *Dublin*

Three hikers came from Knockree
To scale Kippurean heights
And on their homeward journey bound
They found their heart's delight
For as they passed McGuirk's Hill Farm
A notice caught their eye;
And as they nearer did approach,
The word 'Teas' they did espy,
And they were doubly welcome made,
With tea, boiled eggs and home-baked bread.

In July 1949, McGuirk's welcomed well over a hundred visitors, many of them from heavily rationed Britain, all surprised by the amount of food they were served, and by the 'real' butter. The entries this month mainly praise the food, and many lines of doggerel (other than those quoted from this July 1949 entry) rhyme 'tay' with 'Lough Bray' and 'hurray'.

Sketches left by a scout group in July 1947 with the comment, 'Kipure was great but the tea was greater'

11 August 1949

E.F. Coard MRCVS   *5 Terenure Park, Dublin*
[Member of the Royal
College of Veterinary
Surgeons]

God be with the days when I slept in Dunne's old house near here with my brother and Jack Lambert the Poacher. I still get a great thrill when I come out here which unfortunately is all too seldom.

The poacher Jack Lambert was well known in Glencree. As a young man, he was arrested for poaching and, as was common at the time, was told by the judge that he could choose between prison or the British armed services. It seems likely that he joined the Royal Rifles of Canada.

12 August 1949

'Grouse Day' – but no grouse from:
A.R. Whitehead   *Birmingham, England*

> *I can't rival your Irish poets*
> *Who've written in this book,*
> *But I did enjoy my tea,*
> *'Good luck' to the cook!*

On 12 August every year, there was a red grouse shoot on the lands of Mervyn Patrick Wingfield, 9th Viscount Powerscourt. Tom McGuirk remembers many of the men from the valley, the Quinns, the Rogers, the Gallaghers and others, assembling on the road outside the cottage to beat for the guns. George McLaren, the gamekeeper, who lived in a house beside Lough Bray Cottage, was in charge of the shoot: the beaters got a free lunch and a bottle of Guinness.

3 September 1949
Dorothy Price
Liam Price
Robert J. Stopford

We have met Eleanor Dorothy Stopford Price and George William 'Liam' Price before.

Robert ('Bobbie') Jemmett Stopford (1895–1978) was born in Dublin, one of ten children and brother of Dorothy Stopford Price. He joined the Friends' Ambulance Unit at the outbreak of WWI, serving at Ypres, Salonika and Egypt. After the war, he read economics at Oxford and, after a brief spell with the British Overseas Bank, became private secretary to John Simon, 1st Viscount Simon, and spent two years in India, meeting key Indian leaders and laying down the foundations for the end of British rule there. During the rise of Adolf Hitler, he worked in Prague facilitating the transfer of wealthy Jewish families' money out of Austria, Hungary and Germany to London. As war approached, this activity extended to smuggling out Jews. During WWII, he worked in the British Embassy in Washington DC, and then at the British Ministry of Economic Welfare. After the war, he was vice-chairman of the Imperial War Museum in London, and collaborated with the Irish historian R.B. McDowell in writing a biography of his aunt, Alice Stopford Green.

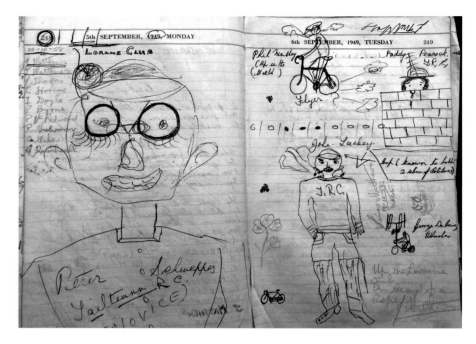

1950

McGuirk's now hosted more visitors from England, Wales and Scotland than from Ireland, and, for these travellers, rationing at home must have made Mrs McGuirk's cakes a real treat. They were particularly impressed by 'real Irish bread and butter' and 'delightful tea'. The rise in the general standard of living for some, while allowing many more people to afford bicycles and motorcycles, was not parallelled by a rise in educational standards and so the quality of handwriting, sketches and poems in the visitors' books can be seen to be deteriorating. Turf-cutting continued on the Featherbeds, and the men working on the bog remained frequent visitors.

9 January 1950

J. Griggs	*Hampton Court, Surrey*
B.K. Till	*Pathé Pictures (on location for 'The Workhouse Ward').*

These two visitors were part of the film crew working on a British Pathé production of *The Workhouse Ward*, a play by Lady Gregory that was first performed in 1909. Ria Mooney was the director; the actors in the 28-minute film are not named but referred to as 'Abbey Theatre Players'. Only one very short sequence, a long, panning shot of Glencree Valley, was ultimately included in the film.

Pathé's *The Workhouse Ward* (1950)

17 March 1950
Eric Bentley   *Theatre Arts, New York*
Maya Rooney   *59 Larkfield Grove, Dublin*

Eric Russell Bentley (1916–2020) was born in England and attended University College, Oxford, where his tutors included J.R.R. Tolkien and C.S. Lewis. Receiving his degree in English in 1938, he received his PhD from Yale in 1941; by 1953, he was lecturing at Columbia University. In 1960, he was appointed Charles Eliot Norton Professor at Harvard. His work as a theatre critic provoked a threat of lawsuits from Tennessee Williams and Arthur Miller. His books of theatre criticism and his own plays, *The Red, White, and Black* and *Lord Alfred's Lover*, were well received, and his translations of Bertolt Brecht were very successful. He died in New York at the age of 103.

11 April 1950
D. MacNamara (graver of images and fancies)
Ernest Gébler (who came back on the 'Mayflower')
Leatrice Gilbert Hart (American parasite)
Loren [sic] Hart (who played 'Pooh-Sticks' in the corner)
Louis Sowden – all the way from South Africa
Dora Sowden – learning to like it
Sybil Shein – Delighted by my revisit

Streets become roads which ribboned over hills
And if upon the mountains found no place
At least to body's, if not heart's [sic]
Great hunger came surcease.　　　　　　*Anthony Cronin*

The strange quatrain is an early work of the poet and author Anthony Cronin, part of this group although not listed, who was born in Co. Wexford and educated at Blackrock College and University College Dublin, from where he received a BA; he was later called to the Bar. He was a cultural advisor to both Charles Haughey and Garret FitzGerald, and was involved in setting up the Heritage Council and the Irish Museum of Modern Art. A founder member of Aosdána, the academy of Irish artists, he was elected its first Saoi (which means 'wise one' in Irish and is the highest honour bestowed by Aosdána).

Desmond Joseph MacNamara (1918–2008) was an artist and writer who was a key figure in Dublin cultural life in the 1940s and 1950s. He was born in Dublin and educated at University College Dublin and the National College of Art, where he studied sculpture. He designed sets and props for the Gate Theatre, the Abbey Theatre and for the film *Henry V* that was shot in Powerscourt, Co. Wicklow, in 1944. His studio in Grafton Street was a meeting place for the cultural intelligentsia of the time, and visitors included Anthony Cronin, John Ryan, J.P. Donleavy, Carolyn Swift and Alan Simpson. He was the model for J.P. Donleavy's character MacDoon in *The Ginger Man* (1955) and was well known for his songs, recitations and stories; his left-wing leanings brought him into contact with the young Brendan Behan, whose literary career he assisted: Swift and Simpson produced Behan's first play, *The Quare Fellow*. The destruction of the Abbey Theatre by fire in 1951 so affected MacNamara's livelihood that he had to move to London in 1957. Late in life he wrote two novels, *The Book of Intrusions* (1994) and *Confessions of an Irish Werewolf* (2006).

Ernest Gébler (1914–1998), author, playwright and television scriptwriter, was born in Dublin to a Czech Jewish father and a

Anthony Cronin in 1974

Dublin mother. His first novel, *He Had My Heart Scalded*, was published in 1946 but, in the same year of his visit to McGuirk's, his novel *The Voyage of the Mayflower* was a bestseller that was later made into a Hollywood movie, *Plymouth Adventure*, starring Spencer Tracy. While in Hollywood, Ernest met and married Leatrice Gilbert Hart, and the couple moved to Ireland and had a son. They divorced in 1952, and in the same year Gébler met the novelist Edna O'Brien and they moved to England, marrying in 1954. They had two sons, one of whom, Carlo, became an acclaimed novelist and literary critic. They divorced in 1968.

Leatrice Joy Gilbert Hart (1924–2015) was the daughter of the silent-film actors John Gilbert (who made ninety films and was divorced four times) and Leatrice Joy. Growing up, Leatrice knew actors such as Jean Harlow, Joan Fontaine, Spencer Tracy, Clark Gable and Ava Gardner. At the age of twelve, she made her first film, *Of Human Hearts*, with James Stewart, followed by other films for MGM, after which she moved to New York, where she sang in a number of operas. She was married five times, and Ernest Gébler was her second husband, with whom she had one son. She didn't like the damp of Ireland and returned regularly to the United States on holidays. After divorcing Ernest, she married the American actor Henry Hart, with whom she had a daughter, Lorin. This marriage lasted for three years, after which she married twice again, and lived to be ninety-one.

Lorin Hart was Leatrice's daughter who later became a folk singer and songwriter. 'Poohsticks' is a game mentioned in A.A. Milne's *The House at Pooh Corner* (1928).

Lewis Sowden (1905–1974) was born in England but lived most of his life in South Africa. He was a novelist, poet, playwright and theatre critic. His play, *The Kimberley Train*, about miscegenation under Apartheid, was highly successful. He moved to Israel with his wife in 1966.

Dora Sowden (née Leah Levitt) married Lewis Sowden in South Africa in 1936.

Sketch left in 1950

28 May 1950
Whit Sunday
Diarmuid Sutton
Ronald Smyth
Dermot Smyth
Barbara McGuire
Ruth Sutton

Over the rugged mountain path,
Dermot driving and having no heart
Did yellow walls sickly bump
Did Ronnie save and hold his breath,
Thinking only of approaching death,
And Barbara did the wireless stump,
While Ruth in wonder gazed
At Mount Pellier through the haze.
And Pamela thinking of approaching life,
Did practise nursing to be Ronnie's wife.
So down the winding hill,
And thinking only of having a fill,
Yonder did McGuirk's we see,
Who came to our aid and gave us High Tea.

1951

The McGuirks' visitors' book for 1951 was mostly destroyed by damp, and Tom McGuirk tells me it is very likely that it contained entries by the crew of another Glencree-based film, *The Gentle Gunman* (1952), well remembered in the valley to this day. It starred John Mills and Dirk Bogarde; Irish actors Barbara Mullen, Jack McGowran and Eddie Byrne also had roles. The film set, with a two-storey, white-washed cottage and a motor garage, built on the Military Road above Glencree, was later demolished.

1952

From the early 1950s onwards, the general tone and content of the entries in the McGuirks' visitors' books are eloquent testimony to the social changes taking place in Ireland at the time. An Irish exile who left the country in 1920 and returned in 1950 would find little change but, in the decade that followed, a remarkable transformation took place, socially and economically, as a new Ireland began to emerge. The country survived social implosion by exporting its unemployed, nearly half a million during the 1950s alone, but radical changes in economic policies, which included the dismantling of protectionism and the utilisation of foreign direct investment, began to create an upsurge in general prosperity. The great flood into the cinemas of spectacular Technicolor and CinemaScope films was followed, from the 1960s, by liberal doses of American culture beamed into homes by Raidió Teilifís Éireann (RTÉ), the new television station, which fed a great increase in expectations.

The expansion of industry and employment followed by the rise in general income affected every stratum of Irish society. Credit was widely extended to the newly waged, and people who could never have previously considered buying such luxuries as a car could do so now, through credit and hire purchase arrangements.

After the war, surplus British Army bicycles flooded the Irish market at very reasonable prices and, as they were available on 'the never-never', one could be off into the countryside within minutes of paying the first deposit. Many new cycling clubs were established, including the Dublin Wheelers and the Orwell Wheelers.

The Lambretta scooter was introduced to Ireland in the 1950s, and the NSU Quickly, a motorised bicycle built in Germany and now available in Ireland, also transformed local travel. Ordinary working people found that they were able to go places that were previously accessible only to the better off.

Arthur McGuirk cut no turf in 1950, and spent most of the year in bed with a mysterious ailment. None of the visitors were aware that Mona suffered from chronic bronchitis and that, sometimes, because there was no other income, she and her family lived near the poverty line and were often cold and hungry. She never let it show, however, and continued to endear herself to visitors.

20 July 1952

Francis Meredith	*Old Mother Lug, God be with the old days*
Elizabeth Meredith	*102 Waterloo Road, Southport*
Ethel Meredith	*4 Eaton Place, Monkstown, Co. Dublin*
Ethel Kellett	*ditto*
T.C. Kellett	*ditto*

Francis Meredith was one of the original members of the Brotherhood of the Lug, a walking club that was founded in 1903; indeed, he was the Grand Master of the club in 1925 when his first visit to McGuirk's was recorded.

1 August 1952
John Keane

Thanks for tea Mrs McGuirk, you are still the same good friend.

This is another example of a singular Mrs McGuirk impressing visitors: it is as if the same Mrs McGuirk who was being congratulated and called a friend in the early 1900s is still there in the 1950s.

Mona McGuirk (second from left) with visitors in the mid-1950s

22 October 1952
N.B.

I predict that in less than 10 years' time there will be a Television Transmitting Station in this area (on Mount Maulin or Kippure).

A visitor identified only by his or her initials left this prophetic note. It wasn't until the mid-1950s that Kippure was identified by a Raidió Éireann survey as a potential transmitter site. The Office of Public Works built an access road to the summit in 1959, and a television transmitting mast had been erected by the summer of 1961. Regular television broadcasts began on 31 December 1961.

An Tóstal postage stamp, 1953

1953

4 April 1953
Sean O'Callaghan
Eileen Fitzgibbon   Co. Cork
Roas Fitzgibbon
Esther Gibney

This Tóstal celebration was a credit to Mrs McGuirk and the Nation.

An Tóstal ('The Gathering') was a series of festivals celebrating Irish culture that ran from 1953 until 1958. It was marked by sporting and arts events, many of them designed to attract tourists. As part of An Tóstal, an international cycle race called the Rás Tailteann was founded by the Republican activist and barrister Joe Christle and named after the ancient Tailteann Games. Held in 1953 over eight days, visiting twenty-one counties of Ireland

The tea room in the 1950s

and covering approximately 1,600 km, it subsequently became an annual event. Trouble occurred on the second day of the 1956 race, which took place in Northern Ireland, when Christle flew a large tricolour from the roof of the lead car. The tricolour had been banned in Northern Ireland under the Flag and Emblems (Display) Act (Northern Ireland) 1954. Officers from the Royal Ulster Constabulary seized the flag when it arrived in Lurgan, Co. Armagh, and hostile spectators pelted the convoy of cyclists at Cookstown in Co. Tyrone.

7 June 1953
Leon Ó Bróin
Pat Lawless

Leon Ó Broin (1902–1990) was an Irish- and English-language playwright and author. He joined the nationalist youth organisation Na Fianna Éireann while still at school and, although not in favour of using violent means to achieve freedom, joined Sinn Féin and was imprisoned in 1921 and 1922. In 1924, he joined the Irish Free State civil service, working mainly in the Department of Finance. He married Kathleen O'Reilly in 1925 and they had six children. From 1948 to 1967, he was head of the Department of Posts and Telegraphs and was responsible for Raidió Éireann and later Raidió Teilifís Éireann (RTÉ). He wrote three plays and more than twenty books, the most important of which was *Dublin Castle and the 1916 Rising* (1966).

1955

For a number of years in the 1950s there are no surviving entries, and for others, there are very few, many of which are of little real interest.

9 October 1955
Professor David H. Greene, New York University – In pursuit of J.M. Synge

David Herbert Greene (1913–2008) was born in Boston and attended Harvard University, receiving a PhD in literature in 1939. He was a navy intelligence officer during WWII, after which he was appointed to the English faculty of New York University. He retired in 1979 but continued to lecture as a professor emeritus until 1985. In the mid-1930s, while still a student, he was assigned to look after the Irish playwright Sean O'Casey, who had been invited to speak on campus. They struck up a friendship that lasted decades, resulting in a voluminous exchange of correspondence. Greene had a passion for Irish literature, and his particular interest was J.M. Synge and his place in the Irish literary renaissance. His book, co-published in 1959 with Edward M. Stephens, *J.M. Synge: 1871–1909*, was a seminal work about the playwright and how he assimilated Ireland's Gaelic heritage into poetic drama.

1958

By the late 1950s, many of the wealthier professional classes had moved on and were no longer represented in the pages of the visitors' books – their leisure time was more likely spent abroad or in more exclusive settings. The percentage of visitors with current, or future, high-profile prominence is much reduced: many of those who scribbled their names from 1950s onwards are less likely to be listed in dictionaries of biography. The final volume of the visitors' books, 1958–60, is in poor condition. While entries still praised the tea and brown bread, there was little of the neatness and style of

Sketch left in 1956

James Cagney on location in Ireland filming
Shake Hands with the Devil (1959)

previous decades, and the quality of drawings and poems continued to decline. The general layout deteriorated further: names were now scribbled any old way, packed together and often difficult to read.

29 September 1958

James Farrell

Ronnie McShane

Eric D. Besche

Peter Tubon

Ardmore Films Again! On Location for 'Shake Hands with The Devil'.

Eric Besche (1914–1983) was a French cinematographer (although he was born and died in England). *Shake Hands with the Devil*, directed by Michael Anderson, was filmed for United Artists in 1958 in Ardmore Studios, and on location in Dublin, Glencree and the Featherbeds. It starred Oscar winners James Cagney and Dana Wynter, together with Don Murray and Glynis Johns, but many Irish actors had small roles, including Noel Purcell, Donal Donnelly, Christopher Cassin, Harry Brogan and Richard Harris, appearing in his second film. Anderson was impressed by Harris, even in a minor part, and offered him a role in his next film, *The Wreck of the Mary Deare* (1959), which took Harris to Hollywood and on to a major acting career. There must have been great excitement in the Glencree area at the time *Shake Hands with the Devil* was being filmed.

Ardmore Studios, on a ten-acre site approximately 19 km south of Dublin, had opened in May 1958 under the management of Emmet Dalton and Louis Elliman. Offering filmmakers in Ireland the opportunity to make films indoors, many first-rate cinema productions have been made there, including *Excalibur* (1981), *My Left Foot* (1989) and *Braveheart* (1995).

15 May 1959
Joseph Lynch

I have had many nice meals and hope to have many more.

Joseph Lynch (1925–2001), better known as 'Joe', was born in Mallow, Co. Cork, and, after attending the North Monastery school in Cork, became a well-known stage, film and television actor. He began acting with the Cork Shakespearean company, the Loft, and in 1947 joined the Radio Éireann Players. He appeared in RTÉ's first radio comedy series, *Living with Lynch*, which began in 1954 and, from the 1960s onwards, he appeared in twenty films, including *The Night Fighters* (1960) with Robert Mitchum, some scenes of which were filmed in Glencree in the same year as this visit. Older readers may remember him from his television roles on *Bracken* and *Glenroe*, and he twice won a Jacob's Award for his television work.

Joe Lynch photographed in 2000

23 June 1959
Ronald M. Delaney

This is Ireland's Olympic champion, Ronald Michael ('Ronnie') Delaney (*b.* 1935), who had won the gold medal for the 1,500 metres at Melbourne three years before, in December 1956. Delaney was born in Arklow, Co. Wicklow, and attended Sandymount High School and the Catholic University School. He started running at school, and got a scholarship to study commerce and finance at Villanova University, a private Catholic university in Pennsylvania. Although he became the seventh runner in the world to achieve a four-minute mile, he had struggled to get on the Irish Olympic team for the Melbourne games. He retired from competitive running in 1962 and worked with Aer Lingus and B&I ferries before establishing his own marketing and sports consultancy.

29 July 1959

Iris Rose *Leytonstone, London*
Joshua Rubens *London*
R.E. Garrett *Iver, Bucks.*

From the 'A Terrible Beauty' Film Unit at Ardmore Studios, Bray.

A Terrible Beauty, released as *The Night Fighters*, was filmed in 1959 at Ardmore Studios, starring Robert Mitchum (complete with a 'begorragh' accent) and Richard Harris and featuring Irish actors Dan O'Herlihy, Cyril Cusack and Joe Lynch. A number of scenes were shot in Glencree: a local cottage was used for a scene where Robert Mitchum staggers, wounded, through the door, and the nearby quarry over Upper Lough Bray is where he dives off the road to avoid a British patrol.

Iris Rose (1930–2014) worked in the film industry as additional crew and in wardrobe departments from an early age, but began to receive credits when she was production secretary on Stanley Kubrick's epic *2001: A Space Odyssey* (1968). She worked on eleven James Bond films, starting with *For Your Eyes Only* (1981), and worked with four 007s: Roger Moore, Timothy Dalton, Pierce Brosnan and Daniel Craig.

Mona (on the left) with visitors in 1959

1960

During a debate in the Senate in March 1945, Minister for Industry and Commerce Seán Lemass said, in relation to rural electrification, 'I hope to see the day that when a girl gets a proposal from a farmer she will inquire not so much about the number of cows, but rather concerning the electrical appliances she will require before she gives her consent.' When Arthur McGuirk was offered a supply, suspicious either of electricity itself or the cost involved, he refused, and McGuirk's continued to rely on oil lamps and on a traditional open fire for cooking.

2 March 1960
Benedict Kiely
Sean J. White
E.J. McDonnell
Paddy Sampson

Writer and broadcaster Benedict Kiely

Benedict Kiely (1919–2007) was an author and broadcaster. Born in Co. Tyrone, he briefly studied for the priesthood but went on to receive a BA from University College Dublin. He joined the *Irish Independent* as a journalist and critic in 1949 and later became literary editor of *The Irish Press*. He was writer-in-residence at Emory University and Hollins University in the United States, as well as visiting professor at the University of Oregon. He became one of Ireland's best-known writers, and his books include *Poor Scholar: A study of William Carleton* (1947) and *Nothing Happens in Carmincross* (1985). He became a favourite on the RTÉ radio programme *Sunday Miscellany*, and in 1996 was named Saoi of Aosdána.

Sean J. White (1927–1996) was a writer, journalist and broadcaster, born in Co. Laois and educated at St Kieran's College, Kilkenny, and St Patrick's College, Kiltegan, Co. Wicklow. He received a BA in English and philosophy from University College Cork and a Higher Diploma in Education from University College Dublin in 1950, followed by an MA, also from UCD, in 1953. As editor of the literary journal *Irish Writing*, founded by David Marcus in 1947, he published new work by Samuel Beckett, Brendan Behan and Thomas Kinsella and, for *The Irish Press*, travelled the country with Benedict Kiely, reporting on local events, traditions and characters, under their joint pen name, Patrick Lagan. In later years, he had a rich and varied career in Bord Fáilte as publicity director for North

America; in CIÉ as Head of Information; as a writer and presenter of documentaries and programmes for RTÉ; and as Adjunct Professor of Irish Studies at the University of Limerick.

Under the name Patrick Lagan, either Benedict Kiely or Sean J. White wrote in *The Irish Press* about this visit to McGuirk's:

Someday I'd like to take Mrs McGuirk down to Dublin and lead her around to some of our big hotels to give a few lessons on the lost art of making a drinkable cup of tea. When I mentioned my thoughts on the matter to Paddy Sampson of Enniskerry, he said, simply and proudly, 'It's a Wicklow person's special blessing to be able to make a good cup of tea.' Arthur McGuirk stood with us and above us while we drank the tea and he had about him the ease and quiet strength of a man who knows and loves the mountains, who has lived his life within the sound of the musical torrents that come out of Lower Lough Bray. Once again to quote Paddy Sampson: 'Arthur looks at you and talks to you with all the shyness of wisdom.'

Turning the yellowing pages of a visitors' book that goes back for 65 years, Arthur showed me the signatures I was looking for. They were written in pencil in the year 1906: J. M. Synge and Frank Fay ... Two miles up the mountain and half a mile from where the Liffey rises, they're getting ready for television. Perhaps someday we'll see and hear Arthur McGuirk on TV telling us about the past of the mountains: about, for instance, his friendship with Joseph Campbell, the Mountainy Singer from the Glens of Antrim.

Down the Glen towards Enniskerry Campbell farmed. 'But,' says Arthur, 'he wasn't a serious farmer. He went on more for the pen, you know. And when he went to the

Sketch left at the end of 1959

States to Harvard he sent me a book of poems I have here in the house.'

One last peep into the visiting book before we descend the mountain. Here's an impromptu quatrain in praise of the high house of McGuirk. It's not great poetry but it's palpably sincere!

From Enniskerry to Lough Bray,
When lay-weary on the way,
Behold that cottage above the Valley,
Mrs McGuirk sure knows how to tally.

6 March 1960

Garry Trimble	*50 Ashdown Park, Monkstown*
Francois de Chazal	*Floreal, Mauritius*
Mary J. Trimble	*50 Ashdown Park, Monkstown*
Mairéad Ní Mhaoilmichil	*Seóirse de Geata*

Garry Trimble (1928–1979) was educated at Belvedere College and University College Dublin, where he studied architecture. He was an accomplished sculptor, and his works include busts of Éamon de Valera, Christy Brown, Richard Harris, Benedict Kiely and the English jockey Lester Piggott. He was a close friend of Charles Haughey and designed his island retreat on the Blasket island, Inishvickillane, Co. Kerry.

26 April 1960
Deirdre O'Shea

Sure 'twas a lovely tea I had here with me own dear white-headed boy, Joe the darlin's name is. But he didn't propose to me yet – an' he after coortin' me like mad, the cad.

The Loraine Cycling Club visiting the tea room in 1959

15 May 1960

50 years ago today
Loraine was christened in Howth Bay
A group of cyclists watched with glee,
As Captain Loraine crossed the Irish Sea
What courage and grit this story holds
Of man's achievement to reach his goal
Marie Keane, aided and abetted by MJB.

This contribution was followed by the signatures of twenty other members of the Loraine Cycling Club.

10 July 1960

Joe Linnane	*Radio Eireann*
G.A. Henry	*Bahana, Enniskerry*
James Plunkett	*Radio Eireann*
John Spillane	*Radio Eireann*

Joe Linnane (1910–1981) was a Dublin-born actor and broadcaster. He was educated at Castleknock College, Dublin and, after a period in amateur dramatics, joined the Abbey Theatre and enjoyed success in the 1933 London production of Lennox Robinson's *Drama at Inish*. In 1941, he performed in BBC Radio's *Irish Half Hour*, aimed at an Irish audience in the United Kingdom. He went on to front a series of shows on BBC Radio and appeared in a number of British films, until he came back to Raidió Éireann in 1953 as their highest-paid employee, presenting the popular programme *Question Time*. Two years after his visit to McGuirk's, he was also presenting programmes for RTÉ, including *The Joe Linnane Show*, and he was a strong influence on the young Gay Byrne, who modelled his on-air persona on Linnane's.

James Plunkett (1920–2003), born James Plunkett Kelly in Dublin's inner city, was an author, playwright and television producer.

His short stories were first published in the literary magazine *The Bell* in 1942, and he contributed short stories and plays to Raidió Éireann in the 1950s. He joined the station in 1955 as assistant head of Drama and Variety, and trained with BBC Television before the launch of RTÉ in 1961. His best-known novel, *Strumpet City*, was published in 1969 and sold more than one-quarter of a million copies, in a dozen languages. The televised adaptation by RTÉ was hugely successful and sold in thirty countries.

James Plunkett

11 August 1960

David Krause	*Providence, Rhode Island, USA*
Valerie Kelly	*Rockfield Drive, Dublin*
James Plunkett Kelly	*ditto*
Vadim Kelly	*ditto*
James S. Kelly	
Ross Kelly	

David Krause (1917–2011) was born in New Jersey of Polish parents and was best known in Ireland for his work on the playwright Seán O'Casey, including *Sean O'Casey: The Man and his Work* (1960) and four volumes of O'Casey's letters. He served in the US Army Air Corps during WWII. The GI Bill allowed him to study at New York University after the war, and he received a BA in literature in 1949, an MA in 1951 and a PhD in 1952. Always interested in Irish literature, he spent time in Ireland every year, marrying Ann Gough, a Waterford woman, in 1966. His first volume of O'Casey's letters was named one of the ten best books of the year by *The Times* in 1975. He also published three books of his own poetry. Valerie Kelly (*d.* 1986) is James Plunkett's wife.

James Plunkett Kelly we have met before.

Vadim, James and Ross Plunkett are Valerie and James Plunkett's sons.

EPILOGUE

Mona McGuirk had been suffering from chronic bronchitis since the 1950s, and the tea room closed in 1961. Her son Tom worked for the Institute for Industrial Research and Standards, but moved to the Forestry Commission in the 1970s. After Mona's death in 1962, her husband, Arthur, lived on in the cottage until 1974, when he went to St Colman's nursing home in Rathdrum. He died there in 1979 and Tom emigrated to Canada in 1991.

In the thirty years since Mona McGuirk died and her tea room closed, there were far-reaching changes in Irish society. After slow economic growth in the 1960s and 1970s, following decades of underperformance, Ireland became gradually more prosperous in the late 1980s. The change was due to many factors, including joining the European Economic Community (now the European Union), the improvement in education levels due to the introduction of free secondary education in 1967, and the generous tax breaks given to multinationals.

Paddy Smith, one of Tom McGuirk's childhood friends in Glencree, was married to Gloria, Tom's wife's sister, and lived near the McGuirk cottage, which had been vacated by Tom in 1991. Gloria had a small business supplying bread and baked goods to restaurants and delicatessens in the Wicklow area, and the idea occurred to her that the old tea room might be revived, so, with Tom's agreement, she set about reopening it. Times had changed, and statutory permissions had to be sought for planning and for preparing and serving food. With considerable investment from Gloria and Paddy, the cottage was renovated, and it was during these renovations that Gloria came across the old visitors' books. Recognising their value, she wrapped them carefully in plastic bags and stored them away.

On 15 August 1993, Gloria opened for business, continuing the McGuirk tradition of producing exceptionally good fare, but she added items such as cheese cake, apple crumble and coffee to the menu. She also had her visitors sign a visitors' book: one of her first visitors was His Excellency the Polish Ambassador to Ireland, Ernest Bryll, and his party. Before the end of that first month, Gloria had catered for over 230 visitors, many of whom had been patrons of the old tea room. A couple on the verge of becoming famous film stars, Liam Neeson and Natasha Richardson, signed in at the end of that first month. They had starred that year on Broadway in the Eugene O'Neill play *Anna Christie*, after which Neeson was cast as the lead in Stephen Spielberg's 1993 *Schindler's List*, which won Best Picture at the Oscars. He and Natasha Richardson were married in 1994. Richardson, the daughter of actor Vanessa Redgrave, was in Ireland at the time of her and Neeson's visit to McGuirk's, filming *Widow's Peak*, which was shot on location in Wicklow, Kilkenny and Dublin. She won a number of awards for her performance in *Anna Christie*, including a Theatre World Award and a Tony Award for Best Performance by a Leading Actress in a Musical. She died after a skiing accident in 2009.

The Military Road, the route that had taken early visitors to McGuirk's, usually on their way south to Glendalough or north to Dublin, was now a relatively busy tarmac road that didn't appeal to walkers, who preferred the heathery open hillsides. By the 1990s, the number of cyclists had decreased considerably, and most visitors now came by car. Gloria could accommodate up to thirty people thanks to using two rooms (there was originally just one), and sometimes the only limitations on numbers was the scarcity of parking spaces along the road.

The number of visitors using the Irish language when signing in had reduced to a tiny percentage. Visitors from abroad had increased greatly in number and, while early in the century there had been very few Germans visiting, a large percentage of overseas visitors in the 1990s were German. There was also a high percentage of Irish families with young children, reflecting the increase in car ownership that had occurred in recent decades.

References in the visitors' books to world events continued to be rare, one of the very few examples being left on Monday, 29 July 1996:

Atlanta Summer Olympics 1996 in progress – Ireland 3 gold medals so far!

The three golds were won by swimmer Michelle Smith: she later became embroiled in a controversy over banned substances but was not stripped of her medals because she never tested positive for any banned substance.

During the years that Gloria ran the tea room, six volumes of visitors' books were filled. By the 1990s, however, the entries had lost much of the romance of the earlier period: there were very few attempts at poetry, and the few sketches were simple, often crude, cartoons. What remained was a long list of names and origins devoid of mystery and personality, without the sense that the visitors were pausing briefly on a journey of exploration and, of course, no one left postal addresses any more.

Business was good but times had changed, and respect for law and property had eroded in the century or more since the tea room had first opened. The south-western suburbs of Dublin city now extended to the foot of the mountains, car theft became common, and for these car thieves, or 'joyriders', quiet mountain roads and places like Glencree were easily accessible. There were eight break-ins during the five years Gloria ran the tea room, some burglars stealing what they could find, others painting graffiti on the walls or simply wrecking the place, and there was one intriguing incident when the burglar took the curtains, the pictures off the wall, and six of each piece of delph and cutlery! Steel shutters and a steel-sheeted door failed to stop them: one burglar opened up the slated roof at the back to get in; others cut through the timber doorframe and lifted the steel door off its hinges. It became impossible to find staff and, with two children to mind, Gloria Smith reluctantly closed McGuirk's doors in June 1998.

The former McGuirks' cottage today

> Farewell, thou little nook of mountain ground
> Thou rocky corner in the lowest stair
> Of that magnificent temple which doth bound
> One side of our whole vale with grandeur rare;
> Farewell! – we leave thee to Heaven's peaceful care,
> Thee and the Cottage which thou dost surround.
>
> from William Wordsworth, 'A Farewell'

BIBLIOGRAPHY

Selected Secondary Sources

Beckett, Samuel, 'Recent Irish Poetry' in *Disjecta: Miscellaneous Writings and a Dramatic Fragment* (London: John Calder, 1983).

Brady, Joseph, *Dublin in the 1950s and 1960s: Cars, Shops and Suburbs* (Dublin: Four Courts Press, 2017).

Bryan, Ciaran, 'Rationing in Ireland, 1939–48', PhD thesis (Department of History, National University of Ireland Maynooth, 2014).

Colum, Padraic, *Arthur Griffith* (Dublin: Browne and Nolan, 1959).

Cowell, John, *Where They Lived in Dublin* (Dublin: The O'Brien Press, 1980).

Crowe, Catriona (ed.), *Dublin 1911* (Dublin: Royal Irish Academy, 2011).

Dictionary of Irish Biography (Dublin: Royal Irish Academy, 2009).

Fewer, Michael, *The Wicklow Military Road: History and Topography* (Dublin: Ashfield Press, 2007).

Fitz-Simon, Christopher, *The Arts in Ireland: A Chronology* (Dublin: Gill & Macmillan, 1982).

Fraser, James, *Guide Through Ireland* (Dublin: William Curry, Jun. and Company, 1838).

Grimes, Brendan, 'Dry plates and wheelmen, amateur photography and cycling, 1880 1900', BA paper (School of Media, Dublin Institute of Technology, 2012).

Gurrin, Brian F., *A Social History of the Wicklow Uplands* (National Parks and Wildlife Service, Department of the Environment, Heritage and Local Government, 2006).

Harrison, Richard S., *A Biographical Dictionary of Irish Quakers* (Dublin: Four Courts Press, 1997).

Joyce, James, *Ulysses* (London: Penguin, 1976).

—, *Finnegans Wake* (New York: Viking Press, 1939).

Kennedy, Finola, 'The suppression of the Carrigan Report: A historical perspective on child abuse', *Irish Historical Studies*, Vol. 32, No. 128 (Nov. 2001).

Kiely, David M., *John Millington Synge: A Biography* (Dublin: Gill & Macmillan, 1994).

Lewis, Samuel, *A Topographical Dictionary of Ireland* (London: Samuel Lewis, 1946).

MacLysaght, Edward, *The Surnames of Ireland* (Dublin: Irish Academic Press, 1978).

Mecredy, R.J., *Cyclist & Pedestrian Guide to the Neighbourhood of Dublin* (Dublin: Mecredy & Kyle, 1891).

Molohan, Cathy, *Germany and Ireland, 1945-1955* (Dublin: Irish Academic Press, 1999).

Montgomery, Bob, *R. J. Mecredy, the Father of Irish Motoring* (Meath: Dreoilin Publications, 2003).

Nowlan, Kevin B. (ed.), *Travel and Transport in Ireland* (Dublin: Gill & Macmillan, 1973).

O'Brien, Eoin, *The Beckett Country: Samuel Beckett's Ireland* (Dublin: Black Cat Press/Riverrun Press, 1986).

—, and Cruikshank, Anne, with Sir Gordon Wolstenholme, *A Portrait of Irish Medicine* (Dublin: Ward River Press, 1984).

O'Keefe, Peter J., *Alexander Taylor's Roadworks in Ireland, 1780-1827* (Dublin: Institute of Asphalt Technology, 1995).

Redmond, Adrian (ed.), *That was then, This is now: Change in Ireland, 1949-1999* (Dublin: Central Statistics Office, 2000).

Rudd, Niall (ed. and transl.), *Horace: Odes and Epodes* (Cambridge, Massachusetts: Harvard University Press, 2004).

Skelton, Robin, *The Writings of J. M. Synge* (New York: The Bobbs-Merrill Company, 1971).

St. John Gogarty, Oliver, *As I Was Going Down Sackville Street* (London: Penguin, 1954).

Thom's Irish Who's Who – A biographical book of reference of prominent men and women in Irish life at home and abroad (Dublin: Alexander Thom & Co. Ltd., 1923).

Thom's Official Directory of the United Kingdom of Great Britain and Ireland for the year 1913 (Dublin: Alex. Thom & Co. Ltd, 1913).

Tobin, Fergal, *The Best of Decades: Ireland in the Nineteen Sixties* (Dublin: Gill & Macmillan, 1984).

Tracy, Frank, *If Those Trees Could Speak* (Dublin: South Dublin Libraries, 2009).

Willard, Frances E., *A Wheel within a Wheel: How I Learned to Ride a Bicycle* (Indianapolis: Woman's Temperance Publishing Association, 1985).

Wood, John, *With Rucksack Round Ireland* (London: Paul Elek, 1950).

Selected Primary Sources

MANUSCRIPT SOURCES

Michael Fewer's Archive: The Diaries of John Healy
Brotherhood of the Lugg Archive, in private hands
Irish Newspaper Archives
The Diaries of Claude Wall, National Library of Ireland
The Journals of J.B. Malone, in private hands
Powerscourt Papers, National Library of Ireland, MS L112

NEWSPAPERS, MAGAZINES AND JOURNALS

Autocar
Cork Examiner
Cycling World Illustrated
Decies: Journal of the Waterford Archaeological & Historical Society
Dublin Evening Mail – Irish Newspaper Archives
Evening Herald
Freeman's Journal – Irish Newspaper Archives

Irish Arts Review
Irish Cyclist and Motor Cyclist
Irish Independent
Irish Times
Journal of the Royal Society of Antiquaries of Ireland
Lady Cyclist
Munsey's Magazine
Wheelwoman

ONLINE

Department of Foreign Affairs, Documents on Irish Foreign Policy
    Houses of the Oireachtas Debates
Royal College of Physicians of Ireland, Lives of the Presidents
    project (online)
Wikipedia

INTERVIEWS

Tom McGuirk, Canada
Gloria Smyth, Enniskerry, Co. Wicklow

PERMISSIONS

INDEX